"*Visioning Multicultural Education: Past, Present, Future* is the book every educator needs to read and implement in their practice. Filled with chapters from today's leading scholars, this book provides a road map for all of those committed to multicultural education as well as outlines how multicultural education needs to change and grow to ensure that its goal of equity can be achieved".

Hoyt J. Phillips III, Deputy Director, Teaching & Learning
Teaching Tolerance: A project of the Southern Poverty
Law Center (SPLC)

"When I walked into my first multicultural education course as a doctoral student 45 years ago, I knew I had found my home. In the intervening years, the field, while staying true to its founding ideals of social justice and equity, has become more inclusive and also more incisive in its critique of the forces that marginalize many of our young people. The authors and editors of this volume, both veteran and emerging scholars, remind us why multicultural education has been, and will always be a transformative project. May it continue its long and splendid journey toward justice and liberation".

Sonia Nieto, Professor Emerita, Language, Literacy, and Culture,
College of Education, University of Massachusetts, Amherst

"As global pandemics, violence, poverty, and environmental destruction wage sinister wars on global communities of color, educational systems continue to struggle against the tide of intersectional oppressions, fostering apathy and ignorance despite the wishes and efforts of isolated educators. *Visioning Multicultural Education* provides a needed series of reflections from the nation's leading scholars, advocates, and critical educators. The authors, founders of the movement for multicultural education, senior scholar-activists, and mid-career educators carrying future generations, come together to provide critical affirmations and lessons learned from past and contemporary struggles, suggesting how educators must transform schooling if we are to survive, and indeed, thrive, as a pluralistic, integrated, socially cohesive society beyond tomorrow. As the authors show, we cannot tinker our way out of each of these global meltdowns; our futures lie in the collective solidarity that multicultural education offers".

Christopher Knaus, Professor, Education
University of Washington Tacoma

"Charting an effective path forward requires an examination of past and current efforts. In this book, the pioneers and esteemed scholars in the field of multicultural education call on us to challenge our thinking, understand current barriers, and examine the practices that continue to limit access to a quality education for ethnically, racially, and culturally diverse students. It is an exceptional and insightful book that is a must-read for educators and administrators".

Faye Snodegress, Executive Director, Kappa Delta Pi,
International Honor Society in Education

"*Visioning Multicultural Education* is a powerful book all educators and community members ***must read*** to better understand the field of multicultural education and its work towards social justice in schools and communities. Written by noted scholars and rooted in intergenerational perspectives, the book provides us an important look back on the foundations of the field and its impact, engages in a critical inquiry of where we are now in our scholarship and advocacy, and provides us a clear roadmap of vision, hope, and action for our future work with schools, communities, families, and, most importantly, the students we serve".

Kevin Roxas, Editor, Multicultural Perspectives, NAME Journal, Professor,
Department Chair, Secondary Education Department,
Woodring College of Education, Western Washington University

VISIONING MULTICULTURAL EDUCATION

Organized by the National Association of Multicultural Education (NAME), this volume explores the organic relationship between the past, present, and future of the discipline. In particular, the book addresses the various forms of recent social upheaval, from educational inequities and growing economic divides to extreme ideological differences and immigration conflicts. Written by a group of eminent and emerging scholars, chapters draw lessons from the past two decades and celebrate present accomplishments in order to ambition a better future through multicultural education.

H. Prentice Baptiste is Regents and Distinguished Achievement Professor, at New Mexico State University, Las Cruces, New Mexico. He was NAME's President (2016 to 2018), and founding member (1990). Baptiste has authored/ edited seven books, and over 125 publications on multicultural education and presented papers internationally, e.g. in Nigeria, Germany, Jamaica, Morocco, Netherlands.

Jeanette Haynes Writer (Tsalagi/Cherokee Nation citizen) is Professor of Curriculum and Instruction at New Mexico State University, Las Cruces, New Mexico. Her areas of scholarship include critical multicultural and social justice education; Tribal Critical Race Theory; Native American education; and teacher education.

VISIONING MULTICULTURAL EDUCATION

Past, Present, Future

Edited by H. Prentice Baptiste and Jeanette Haynes Writer

Routledge
Taylor & Francis Group
NEW YORK AND LONDON

First published 2021
by Routledge
52 Vanderbilt Avenue, New York, NY 10017

and by Routledge
2 Park Square, Milton Park, Abingdon, Oxon OX14 4RN

Routledge is an imprint of the Taylor & Francis Group, an informa business

Library of Congress Cataloging-in-Publication Data
Names: Baptiste, H. Prentice, editor. | Haynes Writer, Jeanette, editor.
Title: Visioning multicultural education: past, present, future /
edited by H. Prentice Baptiste and Jeanette Haynes Writer.
Description: New York, NY : Routledge, 2021. |
Includes bibliographical references and index.
Identifiers: LCCN 2020019948 (print) | LCCN 2020019949 (ebook) |
ISBN 9780367558994 (hardback) | ISBN 9780367558987 (paperback) |
ISBN 9781003095644 (ebook)
Subjects: LCSH: Multicultural education–United States. |
Minorities–Education–United States. | Educational equalization–United States. |
Education and globalization–United States.
Classification: LCC LC1099.3 .V574 2021 (print) |
LCC LC1099.3 (ebook) | DDC 370.1170973–dc23
LC record available at https://lccn.loc.gov/2020019948
LC ebook record available at https://lccn.loc.gov/2020019949

ISBN: 978-0-367-55899-4 (hbk)
ISBN: 978-0-367-55898-7 (pbk)
ISBN: 978-1-003-09564-4 (ebk)

Typeset in Bembo
by Newgen Publishing UK

This book is dedicated to those courageous individuals of the past, present, and future who willingly sacrifice their lives and careers to establish the basic multicultural principles in our schools, governments, and other social institutions for the benefit of all humankind.

CONTENTS

FOREWORD

Gary R. Howard

It is an honor here to express gratitude for the vision and the movement that have inspired, informed, and sustained my work in education for the past five decades, and to the people who birthed that movement, as well as those who continue to expand and deepen its course.

In the early years of my teaching, in the mid-1970s, I asked a question that would determine the trajectory for the rest of my personal and professional life: *How can I bring the lessons and meaning of the Civil Rights Movement into the minds and hearts of my predominantly white rural middle school students?* They, their families, and their community had, for the most part, missed the revolution of the 1960s, which had been so deeply transformative for me as a white college student witnessing the flames of that time while living and working in the Black community in New Haven, Connecticut.

My search for answers to that early question took place in the context of a graduate internship in the Teacher Corps program, a search that led me first to Carl Grant, then to James Banks, and then to Geneva Gay, Carlos Cortés, Sonia Nieto, Christine Sleeter and other founders of the multicultural education movement, many of whose voices are present in this volume. I studied the writings of these eminent scholars and discovered that my question was merely one small part of a much larger body of research and analysis, and a community of social justice advocates who were forging a deep critique and reformulation of what education should look like in a diverse society.

In 1990, this community coalesced around Rose Duhon-Sells' vision for the founding of the National Association for Multicultural Education. Over the years, NAME has been a catalyst for promoting our multicultural vision, debating and clarifying our concepts, refining our analysis, and energizing our activism for social change. Through its national and international conferences and events, combined with the prolific writing of its members, and the nurturing of our personal and professional relationships, NAME has sustained a movement that has consistently pushed education toward substantive reform centered on social justice and critically informed democratic citizenship.

With the support and advocacy of this multicultural education community, I was eventually able, over many years, to create a process for engaging white educators and students in transformative multicultural work. I was then challenged and encouraged by my multicultural colleagues to write about that work, and the writing, in turn, has led to many years of travel and collaboration with educators throughout the U.S. and abroad. None of this would have happened without the intellectual and personal nurturing I received from these colleagues and friends. The intent of multicultural education has always been transformative at multiple levels: the personal, the pedagogical, and the political. My life story, along with the personal narratives of thousands of other multicultural educators, bears testimony to the power of that transformative vision.

Editors H. Prentice Baptiste and Jeanette Haynes Writer have gathered together in this volume the voices of several colleagues from my generation, as well as the perspectives of eminent early and mid-career scholars and activists who are presently shaping multicultural education, and will continue to do so for years to come: Patricia Marshall, Wayne Au, Angela Banks, and Kristen French, co-authoring a chapter with Jeanette Haynes Writer. The topics and themes of these chapters are as diverse and complex as the movement itself. Taken together, these writings form a dynamic intergenerational conversation that clearly and consistently challenges the dominant neo-liberal narrative regarding "school reform"—a narrative that purports to serve the needs of our most marginalized students and families, but actually and insidiously reinforces the dynamics of social dominance, colonialism, Christian hegemony, and whiteness. The multicultural education movement, both today and since its earliest inception, has sought to articulate a counter-narrative, one that is forged in the cauldron of critical analysis and social justice activism. The passion that energizes this counter-narrative clearly resonates with what Martin Luther King, Jr. referred to in his 1963 speech at the March on Washington, as the hope that we might someday "make real the promises of democracy." Multicultural education has always lived in this nexus of critical analysis and hope for real change.

On the long road of history, our multicultural education movement is still young, though many of us have grown older along the way. Wherever you are in your personal and professional journey, you will be informed, affirmed, challenged, and inspired by the chapters in this collection. The authenticity, richness, and clarity of vision offered by the authors gathered here is powerful evidence that the lessons of the past, the challenges of the present, and the hopeful possibilities for the future will continue to harmonize in creative and complex ways. As each of us in the multicultural education movement continues on that path, it will be helpful to remember what James Banks, many years ago, challenged all educators to do: to know, to care, and to act.

NAME ACKNOWLEDGEMENTS

The National Association for Multicultural Education (NAME) would like to thank Dr. H. Prentice Baptiste and Dr. Jeanette Haynes Writer for all of their work on this very important book. It would not have been possible without their hard work and focus. We also appreciate the contributions of all of the chapter contributors. Their voices are vital for this book and the future of Multicultural Education.

Most importantly, NAME would like to express its deep gratitude to NAME Founder Dr. Rose Duhon Sells. Without her vision, strength, and determination NAME would not exist. Thank you, for giving birth to NAME, nurturing the organization, and mentoring its members throughout the years.

Dr. Rose Duhon-Sells, NAME Founder

Cover photographer: Lewis W. Diuguid, Journalist, Author, NAME PAC Chair.

Cover photo art and digitization: Cordero D. Core, M.S., ACS Certified Biochemist, AIChE Certified Chemical Engineer, Podcast Host.

Cover subjects (left to right): Christine Sleeter, NAME Past-President; Leslie Bash, IAIE Vice President; G. Pritchy Smith, NAME Founding Member, Past-Vice-President; H. Prentice Baptiste, NAME Founding Member, Past-President, Editor.

EDITORS' ACKNOWLEDGEMENTS

The title of this book—*Visioning Multicultural Education: Past, Present, Future*—supports the idea that our acknowledgement must be threefold. First of all, we must pay homage to "past" examples of such heroic scholars as Carter G. Woodson, W. E. B. Du Bois, Luther Standing Bear, Gertrude Simmons Bonnin, Ernesto Galarza, Carlos Castaneda, and others who waged an intellectual war against racism and other forms of oppression and institutionalized acts of dehumanization. We stand on the shoulders of those magnificent trailblazers of the past.

Secondly, we evoke our gratitude to the "present" renowned scholars of Multicultural Education, represented in this book. These scholars and others have established Multicultural Education as a discipline with a valid research base and global recognition. Thirdly, we acknowledge with confidence that future emerging scholars will take the multicultural baton and continue to effectively challenge and deconstruct those social problems which dehumanized various powerless groups of people.

H. Prentice Baptiste extends his deepest gratitude to his wife and eternal friend, Dr. Lesley McAvoy Baptiste, for her inspiring, undying support during the production of this book.

Jeanette Haynes Writer thanks her partner, Vincent Larry, for his constant love and support in all she has been called to do. Thanks to Gracho and Ba'hozhoni for their patience and loyalty.

INTRODUCTION

H. Prentice Baptiste and Jeanette Haynes Writer

Multicultural Education is usually conceptualized as an umbrella, that is, an overarching concept for ethnic studies, bilingual education, immigration/migration concerns, Indigenous populations, social justice issues, among others. Multicultural Education is also timeless. There is an organic relationship between the past, present, and future that cannot be ignored, because they inform and impact each other to evolve a vision of a just and affirming world through the accomplishment of an equitable society. This translates to a greater vision for a society of equity and revolutionized education. Therefore, learning from the two decades thus far in the twenty-first century, celebrating present accomplishments, and ambitioning a better future in Multicultural Education is a legitimate goal. The social turmoil of the last two decades highlights the human challenges for the next decade. Specifically, we have witnessed resistance to immigrants seeking freedoms like those Europeans generations before; ethnic, linguistic, sexuality and religious intolerance exacerbated by illusions of making America great again; racial hate combined with *de jure* and *de facto* violence; continued violations of tribal treaties[1] and continued taking of Native lands through settler courts and institutions (Meyer, 2016);[2] and subsidizing the privileged while the poor continue to struggle (Goodman, 2019). Such turmoil ricochets around immigration conflicts, attacks on tribal sovereignty, educational inequities, health inequities, growing economic divides, extreme ideological differences, and other volatile issues. Do we, as multicultural educators, have a vision for addressing these various forms of social upheaval?

The theme for this book, *Visioning Multicultural Education: Past, Present, Future*, prompted Multicultural Education scholars to commence interrogating events thus far in the twenty-first century, to interpret their impact and meaning for the evolution of Multicultural Education. The scholars were asked to:

- *examine and discuss how social issues—immigration, neoliberalism, colonialism, racism, etc., have manifested during the first two decades of the twenty-first century*
- *excavate and reveal how the past has led to the present and how the present manifests the future.*

The concept for the book came about following discussions related to multicultural concerns related to the tumultuous beginning of this decade. We highlight some features of Multicultural Education from past, present, and future challenges; however, it is beyond the scope of this introduction to present a deep or comprehensive view of the numerous challenges. We leave specifics to the authors. Through their chapters, they will exercise a more lucid view from their particular multicultural area of interest and their scholarly expertise.

The Past

The late Barbara Sizemore (1969) stands as one of the first scholars to declare that "multicultural" was a political concept. The political unrest of the 1960s followed the establishment of judicial desegregation rights spearheaded by the 1954 Supreme Court decision Brown v. Topeka (1954). This decision reversed the Plessy v. Ferguson (1896) Supreme Court decision that "separate could be equal," which established the legal foundation for segregation. The 1954 decision led to the task of deconstructing the underpinnings of segregated institutions. It became obvious that the removal of the cornerstones of segregation would meet with great resistance. This resistance was well manifested in housing availability, quality, and location; access to hotel accommodations, and entry to and service at restaurants. However, the greatest resistance was demonstrated in the opposition to and confrontation exhibited in desegregating public schools. The failure of desegregation is unmistakably evident—our schools are more segregated today than in past decades since the 1954 decision (Orfield & Harvard Project on School Desegregation, 1996; Smith, 2004; Tatum, 2017).

The 1960s could be referred to as the decade of civil rights. During this period, major civil rights legislations were passed by Congress and signed into federal statute by President Lyndon B. Johnson (Baptiste, Kamenski, & Kamenski, 2007). These statutes were accompanied by political (i.e., Native American sovereign nations), ethnic, and cultural minority group members demonstrating for their civil and human rights. It became quite obvious as we exited the 1960s and progressed through the 1970s and 1980s that the respective cultures, dignities, and rights of various peoples were not valued or recognized in the operations of societal institutions. These institutions were created by and for those in power, thus, were permeated with policies, practices, and procedures of racism, sexism, and other "isms" along with strategic practices of discrimination. The institutions safeguarded power for society's dominant group to wield; for example, U.S. legal, financial, housing, health care, religious, media, education, and other such institutions continued their flagrant extension of inequities and discriminatory practices.

The Present

For our purpose here, we make the designation of the "present" as consisting of the years from 1990 to 2020. The beginning of this period is marked by the courageous founding of the National Association for Multicultural Education in 1990 and closed by the beginning of 2020, and the frightening and deadly Covid-19 pandemic. In this period multiculturalism has been challenged to broaden its umbrella of coverage of marginalized groups seeking equitable treatment in our global world. Multicultural Education as a process and philosophy (Baptiste, 1989, 1996) has engaged, through its scholars and practitioners, the tackling of social problems faced by constituent groups such as homeless students (Sparks, 2020); LGBTQIA groups (Human Rights Campaign, 2017); people of varying physical, intellectual, and emotional ability statuses (Purlang, n.d.); immigrant populations; and sovereign nation and Indigenous Peoples. Multicultural Education continues to advocate for women's rights,[3] equitable processes and rulings within the legal system, opportunities to learn, maintain, or use one's heritage language, in addition to continuing to battle the oppressive nature of the constricting and marginalizing structures of U.S. social institutions. The ingrained oppressive nature of these institutions, established, protected or led by pernicious powerful leaders, has caused members of these oppressed groups, individually or collectively, to seek redress of these wrongs. As the discipline has matured, Multicultural Education (Multiculturalism) has manifested itself as a global concept, as demonstrated by members of underrepresented, deprived, and oppressed groups seeking redress of their human rights through petitions to governmental entities or United Nations committees, various civil demonstrations, and demands for educational access, quality, and input on educational decision-making processes.

The Future

There are several questions that scholars and practitioners must be willing to entertain for the vitality and continuation of Multicultural Education:

1. Is the concept of Multicultural Education robust enough to face social challenges of the future?
2. Will inclusiveness and equity continue to be fundamental principles of Multicultural Education?
3. Will the political nature of Multicultural Education continue into the future providing a basis for those marginalized groups to access and acquire power?

4. Will various constituent groups be willing and able to accept the incommensurability[4] of differing groups' interests and goals and still stand as allies?

It is our belief that the future will witness a resurgence in Multicultural Education. Cultural communities and sovereign nations that have been marginalized and dehumanized by collectives of political privilege and influence, governments, and governmental entities will seek political power to rectify inequities and meet basic needs. Inclusiveness and equity are ascertained through leveraging political power. Political power is strongly correlated with group power. While we recognize that projects of change are underway, our present social, economic, and environmental climate calls for more. Powerless groups, or "power denied" groups, regardless where located, will begin to unite the members of their respective communities and move toward forming coalitions with other powerless groups to assemble formidable power bases. It is a process that requires continuous commitment, momentum, and coalescing to make headway toward change. Powerless cultural groups must develop a political power base. Because the groups' members lack wealth and land ownership, the usual sources for power, it is essential for these powerless groups to realize that another source of power is their people in a unified front (Sizemore, 1969).

Authored by renowned multicultural scholars, the book consists of nine chapters, divided into two sections. The authors have developed their chapters to focus on the past, present, and future aspects of Multicultural Education, or the issues Multicultural Education is tasked with addressing into the future. The chapters fall into two themed sections: Historical Continuity and Movement Toward Change, and Limits and Transformation. Each of the authors has developed his/her/their chapter from a multicultural perspective, knowledge base or professional expertise to impart a discussion of the past and present. Looking forward, each vision the trajectory of Multicultural Education in years to come in terms of the field at large, the issues or approaches Multicultural Education must take on, or one's personal professional development as a multicultural educator. We encourage others to join us in the process and work of *Visioning Multicultural Education: Past, Present, Future.* We ask that we each not only vision, but bring to fruition a strengthened, refined, yet malleable Multicultural Education future.

Notes

1 See the Smithsonian, National Museum of the American Indian's (2018) *Native Knowledge 360°* website for lesson planning on Native American topics (https://americanindian.si.edu/nk360/). The lesson, "Treaties Still Matter: The Dakota Access Pipeline," assists students and educators to become informed and think critically about the issues surrounding the Dakota Access Pipeline, its impact on the Standing Rock Sioux Tribe, and the Fort Laramie Treaty. This lesson can be accessed at https://americanindian.si.edu/nk360/plains-treaties/dapl

2 As an example of the struggles Native Peoples continue to experience, one can examine the case of the Mashpee Wampanoag, in what is now the state of Massachusetts. The People were declared no longer "Indian" by the U.S. Department of the Interior (Bennett-Begay, 2018). Recently, the U.S. Department of the Interior took the step to take the People's land out of trust because they were not "recognized" as an "Indian tribe" by the U.S. when the Indian Reorganization Act was enacted in 1934 (Lusamba, 2020). Further examples of Native Peoples' battles for legal justice in the U.S. are clearly presented in Walter R. Echo-Hawk's (2010) book, *In the courts of the conqueror: The 10 worst Indian law cases ever decided.*

3 To learn about current issues affecting women and activities to end oppression and move toward equity, see the American Civil Liberties Union (ACLU) and the National Organization for Women (NOW) websites at www.aclu.org/issues/womens-rights and https://now.org/issues, respectively.

4 Tuck and Yang (2018) explain the "ethic of incommensurability" as being "an alternate mode of holding and imagining solidarity" (p. 2). Understanding that we should not expect that all constituent groups have the same interests and goals, "an ethic of incommensurability acknowledges that we can collaborate for a time together even while anticipating that our pathways toward enacting liberation will diverge" (p. 2). The scholars explain that "we can come to understand the gap between our viewpoints" (Tuck & Yang, 2018, p. 2), yet still demonstrate unity.

References

Banks, J. A. (2003). *Teaching strategies for ethnic studies* (7th ed.). Boston, MA: Allyn & Bacon.

Baptiste, H. P. (1989). *Multicultural education and urban schools from a sociohistorical perspective: Internalizing multiculturalism.* In J. L. Burdin (Ed.), *School leadership: A contemporary reader* (pp. 187–203). London: Sage Publications.

Baptiste, H. P. (1996). Internalizing multiculturalism: A typology for the learning environment. In J. B. Boyer & H. P. Baptiste (Eds.), *Transforming the curriculum for multicultural understandings: A practitioner handbook* (pp. 97–127). San Francisco, CA: Caddo Gap Press.

Baptiste, H. P., Kamenski, H. O., & Kamenski, C. J. (2007). Examining presidents Thomas Jefferson, Abraham Lincoln, and Lyndon B. Johnson. In H. P. Baptiste (Ed.), *The U.S. presidency and social justice: Implications for public education* (pp. 93–128). San Francisco, CA: Caddo Gap Press.

Barber, B. R. (1992). *An aristocracy of everyone: The politics of education and the future of America.* New York, NY: Random House.

Bennett-Begaye, J. (2018, September 19). Interior denies Mashpee trust land: 'You do not meet definition of an Indian.' *Indian Country Today.* Retrieved from https://indiancountrytoday.com/news/interior-denies-mashpee-trust-land-you-do-not-meet-definition-of-an-indian-3qLsXhzf2kyptA5oxX4VpA

Brown v. Board of Education of Topeka, 347 U.S. 483 (United States Supreme Court 1954).

Goodman, J. C. (2019, September 5). How to help the poor without subsidizing the rich. *Forbes.* Retrieved from www.forbes.com/sites/johngoodman/2019/09/05/how-to-help-the-poor-without-subsidizing-the-rich/#33ab06f560de

Human Rights Campaign (2017). Trump's administrative abuse and the LGBTQ community. Retrieved from www.hrc.org/resources/trumps-administrative-abuse-and-the-lgbtq-community

Lusamba, J. (2020, March 30). US Secretary of Interior orders removal of the Mashpee Wampanoag Tribe's land from federal trust. *Jurist*. Retrieved from www.jurist.org/news/2020/03/us-secretary-of-interior-orders-removal-of-the-mashpee-wampanoag-tribes-land-from-federal-trust/

Meyer, R. (2016, September 9). The legal case for blocking the Dakota Access Pipeline: Did the U.S. government help destroy a major Sioux archeological site? *The Atlantic*. Retrieved from www.theatlantic.com/technology/archive/2016/09/dapl-dakota-sitting-rock-sioux/499178/

Orfield, G., & Harvard Project on School Desegregation (1996). *Dismantling desegregation: The quiet reversal of Brown v. Board of Education*. New York, NY: W. W. Norton.

Plessy v. Ferguson, 163 U.S. 537 (United States Supreme Court 1896).

Purlang, A. (n.d.). Top 5 disability issues. Center for Disability Rights. Retrieved from http://cdrnys.org/blog/disability-politics/top-5-disability-issues/

Sizemore, B. (1969). Separation: A reality approach to inclusion? In R. L. Green (Ed.), *Racial crisis in American education* (pp. 249–279). Chicago, IL: Follett Company.

Smith, G. P. (2004). Desegregation and resegregation after Brown: Implications for multicultural teacher education. *Multicultural Perspectives* 6(4), 26–32.

Sparks, S. D. (2020, February 10). Number of homeless students hits all-time high: Influx poses challenges for schools. *Education Week*. Retrieved from www.edweek.org/ew/articles/2020/02/12/number-of-homeless-students-hits-all-time-high.html

Tatum, B. (2017). *"Why are all the black kids sitting together in the cafeteria?" And other conversations about race* (20th anniversary ed.). New York, NY: Basic Books.

Tuck, E., & Yang, K. W. (2018). *Toward what justice? Describing diverse dreams of justice in education*. New York, NY: Routledge.

SECTION I

Historical Continuity and Movement Toward Change

The five chapters of this section are interrelated in how they uniquely use historical perspectives to inform us. The contributors' writings in these chapters reflect a passion for a movement toward a positive change.

Geneva Gay's chapter, "The Reaffirmation of Multicultural Education," takes us on an exciting journey from the genesis of Multicultural Education to what could be its future accomplishments. Along the way, she suggests two major areas of reaffirmation: (1) that more attention must be given to educational thoughts and practices that are precedents for Multicultural Education; and (2) continuity and change both serve as a natural complement to Multicultural Education precedents. Gay tells us that the vitality and viability of Multicultural Education rests on nuanced refinements of the established precedents, while at the same time balancing the pressures of educational and societal changes.

In Patricia Marshall's chapter, "The Continuing Multicultural Education of a Black Teacher Educator: Reflections on a Journey Toward My Referent Other-Self," this dedicated, driven learner explores and shares the self-knowledge insights gained when she made a long-term commitment to study a second language. Unexpectedly, her journey to bilingualism challenged her to examine and critique the substructure over which her own longstanding sense of cross-culture competence had been erected.

In "Challenging Racism and Colonialism through Ethnic Studies," Christine Sleeter demonstrates how ethnic studies in U.S. schools attempts to combat the historical amnesia schooling perpetuates regarding colonialism and racism. She reviews processes that dilute how many people understand Multicultural Education, and how that diluted understanding is reflected in white dominant curricula. The chapter provides two examples of how ethnic studies praxis has positively impacted students.

Carl Grant's creatively written chapter, "Imagining: 'A Letter on Racial Progress'—James Baldwin's Keynote at the 30th Annual NAME Conference—Evolution of Multicultural Education: 21st Century," carries us on an imaginary trip with the iconic James Baldwin as the keynote speaker at NAME's thirtieth anniversary conference in Montgomery, Alabama. Readers become audience members, and envision Baldwin describing the history of racial progress in America, as told through his observations of W. E. B. Du Bois and Martin L. King. Baldwin's speech imparts important knowledge about the past, signaling there is still much work to be done.

In "Truth, Land, and Sovereignty: Native American Intellectual Activists, Their Critique of Settler Colonialism, and the Unsettling of Multicultural Education," Jeanette Haynes Writer and Kristen French bring to our attention Gertrude Simmons Bonnin, Charles Eastman, and Luther Standing Bear, three Native intellectual activists of the early twentieth century, and urge us to include them as Multicultural Education antecedents and foundational scholars. Biographical sketches of the three intellectual activists concisely capture their educational and life experiences to explore the harmful nature of settler colonialism. To bring forward Indigenous futurities, the authors make recommendations for Multicultural Education based on the words and work of the intellectual activists.

1

THE REAFFIRMATION OF MULTICULTURAL EDUCATION

Geneva Gay

Introduction

The genesis of present-day Multicultural Education long preceded its origins in the mid-twentieth-century Civil Rights Movements. Like recurrent efforts in the broader society by various marginalized groups to eliminate economic, residential, and political inequities and powerlessness, Multicultural Education was (and is) similarly intended, but specifically targets teaching and learning. In effect, it is a pedagogical civil rights initiative of and for different ethnic, racial, social, and cultural groups within specified nation states. In this way the beginnings of Multicultural Education were a continuation of historical equality efforts among disenfranchised populations, and to advance U.S. democratic ideals within the educational enterprise. It challenges educational systems to fulfill the promises of rights and opportunities embedded in canonical claims that U.S. society and culture are synergies of diversity.

In reaffirming Multicultural Education more explicit attention should be given to its historical foundations. They are deeply ingrained in the "origin story" of the United States. Contrary to tendencies that limit analyses of its demographic imperative primarily to the mid-twentieth and twenty-first centuries this is too myopic. This short-sighted vision overlooks some important information that should be included in shaping Multicultural Education for the future. In fact, ethnic, racial, and cultural diversity (the bedrocks) of Multicultural Education have been prominent in the construction of the United States from its very beginnings (if not before). It has been both productive and problematic (Barber, 1992; Geraghty, 2018; Sowell 1981).

In explaining the continuing presence and power of this plurality in shaping the "American experiment," Geraghty (2018) said, "Americans who are not 'white' … have had an integral role in the country's victories, breakthroughs, turning points, innovations, and triumphs of history (and indeed, some of its mistakes, failures, and uglier moments, too) …" (n.p.). Sowell (1981) added that "The mixture of unity and diversity runs through American history as through American society today. No ethnic group has been wholly unique, yet no two are completely alike" (p. 4).

Reclaiming these historical legacies and understanding the persistence (and sometimes problems, too) of ethnic, racial, and cultural diversity in the U.S. should be much more prominent in future Multicultural Education policies, programs, and practices. So, Multicultural Education is like another chapter in this long history of how to engage diversity most effectively. Such an acknowledgement does not diminish its necessity and significance; it just means that by understanding its historical legacies, contemporary and future efforts can make more worthy contributions to realizing its intentions and potentials.

Multicultural Education initially began in the United States, and targeted formal pre-collegiate education for racial minority groups. In the intervening years its boundaries have broadened to include other identity groups, locations, forms of oppressions, levels of education, and other sites of human engagement. Now Multicultural Education (or some derivatives or facsimiles of it) is being promoted in other countries throughout the world, and in other industries such as health care, social work, religion, media, entertainment, and higher education. This growth itself is a form of reaffirmation.

Like other "civil rights" goals and initiatives that have not been fully accomplished yet, this is also true of Multicultural Education. This alone is reason enough for its reaffirmation, but not necessarily its historical replication. As Gay (2018) explained,

> Students … from ethnic, racial, cultural, and socioeconomic backgrounds different from the dominant Eurocentric, middle class group still are not receiving proportional, equitable, high-quality educational opportunities and performance outcomes. U.S. society continues to be plagued by resource inequities, and human indignities toward diverse populations and communities. Racism, homophobia, classism, and other forms of inequity and oppression are still rampant.… Attending to ethnic, racial, and cultural differences in schools and society too often involves little more than some cosmetic tinkering, rather than any substantive and significant changes. The traditional status quo and historical centers of power and privilege have not been significantly transformed.
>
> *p. xxix*

Given these realities if Multicultural Education were not reaffirmed this would be an atrocity for the equity, justice, and human dignity of marginalized ethnically, racially, culturally, and socially diverse students within educational contexts.

Explicating Precedents

Different groups denied their human rights to fairness, representation, justice, and access to quality education directly pertinent to their particularized needs have always resisted associated oppression, exploitation, and exclusion, and have done so in many ways and on many different platforms. Often these efforts have been constituent-specific, in that the leading actors and activities used their primary referent group orientations to give functional or operational meaning to conceptual ideals. Thus, invariably early African American activists referenced their own ethnic group in articulating their advocacy for educational relevance, inclusion, and equality. Mexican Americans did likewise for Mexican Americans, and so did Native Americans for Native Americans, and Asian Americans for Asian Americans. Middle-class Whites crafted educational systems and agendas for middle-class White youth.

As the parameters of Multicultural Education expanded to include other forms of oppression and "minoritization" (such as gender and alternative sexual orientations) their primary advocates were members of these groups, or had a personal affinity towards them. This "self-referencing" in Multicultural Education ideology and actions has become more eclectic over time, but without sacrificing specific group needs and orientations; nor should it. Ethnic, racial, gender, social, and cultural group self-referencing should not be perceived as negative or exclusive. Rather, it should be considered as a normative point of departure in imagining educational transformations, and should continue to be evident in future iterations of Multicultural Education. After all, other education theorists, practitioners, and reformers are often motivated by and speak from the standpoints of strong identity affinities (real, vicarious, or symbolic).

Multicultural Education did not emerge out of osmosis in the early 1970s. Precedents for it existed across time and various constituencies, but their connections to the Multicultural Education we knew then and now are not as explicit as they should be. Making these more so in future iterations will enhance its credibility. Connecting Multicultural Education to historical precedents and concurrent ones in education and other disciplines also will contribute significantly to dispelling assumptions of some that this is a fad or short-term diversion that will not prevail in the long run, or can be accomplished instantaneously.

The fallacy of these assumptions should be clearly dispelled in the reaffirmation of Multicultural Education. The contributing authors to *Becoming Multicultural Educators* (Gay, 2003) may be helpful in this undertaking. The personal stories of these authors, individually and collectively, present compelling explanations and examples of why becoming and being multicultural educators is a *continuing developmental process*. While this may be obvious for those experienced in the field, it seems to escape the attention of many novices. The haste to act without adequate prior preparation and to expect immediate "universal" success may indeed compromise the integrity of what Multicultural Education is all about, as well as discourage potential advocates from persisting. Although the needs that Multicultural Education addresses are urgent, too much haste in action could be more problematic than promising. This creates a dilemma that has to be dealt with even if (or when) resolutions are not readily apparent and easily achievable. Hence, reaffirmations need to be unequivocal and crystal clear about the practical realities related to continually building applied multicultural competencies and capacities.

Undoubtedly, parents and communities of various racial and ethnic ancestries routinely teach their children their own cultural heritages, community rules, and regulations, and life skills beyond the boundaries of formal schooling. In addition to being a normal human process, sometimes these teachings were necessary because of limited access to formal educational systems. Other times they were formalized as alternative school structures because different ethnic communities wanted to ensure their cultural survival and address their special needs as they adapted to different living environments in the U.S. The results were the cultivation and perpetuation of "socio-cultural funds of knowledge" similar to those observed by Gonzalez, Moll, and Amanti (2005) in the homes and communities of Mexican Americans. And, of course, African, Asian, and Native American families and communities also informally taught their children their cultural heritages and how to navigate marginality in mainstream U.S. society before and during their entry into formal education systems. These ethnically diverse informal educational strategies may be challenging for formal educators to access, but this difficulty does not invalidate their significance. Powerful lessons may be learned from them that can enrich and complement Multicultural Education efforts. But we will not recognize, or know how to benefit from these alternative ethnic educational legacies if we continue to largely ignore them.

Nor did early generations of multicultural educators come to their advocacies with blank scholarly and experiential slates. Prior ideologies, experiences, and actions probably influenced their thoughts and proposals for educating underserved student populations on some level, even if these precedents were not specifically named or deliberately evoked. Just because these individual, institutional, and ideological predecessors did not use the nomenclature (i.e., "multicultural education") does not mean that the influence was not conveyed through their analyses of the need for a better-quality education and life for individuals and communities pushed to the margins of U.S. mainstream society, and how this might be accomplished. Other times these connections came through advocates' memories of their own less than culturally validating school days, and a desire to prevent similar experiences from being foisted upon another generation of "marginalized" students. Some more formal precedents existed in the reasoning of scholars of color in other disciplines, such as literature, psychology, sociology, philosophy, politics, and the arts.

One example of anti-oppression and educational equality of various marginalized populations that predated the actual beginnings of Multicultural Education is alternative ethnic schools. As different immigrant constituents arrived in the U.S., invariably, they grappled with educating their particular members when the prevailing systems failed to do so adequately. It was not uncommon for them to create compensational initiatives. Sometimes separate institutions (such as ethnically specific language and cultural schools established by and in different immigrant communities, street-front academies, ethnic-heritage colleges and universities, gender-specific schools and colleges, political activism training camps, etc.) were created. Other times these efforts were formulated as alternative pedagogical ideologies (such as different variations of ethni-centricism—Afro-, Latino-, Chino-, Indigenous-). Even segregated schools often crafted educational practices to meet the social, cultural, emotional, and academic needs of their constituencies, despite operating under extreme resource limitations and harsh racist policies (Jones-Wilson, 1981; Siddle Walker, 1996).

But whatever the form these efforts took, different ethnic groups have repeatedly raised issues of educational inequities and sociopolitical injustices across time, and advocated for their resolution. These legacies are not as visible in Multicultural Education thought and action as they should be, or at least the lessons learned from them, so that they become foundations for building forward instead of engaging in uninformed repetition. For example, in a study entitled "After-school institutions in immigrant Chinese and Korean communities: A model for others?" Zhou and Kim (2007, n.p.) noted that

> Chinese-language schools have been an integral part of the Chinese immigrant community in the United States, and in the Chinese diaspora worldwide.... Today, ... [t]he majority aim not only to maintain language and culture, but also to serve the educational needs of immigrant children.

Many of the most powerful and compelling of these historical critiques and transformative possibilities for educating ethnically, racially, culturally, and socially diverse students have been offered by scholars of color. A few graphic examples of these from the African American experience were provided by Carter G. Woodson's (1933) *The Mis-education of the Negro*; Ralph Ellison's (1952) *Invisible Man*; James Baldwin's (1963) "A Talk to Teachers"; Mary McLeod Bethune's (1955) "My Last Will and Testament"; W. E. B. Du Bois' (1940) *Dusk to Dawn*; Lerone Bennett, Jr's (1975) *The Shaping of Black America*; and Molefi Asante's (1988) *Afrocentricity: The Theory of Social Change.*

Similar "insider perspectives" on educational, social, and political problems and corrective possibilities for Asian, Native, and Latinx Americans also predated the beginnings of Multicultural Education so named; others occurred concurrently. Among these from Asian Americans' perspectives are Young Pai's (2001) *Cultural Foundations of Education*; Ronald Takaki's *A Different Mirror: A History of Multicultural America* (1993) and *Strangers from a Different Shore: A History of Asian Americans* (1989); Stephanie Cham's (2018) *Patsy Mink*; and Erika Lee's (2015) *The Making of Asian America: A History*; and from Latino Americans, Rodolfo "Corky"

Gonzales' (1967) epic poem "I am Joaquin [Yo Soy Joaquin]"; Rodolfo Acuna's (1972) *Occupied America: The Chicano's Struggle Toward Liberation*; Rudolfo Anaya's (1972) *Bless Me, Ultima*; and Piri Thomas' (1967) *Down These Mean Streets.* Prior and concurrent arguments and ideas about equity and empowerment for marginalized groups similar to those underlying Multicultural Education are presented by Native Americans' writings as well. Among them are Vine Deloria, Jr.'s (1969) *Custer Died for Your Sins: An Indian Manifesto*; Vine Deloria, Jr. and Clifford Lytle's (1983) *American Indians, American Justice*; Sarah Janda's (2007) *Beloved Women: The Political Lives of LaDonna Harris and Wilma Mankiller*; and Dee Brown's (1971) *Bury My Heart at Wounded Knee.*

European Americans also have made contributions that are significant precedents for Multicultural Education. Sociological, historical, and political analyses of ethnic, racial, and cultural diversity in the U.S. over time, and how the country has responded to it, are especially beneficial for informing future versions of Multicultural Education. They provide compelling evidence about the reality of ethnic and cultural diversity throughout the country's history, and the rightness of it being honored and perpetuated within and through educational policies, programs, and practices. While these precedents may not affirm Multicultural Education per se, they do confirm the historical legitimacy of some of its major foundations. Resources particularly helpful in supporting these claims, and from the perspective of majority group (European American White) scholars, are James Loewen's (1995) *Lies My Teacher Told Me: Everything Your American History Textbooks Got Wrong*; Jim Geraghty's (2018) "America Was Always Diverse"; Howard Zinn's (1980) *A People's History of the United States*; Jack Eller's (2015) *Cultural and Diversity: So Many Ways to Be American;* Susan Mizruchi's (2008) *The Rise of Multicultural America: Economy and Print Culture, 1865–1915*; and Gary Gerstle's (2015) *American Crucible: Race and Nation in the Twentieth Century.*

First- and second-generation multicultural educators also were influenced by concurrent political thought and action. Many of them were coming of age chronologically, intellectually, culturally, and politically during the 1960s and early 1970s during large-scale civil rights activism. After all they were surrounded by and/or immersed (literally or vicariously) in these activities. It was natural for their political experiences to influence their educational ideas and actions given the prevailing emphases on liberation and empowerment of oppressed and marginalized groups. Consequently, their action platforms became liberating students from psychological and intellectual captivity.

There are hints of these connections in the existing body of Multicultural Education scholarship but much more explication is needed. Including specific and detailed accounts of some of these "rites of passage" and how they shaped educational thoughts and proposals for action will enhance the credibility and feasibility of future Multicultural Education efforts. For example, including some of these personal stories may provide valuable insights for novice multicultural educators who often ask their seniors questions like, "What compels you to continue your involvement in and advocacy for Multicultural Education, and how do you do so in the face of persistent resistance?"

These "kindred" scholars and educators most often did not explicate specific pedagogical strategies. But their philosophical beliefs and sociocultural analyses of pervasive inequities suffered by their referent groups of concern are highly compatible with the fundamental claims and catalytic motivations of Multicultural Education. These should be intentionally explicated in future iterations of Multicultural Education. A graphic case in point is Carter G. Woodson's reasoning for why a radical shift was needed in educating African American youth academically, culturally, ethically, racially, economically, and politically. In his 1933 introduction to *The Mis-education of the Negro* Woodson argued cogently that

> every individual of the social order should be given unlimited opportunity to make the most of himself. Such opportunity, too, should not be determined from without by forces set to direct the proscribed element in a way to redound solely to the good of others but should be determined by the make-up of the Negro himself and by what his environment requires of him.
>
> This new program of uplift ... should not be decided upon by the trial and error method in the application of devices used in dealing with others in a different situation and at a different epoch. Only by careful study of the Negro himself and the life which he is forced to lead can we arrive at the proper procedure in this crisis.... Herein, however, lies no argument for the oft-heard contention that education for the white man should mean one thing and for the Negro a different thing.... [I]t is merely a matter of exercising common sense in approaching people through their environment in order to deal with conditions as they are rather than as you would like to see them or imagine that they are. There may be a difference in method of attack, but the principle remains the same....
>
> *pp. ix–xii*

This powerful statement reverberates across time and groups in trying to meet the challenges of educating diverse marginalized students. But for some periodic language usage Woodson could be talking about Multicultural Education concerns of today. Among these are multidimensional negative consequences of educational programs and practices that ignore or denigrate the sociocultural funds of knowledge, identities, heritages, and experiences of ethnically and racially diverse students of color; engaging in mind manipulation; promulgating stereotype threats; perpetuating epistemological racism; and attempting to separate racial minority students from their existential contexts as a precursor to teaching them. Woodson makes it clear how damaging and ludicrous such attempts are. His capstone statement to the effect that general educational principles should prevail across time, circumstances, and consumers, but teaching methodologies should be specific to and for diverse students, is the essence of contemporary Multicultural Education!

The current focus among educators on the psychosocial and emotional wellness of students, coping with trauma, and developing competencies in these areas is fortuitous for reaffirming Multicultural Education. Conceptually and theoretically Multicultural Education has always been more inclusive than academic achievement. It recognizes that learning is affected profoundly by psychological, social, and cultural variables. But, these often are not employed consistently and correctly in practice. To some educators these connections are obvious, but to others they are obscure. Brackett and Simmons (2015) provide some compelling explanations for dealing directly with emotions in teaching and learning. Although they do not mention students of color specifically, logic suggests that these influences are probably even more compelling for marginalized, underprivileged, and underachieving students. They explained that "Emotions can either enhance or derail classroom performance. Interest and amusement, for example, harness attention and promote greater engagement. Boredom, anxiety, and fear disrupt concentration and interfere with the ability to learn" (Brackett & Simmons, 2015, p. 24). Beyond being successful learners, students of color need to be healthy (holistically!) human beings. Thus, cultivating these needs and related skills more intentionally is another invitation and challenge for the reaffirmation of Multicultural Education.

Continuity and Change

The reaffirmation of Multicultural Education also needs to attend to both continuity and change. Every educational paradigm needs to have both foundational stability and developmental fluidity to preserve its vitality and credibility. In other words, as the ecological settings in which it exists change so must Multicultural Education. Yet, the changes need to renew rather than replace its ideological values and beliefs if it is to maintain its disciplinary integrity. Carter G. Woodson's comments about general principles of educational quality prevailing across constituencies, times, and circumstances while implementation practices being specific to these contexts are apropos here.

Problems occur in actualizing this advice when developmental, occupational, and generational gaps exist between theorists and practitioners. Different demands on their professional time also can be problematic in maintaining contextual cohesion and coherence in Multicultural Education. Theorists seem to have more time to revise and refine ideological conceptualizations while practitioners often have to accommodate immediate political and experiential exigencies. They may excerpt some aspects of the ideological foundations of Multicultural Education rather than attending to the composite. For example, practitioners may see demands of standardized testing as taking time and effort away from doing Multicultural Education. Conversely, theorists (and conceptualizers) may consider these as revealing or creating more gaps in educational outcomes for many students of color, and therefore reinforcing the need for more, not less, Multicultural Education. Both sides of this dilemma have some validity, and the tension between them is significant support for the reaffirmation of Multicultural Education for and within shifting contextual realities.

Another area of change that demands the reaffirmation of Multicultural Education is shifting targeted audiences. It is not sufficient to simply claim that Multicultural Education is good for all students. Statements like this are too vague to be of much value for educators responsible for implementation. Rather, future Multicultural Education thoughts and actions need to elaborate how it is nuanced somewhat differently for various settings and circumstances. For example, current scholarship is not as informative as it needs to be about how Multicultural Education is configured for different constituent groups and learning environments, such as in school settings comprised mostly of diverse multiethnic students of color; or few students of color in schools populated by mostly majority students; or single race informal daycare centers or dominant ethnic heritage colleges compared to predominantly White ones.

Undoubtedly, various racial, gender, and socioeconomic groups experience prejudices and discrimination, but the actualization of these has some aspects that are unique to particular groups. Simply put, sexism and racism are not identical. Nor is xenophobia toward immigrants from different countries the same; nor is sexism directed toward females from various ethnic, racial, and cultural groups. This variability demands diversity in establishing its validity, and maximizing its effectiveness in practice. As Multicultural Education continues to grow its broad-based claims and commitments, more specificity is needed about how they are manifested among various constituent groups. These kinds of details are needed to better facilitate translating Multicultural Education ideas into actions, and to prevent ideological distortions and inaccuracies from occurring.

Other areas of specificity are needed, too, such as when, where, and how to teach content about different ethnic, racial, and cultural issues and experiences. Current suggestions tend to be highly compatible with key conceptual principles of quality education and democratic values, but not as much so for the practical realities of different levels of education and areas of study and teaching. For example, there is a high level of agreement in scholarship that teachers in all levels of the educational enterprise need to make their content and instructional styles more relevant to students from different ethnic groups. But, what does this mean pragmatically for college engineering teachers, or teaching reading readiness to kindergartners, or high school science teachers? What does this look like in actual practice for immigrant Latinx students and those who are long-time citizens; or Vietnamese American students; or African American students; or students of various Indigenous groups; or 1.5 generation immigrant students from different cultural, linguistic, national, and experiential backgrounds; or White students attending schools in economically privileged communities; or different ethnic students in diverse rural settings? Nor is adequate attention given to students of color who are *not academically* at risk, but may have identity, self-acceptance, and inclusion challenges regardless of their learning locations.

Some scholars do analyze minority students living in, learning in, and navigating these institutional environments, but these issues have not gained the prominence in Multicultural Education that they deserve. When they are addressed, the priority attention invariably is on academic achievement. There is no question about the importance of this but there are other areas of personal growth and development that merit attention on their own, such as psychological health, cultural and linguistic maintenance, coping with marginality, and navigating multiple cultural and personal identities.

A related change currently occurring in practice that needs much more explication in future iterations is the increasing "globalization" of Multicultural Education. Gay (2018) explains some of its dimensions in relation to cultural responsiveness, a derivative of Multicultural Education. The field is growing geographically and conceptually, both internally and externally, but not as well as it might for different locations of practice. It is no longer only a pedagogical enterprise, strictly an educational enterprise, or restricted to the United States. Instead, virtually all aspects of the educational enterprise are recognizing the need for and declaring multicultural implementation efforts; other professions are embracing the idea and attempting to act in accordance, and other countries are developing variations of Multicultural Education, but too often attempting to follow United States examples in thought if not action. While this is encouraging, it is also problematic because the efforts may not be as conceptually accurate as they should be.

It is not clear whether these other "domains of interest" are reading Multicultural Education scholarship as produced by long-term leading "origin" scholars in the field as carefully and deeply as they need to. They may be operating on 'fictionalized" and abbreviated rather than authentic and comprehensive meanings of Multicultural Education. These distortions may result more from "crossing epistemological borders" than intentionality but the results are the same—the efforts may not be genuine, and could have detrimental effects on sincere Multicultural Education advocacy efforts. In the reaffirmation of Multicultural Education the problems and potentialities of this "growth dilemma" need to be addressed. To do so most effectively may require some cross-disciplinary and cross-national collaboration and contextualization.

Future multicultural educators also need to be much more aggressive about demanding disciplinary integrity. This does not mean expecting everybody within the discipline to speak in a uniform voice. This is not possible; yet there are some "conceptual standards or disciplinary truths" that should be reaffirmed. The simple fact is Multicultural Education cannot be everything for everyone; it is not a catch-all or a panacea for every conceivable form of educational inequity and irrelevance. If it is imagined so, it will lose its disciplinary integrity and vitality. Yet, the field is expanding, and rightfully so since the growth of ideas and organisms is necessary for their perpetuity. Nor is Multicultural Education a stop-gap or temporary interlude. As long as students continue to be (and increasingly are) ethnically, racially, and culturally diverse, Multicultural Education is here to stay. It is the "new education norm." There is an undercurrent in some school practice-based discourse that Multicultural Education is something that will be completed at some point in time, and then educational systems can move on to something else. In fact, multiculturalism is inherent in the origins and evolution of the United States, and is likely to be inseparable from its continuing development. Throughout time it has been both problematic and generative (and probably will continue to be) (Barber, 1992; Geraghty, 2018).

In the reaffirmation of Multicultural Education the fantasy that it is a new and temporary fad needs to be dispelled deliberately and aggressively. This can be done by revealing the long historical reach and normalcy of its foundational source (dealing with the ethnic, racial, and cultural diversity within *national* boundaries). Also, how and why Multicultural Education is highly congruent with the nature of the human condition, and the mission of educating "the public," which is demographically, experientially, and socially diverse. As societal and broader educational settings and circumstances shift, so must how Multicultural Education is nuanced. At first glance this statement may appear to be contradictory, but it really is not.

These complementary (although seemingly contradictory) dimensions need to be explained more clearly and extensively. Without such explanations these perspectives could compromise the potential strength, and invite some educators to resolve the apparent dilemmas by seeking "practice-based common denominations" or "best Multicultural Education practices" for everyone. To do so would contradict its fundamental purpose of placing *specific* ethnically, racially, culturally, and socially diverse issues and experiences in the center of educational endeavors. In fact, the best quality education for the greater number of students is not possible in the absence of these diversities.

Another element of the continuity–change spectrum that deserves attention in the reaffirmation of Multicultural Education is some different discussions about privilege, power, and powerlessness; oppression; racial and ethnic prejudices, discrimination, and racism. These are persistent concerns and they are already prominent in Multicultural Education discourse, but there are some dimensions of them that are only alluded to, rather than explicated in detail. Most explicit examinations of these now occur from a unidirectional, vertical perspective. That is, the "majority–minority" spectrum in which minority populations (groups of color) are victimized and marginalized by the power, privilege, and prejudices of members of the majority population. While many of these groups are "minorities" in their diaspora locations, they often are members of "the majority" in their ancestral countries of origin. For instance, Somalis in the U.S. and in Somalia; or Jamaican Americans in the U.S. and in Jamaica; Mexican ancestry individuals in the U.S. and in Mexico; and Han Chinese in the U.S. and in China. There are passing references to minority groups' prejudices and discriminations toward majority Eurocentric Whites and toward other minority groups within the U.S., but typically these are not elaborated. These are oversights that should be explained in detail in future versions of Multicultural Education.

Undoubtedly, some members of different ethnic minority groups have prejudicial attitudes and behaviors toward majority populations in different countries engaged in some form or another of Multicultural Education. The same is probably true about different minority group members' perceptions of other minority groups. These attitudes and behaviors need to be admitted and explained without equivocation if the struggle against human indignities, oppressions, and exploitations is to be effectively implemented. It is not enough to indict mainstream institutions for perpetuating these atrocities because individuals create and facilitate institutions. At the point of action, general claims limit corrective effects; conversely, specificity cultivates more tangible results. Therefore, it is important for more attention to be given to both *specific* problematic and productive minority–minority relationships as manifested by individuals, institutions, and groups. Current Multicultural Education discourse concedes this importance generally, but *specific* actual details about who, what, when, why, and how are still too sketchy.

This is becoming increasingly more important as "minority" populations in the United States and other countries around the world are increasing demographically, are more mobile, and their presence and influence are more evident. For example, in the last decade Asian ancestry individuals in the U.S. had the largest percentage increase of all ethnic groups. China now readily admits to having 55 different minority groups, many of whom are beginning to demand recognition, inclusion, and representation. Indigenous populations in Canada, the U.S., Australia, and New Zealand are pursuing more constructive and collaborative relationships with each other, along with coalesced equity demands from the majority populations in their respective countries. Some similar issues are apparent among different ethnic and racial minorities in large cities throughout the United States who live in close proximity to each other, and whose children attend the same schools. So, as we craft future educational conversations about combatting racism, discrimination, and prejudice, and redistributing educational power and privilege, these minority–minority dynamics, and the upward directions of these from minority toward majority, need to be elaborated. These examinations should not replace continuing analyses of majority-driven inequities and exploitations of minorities. Rather, they should extend the dialogue by recognizing that sometimes minority groups victimize too, even as they are being victimized.

Often conversations about key Multicultural Education concepts like privilege, power/powerlessness, and marginality seem to imply that these conditions are universal and permanent, when, in reality, they are task- or situation-specific and fluid. Thus, contrary to many prevailing assumptions, "the margins" are not always barren, desolate, and perpetually hopeless places and states of existence. Instead, there is much ingenuity and productivity even in the midst of limited material resources. Within their own communities, and by their own cultural standards, many African Americans who are otherwise thought to be marginalized and powerless, are not; in their own contexts they are part of their own mainstream, and possess much appropriate social and cultural capital. When these same individuals leave their "home-bases" and have to operate in "other people's worlds according to other people's standards" they may indeed be powerless and marginalized. Individuals proficient in Spanish, Chinese, Korean, or Navajo are privileged and powerful in their respective linguistic and cultural communities, but may be "at-risk" when they are operating in other language environments such as English-only U.S. schools.

These ideas about individual and cultural competence being contextual or situational are discussed to an extent in current Multicultural Education discourse, but not enough, and usually as contingent to academic achievement (i.e., strength-based, asset- and growth-minded teaching and learning), rather than as worthy competencies in their own right. Therefore, reaffirmations of Multicultural Education should be more diligent about articulating the fluidity and contextuality of skillsets that ethnically diverse students already have and others they need to develop for what purposes. More articulated emphasis needs to be given to the reality that students are complex human beings who need *repertoires* of knowledge and skills that can serve many purposes and places because, simply put, they do not live all their lives all of the time in the same places and in the same ways. In effect, their versatility enhances their humanity. This complexity demands more plurality in recognizing students' current capabilities and in cultivating future ones.

Another connection that needs to be made more explicit by the next generation of multicultural educators is interrelatedness of some canonical educational principles and those of Multicultural Education. These are values and beliefs that are more specific to the education enterprise than more abstract notions (such as democracy, equity, and empowerment). They include beliefs that high-quality educational practices build on students' prior frames of reference; expand their horizons; affirm what they already know before introducing new knowledge; use developmental appropriateness content and methodologies; and maximize individual potential. Generally, educators seem to assume that the intended recipients of these ideas in action are "universal students." What do they actually mean and look like in practice for "real students" who are not replicas of each other? These ideas and values are embedded in Multicultural Education thought and practice. But if educators are hesitant about dealing directly and explicitly with race, class, ethnic, and cultural diversity in their thoughts and actions, and are not accustomed to reading the subtexts (implied meaning) of multicultural scholarship, they may not make these connections. Sometimes even teachers read but don't understand, look but don't see, and listen but don't really hear what others may consider obvious. Future multicultural efforts should make these conceptual, ideological, valuative, and methodological interconnections more explicit rather than assuming they can be inferred or extrapolated.

A related need is explicating how Multicultural Education translates general educational ideas and values into pedagogical actions that include multiple cultural and ethnic perspectives and experiences. Again, these are exercises in continuity and change. An idea to illustrate this is "the migration story" as literal experience and conceptual metaphor. Migration as an education issue is gaining in prominence as more and more people leave their native countries and resettle in others. But, this "migration" also involves some groups in their own countries and cultures. Rural residents in many countries are "migrating" to urban areas; twenty-first-century global migration is occurring in directions and from cultural sources that defy historical precedents; ethnically and racially diverse students are perpetually navigating and crossing cultural borders in their routine educational endeavors. Placing these educational challenges in a framework such as this may make Multicultural Education more palpable for the reluctant, the unconvinced, and even the recalcitrant.

For purposes of this discussion a final change and continuity element in the reaffirmation of Multicultural Education is elaborating its instrumental or utilitarian value. Some of this is already being done, but more is needed. At its essence Multicultural Education is a mechanism for accomplishing other outcomes rather than being an end in itself. On one level this is obvious because it is typically associated with achieving educational equity, social justice, improving the academic achievement of underperforming minority students, and combatting racism and other forms of oppression. Often these goals are justified on the basis of the inherent merits and ethics of Multicultural Education. Less attention is devoted to the *processes* of multicultural teaching and learning as mechanisms for improving the quality of other aspects of the educational enterprise. Its instrumental value at the process level is usually attached to including more content about different ethnic and cultural peoples and experiences in various subjects taught in schools. Certainly this is a continuous need and it should be reaffirmed, but there are other aspects of teaching that should be emphasized as well. These involve explaining how Multicultural Education can contribute to the *processes* of teaching and learning math or science or reading or engineering or social studies or writing or computer science or critical thinking or civic efficacy even in the absence of specific culturally diverse subject-based content.

These explanations may counter claims made by some educators that the subjects and skills they teach are culture-free and therefore they are exempted from having to do Multicultural Education. Of course, there is no such thing; all subjects taught in schools and colleges are culturally influenced. Even if they were not, the teachers and students engaged in the teaching and learning processes do so through ethnic, racial, and cultural filters. So the need for Multicultural Education is unavoidable. If it can be demonstrated that Multicultural Education improves the quality of whatever and whomever one teaches (for both students and teachers) then such claims are further invalidated. However, to be most effective these arguments should explicitly connect Multicultural Education to the performance quality of various specific domains of teaching, learning, and other kinds of human functionality.

Conclusion

The reaffirmation of Multicultural Education is paramount because it is still a work in progress since much of what it hopes to accomplish is still unfinished. This is likely to be a perpetual state of affairs as societal and educational inequities continue to exist and evolve, and the corollary need for Multicultural Education to keep pace with these changes. Even when, or if, it becomes the normative or "regular" way of doing teaching and learning, periodic updates and modifications will still be needed. This is a normal part of keeping any kind of educational innovation vibrant, relevant, and recent. These reaffirmations, as argued earlier, are more likely to be nuance refinements rather than substantive revisions of fundamentals. The challenge will be to keep pace with the rapidity of social, cultural, and demographic changes in the multiplicity of contexts that surround educational enterprises and other domains of human functionality within different societies.

Recently Dena Simmons (2020) identified some equity challenges and invitations that are a clarion call to educators. They resonate with the reaffirmation of Multicultural Education. She said,

> To overcome [a] history of exclusion [and inequality] we must … commit to eradicating not only the racist remnants but also … present manifestations … this means understanding how our identity, power, and privilege play out in our instruction, classroom management, and relationships, and ensuring no harm is done. It means … calling out inequity and racism when we see it—every single time …
>
> *p. 89*

That is, creating schools and classrooms where Multicultural Education is **live in everything all the time**!

References

Acuna, R. (1972). *Occupied America: The Chicano's struggle toward liberation*. San Francisco, CA: Canfield Press.

Anaya, R. (1972). *Bless me, Ultima*. New York, NY: Warner Books.

Asante, M. T. (1988). *Afrocentricity: The theory of social change*. Trenton, NJ: Africa World Press.

Baldwin, J. (1963, December 21). A talk to teachers. *Saturday Review*. Reprinted in *The price of the ticket: Collected non-fiction, 1948–1985* (pp. 1–4). New York, NY: St. Martin's Press.

Bennett, L., Jr. (1975). *The shaping of Black America*. Chicago, IL: Johnson Publishing Company.

Bethune, M. M. (1955). My last will and testament. Retrieved from https://freemaninstitute.com

Brackett, M. A., & Simmons, D. (2015). Emotions matter. *Educational Leadership, 72*(2), 22–27.

Brown, D. A. (1971). *Bury my heart at Wounded Knee*. New York, NY: Holt, Rinehart, & Winston.

Cham, S. (2018). *Patsy Mink*. Mankato, MN: Capstone Press.

Deloria, V., Jr. (1969). *Custer died for your sins: An Indian Manifesto*. New York, NY: Macmillan.

Deloria, V., Jr., & Lytle, C. M. (1983). *American Indians, American justice*. Austin, TX: University of Texas Press.

Du Bois, W. E. B. (2017). *Dusk of dawn*. New York, NY: Routledge. (Original work published 1940.)

Ellison, R. (1952). *Invisible man*. New York, NY: Random House.

Gay, G. (Ed.) (2003). *Becoming multicultural educators: Personal journey toward professional agency*. San Francisco, CA: Jossey-Bass.

Gay, G. (2018). *Culturally responsive teaching: Theory, research, and practice* (3rd ed.). New York, NY: Teachers College Press.

Geraghty, J. (2018, December 14). America was always diverse. Retrieved from www.nationalreview.com

Gerstle, G. (2015). *American crucible: Race and nation in the twentieth century*. Princeton, NJ: Princeton University Press.

Gonzalez, N., Moll, L. C., & Amanti, C., (2005). *Funds of knowledge: Theorizing practices in households, communities, and classrooms*. Mahwah, NJ: Lawrence Erlbaum Associates.

Gonzales, R. (1967). I am Joaquin (o soy Joaquin). www.atinamericanstudies.org. Film (1969). Retrieved from www.dailymotion.com

Janda, S. E. (2007). *Beloved women: The political lives of LaDonna Harris and Wilma Mankiller*. Dekalb, IL: Northern Illinois University Press.

Jones-Wilson, F. C. (1981). *A traditional model of educational excellence: Dunbar High School in Little Rock, Arkansas*. Washington, DC: Howard University Press.

Lee, E. (2015). *The making of Asian America: A history*. New York, NY: Simon & Schuster.

Mizruchi, S. L. (2008). *The rise of multicultural America: Economy and print culture, 1865–1915*. Chapel Hill, NC: University of North Carolina Press.

Pai, Y. (2001). *Cultural foundations of education* (1st ed.). Upper Saddle River, NJ: Merrill.

Siddle Walker, V. (1996). *Their highest potential: An African American school community in the segregated South*. Chapel Hill, NC: University of North Carolina Press.

Simmons, D. (2020). Who has the privilege to be empowered? *Educational Leadership*, 77(6), 88–89.

Sowell, T. (1981). *Ethnic America: A history*. New York, NY: Basic Books.

Takaki, R. T. (1989). *Strangers from a different shore: A history of Asian Americans*. New York, NY: Little, Brown & Company.

Takaki, R. T. (1993). *A different mirror: A history of multicultural America*. New York, NY: Little, Brown, & Company.

Thomas, P. (1967). *Down these mean streets*. New York, NY: Knopf Doubleday.

Woodson, C. G. (1933). *The mis-education of the Negro*. Philadelphia, PA: Hakims' Press.

Zhou, M., & Kim, S. S. (2007). After-school institutions in immigrant Chinese and Korean communities: A model for others? Retrieved from www.migrationpolicy.org

Zinn, H. (1980). *A people's history of the United States*. New York, NY: Harper & Row.

2

THE CONTINUING MULTICULTURAL EDUCATION OF A BLACK TEACHER EDUCATOR

Reflections on a Journey Toward My Referent Other-Self

Patricia L. Marshall

Introduction

Some weeks before I began writing this chapter, I led a group of graduate students in an exercise that subsequently prompted me to think more deeply than I had theretofore about my work as a multicultural teacher educator. The exercise required them to create a list of concepts and qualities they associate with what it means to be a good teacher. Many of the students had taken a multicultural education course I had taught the previous semester and so I was pleased to see that their lists included such ideas as knowledge of diverse subject matter, caring, and cultural relevance. A few even mentioned social justice and political consciousness. Curiously absent from all lists were *introspection and humility*, both of which, on some level, speak to gaining insights into the self.

As I began writing this chapter it occurred to me that these latter two qualities are especially relevant in the critical multicultural teacher educator identity; they tug at the conscious in ways that invite us to seek a deeper level of authenticity. Likewise, both dare us to present evidence to ourselves that we do *walk the talk* of the lessons we would have our students learn and internalize. In this chapter I detail my quest to acquire bilingualism as part of my own continuing multicultural education. My commitment to this goal prompted a level of humility and introspection that challenged me to explore and critique the authenticity of perceptions I had long held about my critical multicultural identity and the notion of *other* as related to my sense of cross-cultural competence. I interrogate the basis of the latter (i.e., *other*) and describe how, ultimately, my journey has put me on a path toward my *referent other-self*. I conclude this chapter with implications my journey presents for multicultural education as a social justice project in the twenty-first century.

On Aligning My Multicultural Identities

I am a black African American woman[1] who is deeply committed to multicultural education. A significant part of my professional work involves teaching graduate courses wherein my students and I explore diversity, equity, and social justice issues that confront education professionals in contemporary U.S. public schools and institutions of higher education. Another feature of my work, however, is that I study issues that challenge teachers to enact authentic equity pedagogies in service to delivering high-quality instruction to youngsters from historically marginalized communities. I have learned many lessons from my work and, over the years, have adopted precepts in relation to multicultural education as a social justice project. One of the more significant is that, at some point, the analytic lens and mature critical gaze[2] of the multicultural teacher education scholar must be turned inward. Put differently, I believe those of us who teach, study, and write about our professional activities in service to promoting the multicultural development of others, must accept the project's ultimate challenge. It is the challenge, the dare as it were, to engage in reflection on and study of the multicultural self.[3]

For me, the heft of that challenge presented itself when I began formal study of the Spanish language with the goal of becoming bilingual. My subsequent journey, which recently entered its ninth year, quite inadvertently led me to interrogate the nuances around the notion of *other* as a central feature against which I had conceptualized my critical multicultural identity. My interest has been steadied on exploration of the implicit albeit subconscious notions of this concept and its presence in my self-perceptions (my identity as it were) as a multicultural, cross-culturally competent person. Through my quest to become bilingual, mine has become a counter-hegemonic project encompassed in a self-study of both my professional and personal growth. It involves my critical embrace of something I now characterize as *the referent other-self.*

Questing Bilingualism: A Journey from the Personal to the Professional and Back Again

In the beginning, my decision to study Spanish was simply a plan for personal improvement. Commencing as it did after a brief trip to Puerto Rico in January 2012, the plan might even have been characterized as a New Year's resolution.[4] I contacted the Department of Foreign Languages and Literatures at the university where I teach and, in a telephone conversation with the Director of Undergraduate Programs (DUP) for Spanish, I inquired about the possibility of being permitted to *follow along* in an undergraduate course. I shared with the DUP that I am a professor at the university, explained my interest in Spanish, and then detailed my previous experience with language study.[5] Although I had a well-preserved confidence in my ability to learn Latin-derivative languages, I thought it best to proceed with caution. It had been a while since I'd taken a language course; moreover, I was moderately aware of some of the complexities surrounding second language acquisition.[6]

The DUP was encouraging. He advised me to visit the language lab on campus to complete a Spanish language proficiency test, and he indicated that through a computerized assessment I would learn which course would be most appropriate for me. I followed up the very next day and, based on my performance, the computer opined that I should start with FLS 101, the most basic Spanish course offered at the university. Humbled but not deterred, I shared the results of my placement test with the DUP and also learned that he was the instructor for FLS 101. The DUP agreed to let me follow along in his course which, to my delight, was offered as an online experience.[7] I purchased the required textbook and electronic course pack at the university's bookstore. My plan for personal improvement had officially begun.[8]

Almost immediately, I recognized that my language study experience had implications for my professional work as a multicultural teacher education scholar. Indeed, I started keeping a journal to record thoughts and reflections on the experience. For example, I found myself thinking differently about students in my own courses. Throughout my career, the vast majority of my students had counted mine as the only multicultural education course they ever took in their entire degree program.[9] As such, the readings and learning activities I assigned had always been selected with the goal of providing students a solid introductory background in multicultural education. Though I have offered personalized assistance, many international students in my courses for whom English was not their first language have struggled with the readings I assign. The semester I began my Spanish studies, my empathy for them became more intimate. My personal improvement plan had morphed into a professional development project for which I eventually would formulate ideas about how I could study my experience.

That first semester concluded on a positive high note. Rather than continue to simply *follow along*, that summer I enrolled formally at the university for my second Spanish course (FLS 102), followed by a third course (FLS 201) the subsequent fall semester. Through my study of Spanish, I was beginning to re-examine something that had been at the core of my thoughts about being a multicultural teacher educator, but which I had never named or fully articulated. In an awkward take on the phrase "the personal is political" made popular in 1960s feminist circles, I came up with *the professional must reflect the personal must inform the professional.* With this as my backdrop, I recognized that my personal plan had morphed into what I loosely reconceptualized as a self-study/autoethnography. At its core was my desire to excavate and interrogate the anchor component that allowed me as a multicultural teacher educator to also self-identify as a cross-culturally competent person.

Fieldnotes of a Multicultural Educator Incognito

Spring semester 2013 was the first anniversary of my journey toward bilingualism. I was registered in my fourth course (FLS 202) and this also marked the official start of a new role for me on campus. My studies had reached the intermediate level and this meant the convenient flexibility of online offerings that characterized my first three courses had now given way to the rigid timetable of the university's campus-based course schedule. This new reality was coupled with the fact that the courses I taught met on campus in the late afternoon/early evening hours one night per week. For years I rarely came to campus prior to 16h00[10] but over the next two years this would all change as I assumed a *dual identity* in my academic community. At night I was a full professor, but during the day I was a casually-dressed undergraduate student complete with waterproof backpack. I attended class on campus and routinely went to the library to study and complete my homework. Contemporary university student populations are tremendously diverse along multiple axes including age. Thus, although I was at least a full generation and a half older than nearly all of my classmates, I was not an oddity in my role as undergraduate student. Still, a few issues accompanied the transition from online to campus-based courses, and they made me somewhat uneasy with my dual identity.

For example, a couple of semesters my Spanish courses fell on the same day of the week as the courses I taught. When that happened, I attended my Spanish course session in the morning and studied in the library for about two to three hours immediately afterwards. Then, I would go home to change clothes, and return to campus in the late afternoon to teach my own courses. I made a conscious decision *not to reveal* my professional identity to my undergraduate classmates. My job as a professor, I reasoned, was irrelevant to my role and responsibility as a student in my Spanish courses. Moreover, I sought to immerse myself thoroughly in my role and identity as an undergraduate student. It seemed to me that to disclose that I was a professor on campus could serve only to change the dynamic of the various Spanish courses in which I'd enrolled, and unnecessarily complicate (and perhaps even diminish) my interactions with my classmates. In a word, I wanted to be *accepted* by my peers and to be fully incorporated into the milieu of each Spanish course I took. Even so, being incognito in this way made me constantly aware of my surroundings on campus. Whereas before I freely entered spaces as Dr. Marshall, now I deliberately eschewed my title and instead introduced myself to all as Patricia. A curious scene that often played out in my head involved me inadvertently being "outed" to my undergraduate classmates by a colleague or even one of my own graduate students. In hindsight it is somewhat comical how absorbed I became with trying to eliminate any grounds for my undergraduate classmates to reject me as being one of them. In time it was clear that my concerns were overblown because, though not always the case, the courses I taught were rarely scheduled in the same buildings where my Spanish courses were held.[11] When my twice-weekly Spanish course sessions concluded, my classmates and I would disperse into a sea of other students. With a physical campus space in excess of 2,000 acres and a student population of nearly 34,000, my effort to be incognito was virtually assured.[12]

Community Service and Commendations

I was constantly challenged and enlivened by my studies of Spanish, and my commitment to my coursework was total. Indeed, there were times I was consumed to the point that my other professional work seemed like an annoyance and imposition on my Spanish studies. As my knowledge grew, I became acutely aware of my need for opportunities to use my emerging language skills in authentic, real-life settings. Through my contact with an undergraduate student conversation partner I had hired at the start of my second course, I learned of a campus group called *Voluntarios Ahora en Raleigh* (VOLAR). Organized by an Associate Professor in the Spanish program area, VOLAR was a dual-focused grant project developed to offer authentic oral language opportunities for undergraduate students who had reached the intermediate (or above) level in their study of Spanish. The other focus of VOLAR was to provide service (via unpaid volunteers) to organizations, groups, and businesses in the local Latinx community. I attended the fall 2013 kick-off meeting of VOLAR and learned that most of its volunteering options involved assisting with one-time local events such as cultural/music festivals, food fairs, and so on. Yet there were other options that required students to commit to volunteer for a minimum of three hours weekly with a single organization. Rather than intermittent activity with multiple groups, these latter opportunities required students to agree to a semester-long commitment of service to one organization from among a selection. For two different semesters (and briefly over one summer) I chose the latter option and served as a volunteer at the Mexican Consulate. Another opportunity I seized occurred during my sixth semester of study, when I trained for several weeks to be a volunteer for a literacy program directed at Latinx children in elementary schools. Unfortunately, I did not engage in actual work with the latter activity due to changes made by its director. Later on, and outside of my participation in VOLAR, I volunteered as a teacher's helper and read stories in Spanish to Latinx youngsters.

My hours of commitment to VOLAR were considerable. And at the conclusion of the first semester of my participation, I attended a special dinner in honor of students who had volunteered the most hours for that semester. There were five of us students and two professors. The lead professor, whom I had not met previously, welcomed and congratulated me on my service to VOLAR. She then asked, "Patricia, what is your major?" I smiled and decided to out myself in the presence of undergraduate students for the first time. A year later I would be commended again for outstanding service to VOLAR as well as to another undergraduate campus-based Spanish-language organization that provided service to a public school and for which I had served as a volunteer. That time, my commendation was part of the formal end-of-spring semester honors ceremony of the Department of Foreign Languages and Literatures. The Department Head and numerous faculty members were present along with the Dean of the College of Humanities and Social Sciences. Tens of students from various language majors were receiving honors and recognitions, and scores of parents and other students were present in the audience. When my name was called, I walked to the platform and shook the hand of the Department Head as I received two certificates for my "outstanding service." Each was suitable for framing. It was at that formal ceremony that I finally met, face-to-face, the DUP of the Spanish language program. He congratulated me on my service awards, and he seemed pleasantly surprised to see that my interest in studying Spanish had progressed far beyond my initial request to simply *follow along*.

Adventures of Studying Abroad

The central goal of my journey at its outset was for me to gain full literacy in the Spanish language; however, my speaking skills seemed to be advancing at a much slower rate than my reading or writing skills and this became a major source of stress for me. The VOLAR activities had offered useful oral language opportunities, but they fell far short in promoting demonstrative advancement in my speaking abilities. More than ever I wanted an extended immersion experience, and I found a path to that through my university's five-week Study Abroad program. In May 2013 I enrolled at the Universidad de Costa Rica as an undergraduate student. To take in the experience as fully as I could, I also lived with a local host family.

The group I traveled with consisted of eight undergraduate students from my home university. Each of us had reached the intermediate or advanced level in our studies of Spanish and through study abroad we could take up to two courses and earn six undergraduate credit hours.[13] The *faculty coordinator* for our experience was an advanced doctoral student who also was an adjunct member of the Department of Foreign Languages and Literatures. I had met her a year prior when she served as instructor for my second online Spanish course. About a month before our group's departure, we were required to attend a meeting to receive information about the rules for student participation in the Study Abroad program. We also were given information about the Universidad de Costa Rica and our local host families. At the faculty coordinator's request, we introduced ourselves and shared our reasons for participating in the Study Abroad program. When my turn came, I shared that I am a professor on campus and that my reason for participating was to study my own experience of learning Spanish. My other reason (which I did not disclose) was to gain insights, from the perspective of my status as a student, about the Study Abroad experience itself. We were all excited (and more than a little anxious) about meeting our Costa Rican host families. According to the background information we each received, I learned that my "host parents" were a middle-class family consisting of an accountant and a Tupperware sales manager. At only eight years my senior, they were my generational contemporaries.[14]

There were six females (including me) and three males in our student group and each of us was assigned our own host family. The families lived in different parts of the province of San Jose which meant we had to use public transportation to travel to and from the university each day. On most weekends, our entire group met up at a central location for different excursions that had been pre-arranged by our faculty coordinator. There were two other African American female students in the group. One was my partner during many of the whole-group activities (including ziplining and rappelling) over the five-week period. She was also my roommate for a short overnight excursion that I and three other female students took to Límon, home of the Afro-Costa Rican community. Studying abroad in Costa Rica was the highlight of my journey to that point in that it allowed me to use my emerging language skills in a manner not required of me theretofore. The experience of traveling with a group of undergraduates was an adventure too, but at times it also had been challenging. Still, the immersion that came with being in a country where the dominant language is Spanish was invaluable and so I participated in a second experience the following summer.

My second study abroad was arranged external to my university and was organized by a private company that runs an international chain of language schools. The setting of this second immersion experience was Ecuador and, different from Costa Rica, its duration was eight weeks. This time I participated in small-group as well as one-on-one lessons in Spanish daily, but was free during the weekends. School staff arranged occasional day-trip excursions or put me in contact with local travel agents who could arrange them for me. Like my first study abroad experience, the second included a *homestay* wherein I lived with a local host family. This time my family was an upper middle-class couple whose grown offspring were no longer living at home. The patriarch was a retired former military official and the matriarch a stay-at-home mom. On two different occasions I traveled with them for extended family get-togethers.

My reflective journal entries reveal that at the outset of each of my immersion experiences my concerns were centered almost obsessively on whether I would notice demonstrative growth in my oral language abilities. *Would I be able to speak Spanish at the end better than I did at the start of the experience?* The fact is, it was a long time before I noticed a difference in my speaking abilities. Growth in oral language fluency is so gradual that often it is imperceptible to the learner. Rather, it is our listeners, the compañeras y compañeros we meet along the way, who must be counted on to deliver the news of progress. Curiously, I was often psychologically unprepared to accept that news. A painfully insecure and contrarian internal voice was always at the ready to cast doubts on its sincerity. Learning a second language at this stage in my life offered a window into my soul.

A Different Reflection in My Mirror

As I entered the third year of my journey it was clear that my commitment was solid; learning Spanish had become the embodiment of my own continuing multicultural education complete with personal and professional dimensions. On the one hand, I was taking on a new personal identity accompanied by requisite demands for me to expand my knowledge and worldview; while on the other I was developing a new curiosity about my own pedagogy. For the next leg of my journey I wanted to explore how I would use my emerging personal identity and extant professional skills *living and working* outside the U.S. context. To look into that mirror, I applied for a Teaching and Research Core Award through the Council for International Exchange of Scholars. The experience I sought, which required a full academic year commitment and at least intermediate-level fluency in Spanish, would constitute my longest language immersion experience to date. Some five months after submitting my application I would learn that I had been selected to be a Fulbright Scholar to Ecuador.

I was a visiting scholar at the Universidad San Francisco de Quito, an elite liberal arts institution where a high percentage of the students have some degree of Spanish-English bilingualism due in part to a two-year English language requirement in the curriculum. In brief, my Fulbright project comprised teaching a multicultural education/diversity course structured as a comparative study of schooling in the U.S. and in Ecuador. A twist that I incorporated into my research plan was that I would have to teach the first half of the course in English exclusively, and the second half in Spanish exclusively. One of my objectives was to examine the criticality the students brought to engagement with the third-rail issues of racism/white supremacy and economic class oppression in schools of two different, yet in ways quite similar, national contexts.[15] Another objective, which in some ways was more important to me, was to explore how I enacted culturally relevant pedagogy and how, in my day-to-day life, I exhibited cross-cultural competency outside the U.S. context. Findings from my Fulbright grant studies are being and have been shared in various contexts (Marshall, 2018, 2019).

Unpacking the Evolution of the Multicultural Self

When I made the commitment to become bilingual, I also challenged myself to revisit my identity as a critical multicultural educator/social justice advocate. In turn this prompted me to engage in a kind of excavation activity vis-à-vis my own sense of cross-cultural competence, one of the pillars upon which that identity has been erected. As I see it, laying claim to a critical multicultural educator/social justice advocate identity offers some insight into what a person does for a living, yet it should also speak to that same person's way of being in the world. For me, the latter includes my ongoing intentional efforts to deepen my knowledge about myself and others. It also encompasses my enactment of behaviors that open me to authentic and respectful interface with those whose identities, worldviews, and experiences are both similar to and different from my own. Making the claim to the identity demands recognizing the various axes of power and influence within a given society, along with how the first-level social, political, and economic institutions support the perpetuation of that society. It means acknowledging the interlocking nature of oppressions (Cho, Crenshaw, & McCall, 2013) routinely endured by the minoritized and marginalized members of that same society as they interface with those institutions, and resolving not to add to the oppressions. Ultimately, it means working independently and in coalition with others to end the suffering that oppressions engender. My multicultural educator/social justice advocate identity, perhaps not so dissimilar to that of others, has been shaped and re-shaped by my journey. In this regard, it presents as a perpetual state of being-in-becoming.

My effort to become bilingual represents the most consequential leg of my journey to date in that it has had a profound impact on how I think about myself and it has provoked my curiosity about the evolution of the identities of colleagues and friends I have met along the way and with whom I have felt a strong sense of connection and similitude in our multicultural education/social justice advocacy. A question that has absorbed my thoughts is, *what is the basis of their sense of cross-cultural competence?* In the interest of transparency, I will disclose here that I have been troubled by my own speculations over whether cross-cultural competence is *passé* as a focus of contemporary critical multicultural education scholarship. In this regard I have wondered if the concept itself is what Santos (2014) termed a rear-guard construction of a forgotten theme. Perhaps it is too closely associated with ubiquitous albeit narrow diversity foci mocked by some and widely denounced by other critical multicultural education scholars as a neo-liberal project appropriated by conservative interests. But for me in some ways it is as difficult to imagine the spotlighting of cross-cultural competence as central to contemporary critical multicultural education discourse as it is to imagine contemporary critical multicultural education discourse without an exacting and pointed analysis of how notions of cross-cultural competence present among its vanguards. These contradicting speculations notwithstanding, my interest in the cross-cultural competence of critical multicultural education/social justice advocates (whether self-described or celebrated) persists. Moreover, it has caused me to want to try to open a discourse around this issue.

The fact that I'm sharing this interest in a chapter of an edited book coinciding with the 30th anniversary of the founding of the National Association for Multicultural Education (NAME) has a certain immediacy and relevance. This is particularly the case since the NAME anniversary also happens to coincide with a U.S. presidential election year. As I write, candidates for the presidency are pledging to replace a dangerously regressive incumbent administration that has actively fomented white racist nationalism and anti-immigrant sectarianism on both the domestic and international fronts. This couples with a viral pandemic public health crisis throughout the world now abutted by comments from the current U.S. administration that have stoked a rise in racist assaults against Chinese Americans and other Asian Americans stateside.[16] In this climate, it is not by chance that those now vying for the U.S. presidency want to demonstrate some modicum of cross-cultural competence. The fact is, a powerful rainbow electorate demands that they do. By the same token, I believe this urgency must resonate at the mezzo-level with those of us who take up the mantle of the social justice project that is multicultural education. The irony is not lost on me that I seek to learn Spanish in a twenty-first-century U.S.A. where its native speakers are physically attacked in public spaces for daring to do so.[17] As I stand in solidarity against the racism and terrorism directed at members of the Latinx and Asian American communities, and as I seek to speak the second most spoken language in the world, the words of Freire (1970) ring loudly: "[t]hose who authentically commit themselves to the people must re-examine themselves constantly" (p. 42). My quest to become bilingual has brought me to a place where I am drawn to re-examine my own claim to cross-cultural competence, and in the process I have chosen to unpack the notions of *other* that have been at its core. When I entered into this phase of my journey, I recognized that re-examination takes courage and a steadying of the spirit for there is a very real possibility that we might not like what we see.

Troubling the Prototype Other

I was born and raised in an all-black urban community in one of this country's historical megalopolises. The branches of my family tree in the U.S. extend at least nine generations. Until I entered university, I attended schools where all the students and nearly all of the teachers (but none of the administrative staff) were also black. This was my reality even though pre-collegiate schools throughout the land had been declared legally desegregated before I was even born. My earliest memories of interfacing with *the other* are associated with two class fieldtrips when I was in the fourth grade. Most of the particulars of the first fieldtrip have faded from my memory over time, but I do remember the parental permission slip I brought home for my mother to sign. It indicated that our class would be visiting a Jewish synagogue. That was the first time I had ever heard or seen the word *synagogue*. For the second fieldtrip, our class visited an all-white elementary school located in a suburb far from our neighborhood school. Here my memories are clearer in that I remember my classmates and me sitting in a classroom with those other children for a lesson taught by their teacher. Afterwards, we played games with them on their school's grassy playground area that contrasted sharply with the all-concrete play area at our school. Also, we ate lunch with them in their cafeteria. I have absolutely no recollection of what the parental permission slip said was the purpose of that second fieldtrip, but I do know those children never visited with us in our school. Those experiences, along with the odd lyric of a catchy ditty[18] that was played every year on a popular radio station during National Brotherhood Week, helped shape my earliest understandings of amorphous concepts that would later hold importance in my work as a professional. Against that backdrop I absorbed direct and subtle lessons about possibilities and difficulties of finding common ground with those who did not "look like me."

The years passed and my conception of what constituted "like me" became far more complex, intersectional, and in turns nuanced and intermittently contradictory. My quest to become bilingual provoked a degree of humility that prompted me to reflect critically on my encounters with *the other* years prior, and to explore how those encounters had shaped how I conceptualize and enact my own sense of cross-cultural competence. I focused on my once all-black world, recognizing that it had been firmly grounded in social axes binaries, the most salient of which was race. Not only had this early reality shaped my sense of self, but it had greatly informed my sense of the other. Particularly troubling for me was uncovering that over the years my notion of cross-cultural competence had been dominated albeit subconsciously by honing my abilities to engage on multiple levels with an essentialized *other* personified largely as a *white prototype.*

Through my reflections I surmised that many of the skills, the knowledge, and even attitudes I acquired had been in preparation for interaction with white people and *whiteness* writ large. Both were interpreted and in many ways experienced as the polar opposite of my all-black early life and worldview. Whereas life in my family and community was accessible and affirming, whiteness and white prototype were understood as aloof and threatening. Through this lens, preparation for interface with both was, for nearly all intents and purposes, a veritable project in subversive neutralization taken up for protection and self-preservation. My reflections revealed to me that over the years the prototype white other had been reified by direct but largely superficial interpersonal encounters with white people and through cultural and institutional interfaces with a ubiquitous whiteness or *counter-me* that was perpetually cloaked in the specter of peril. Too often I interpreted and experienced these interfaces and encounters as inherently oppositional and thereby potentially destructive. Labor historian David Roediger (1994) noted that, "[i]t is not merely that whiteness is oppressive and false, it is that it is *nothing but* oppressive and false" (p. 13). My reflections highlighted for me that a certain impenetrability accompanied both my early and later interfaces with whiteness as cultural and institutional reality. And because they were seen and experienced through the exclusive lens of a racial binary, interface with the prototype other effectively muffled the nuances, multi-dimensional complexities, and intersectional realities constitutive of the very cross-cultural competence I sought.

When I think about the early and intermediate legs of my journey to where I am now, I am brought up short by a deeply entrenched belief I once held about black cross-cultural competence. Essentially it holds that *any* black person who successfully navigates the ubiquity of whiteness and white supremacy in its varied manifestations, ranging from micro-aggressions to outright and unmitigated devaluation, omission, and erasure across the spectrum of interfaces, can most certainly claim to be *cross-culturally competent*, if only by default. I did not hold this belief in isolation. Rather, for most of my life it was reinforced through my interactions with other black people irrespective of their social background or educational status. To a very real extent it could be said to constitute a by-product of the double-consciousness described so poignantly by W. E. B. Du Bois (1903/1989). Acquiring cross-cultural (read, racial) competence has always been in service to protecting body and psyche from assault that too often has been part and parcel of black entry into white spaces. It was not until I fully embraced my commitment to become bilingual that the possibility of a different, complex, and succoring notion of *other* presented itself in a manner that was palpably luring.

Moving Forward: Walking with a Referent Other-Self

During the course of my language study I have been able to topple the prototype other from the prominent perch it once held in my subconscious conception of my own cross-cultural competence. In its place is a new reality, a *referent other-self*, that has buoyed me during some of the more challenging legs of my journey toward bilingualism while standing in sharp contrast to whiteness and a narrow notion of the white other. The referent other-self is partial, unfinished, and the obverse of prototype. As *referent* it is an ancillary positive energy force, while as *other-self* it connotes unobstructed interface with the perpetuity of *becoming*. To be sure there is the ever-present possibility for tension inherent in the notion of referent other-self. My sense is the tensions derive in part from the independent and the intersecting complexities that come with performance of the multiple facets (salient and subterranean) of personal and group identities. In light of this I demur to any suggestion, implied or otherwise, that a reciprocal comradeship presents spontaneously between me and those I might perceive as referent other-self. In short, I know that the *other* for whom I perceive *simpatía* won't necessarily perceive it for me. But be that as it may, what makes the very idea of a referent other-self so appealing for me is the complete absence of obligation and coercion. The referent other-self has no real or implied punitive authority, power, or privileged standing to insist upon its necessity and centrality in my life. Rather, the referent other-self holds sway and significance for me solely because I make it so. Hence, in the end the referent other-self is a psychosocial space that promotes and facilitates regeneration.

Through re-examination of my claim to cross-cultural competence, and critical reflection on my encounters and interactions with the *other* over years, I have been able to unpack how the hegemonic race regime that is whiteness introduced and entrenched a unidimensional notion of other in my subconscious. Most significantly, however, I have uncovered how its most insidious element, the prototype white other, had for too long dulled my senses to the *referent other-selves* all around me. The relative recent appearance in and impact of the referent other-self in my most conscious enactment of cross-cultural competence reveals that prior to now I have been living in a veritable state of *talk/walk mismatch* vis-à-vis my identity as critical multicultural educator/social justice advocate. Currently, I experience the *referent other-self* as multi-dimensional. It extends along the gender identity spectrum, is ethnically and linguistically diverse, pluri-national, and geospatially diasporic. Clearly distinguished from my earlier all-black world and experience, its resonance is unyielding. Where the *prototypical other* had been irredeemably oppositional and subtractive, the *referent other-self* is affirming and generative.

Conclusion

This essay has offered a glimpse into one black teacher educator's continuing multicultural education that, over the past eight years, has been dominated by efforts to acquire English/Spanish bilingualism. It is a rendering of how the multicultural education identity consists of so much more than the courses taught; the students whose awareness is raised and social justice consciousness awakened; the keynote address delivered; and the book published. Rather, at its most fundamental the multicultural education identity is about the authenticity of the life we live. I have told my story herein, and in its detailing, I challenged myself to explore the alignment between my professional and personal identities as a teacher educator whose scholarship has focused on diversity and equity in schools and communities. In telling my story, I shared features of how I critiqued my own longstanding claim to cross-cultural competence. The latter emerged as both a personal and scholarly interest for me when I began travelling to countries in *el mundo hispano*[19] and started to build relationships with people whose backgrounds and contemporary realities and circumstances were different from mine, but not foreign to me. As noted earlier, for those of us who take on the project that is multicultural education and its social justice advocacy agenda, I believe at some point re-examination of the self is a critical necessity. For me the analysis and critique that accompanied my most recent re-examination was somewhat troubling and, initially, I struggled with whether to tell certain parts of my story. In the end, I found telling those parts was important to my growth. Nevertheless, I did make a conscious decision to save in-depth critique of *other parts* of my story for another essay.

For example, throughout my period of formal course-taking, it was always noteworthy to me that the instructors of my Spanish classes would emphasize *mestizaje* (i.e., the tri-partite African/European/Indigenous mixture) as an endemic element of the cultures, histories, and identities (if not biological lineage) of the people of Latin America.[20] At the same time, however, in all my courses (particularly those focused on Latin American literature), there was scant focus on the influences of the Indigenous populations beyond brief studies of Bolivia. Likewise, there was a disturbing absence of both the historical influence and the contemporary physical presence of the African diaspora. It was particularly troubling for me as a black woman to experience across more than ten courses in Spanish that not one instructor devoted class time to or incorporated specific content about *Afro-Latinidad*. Indeed, in my dual role as student/incognito professor, I was compelled to try to fill in that gap in a class presentation to my student peers. It happened when the instructor assigned us students to do research on some aspect of the culture of a country of our choice, and deliver a short in-class presentation. My classmates' presentations focused on foods, festivals, and holiday celebrations. I chose Venezuela, and gave a brief report on historic and contemporary Afro-Venezolanos. One factoid in my presentation focused on Pedro Camejo, known by the sobriquet "El Negro Primero" because in Venezuela's war for independence from Spain Camejo was always the first soldier in battle. A public statue of him is situated in the Plaza Carabobo in Caracas, and as late as 2013 he was the only Afro-Venezolano ever so honored.[21]

In view of this and other experiences, an important part of my story that I am currently writing about for another context includes how throughout my journey I have grappled with what has struck me as the erasure of blackness in my studies of Spanish. My current interests lie in how Afro-Latinidad is (not) situated in U.S. teacher education discourses germane to the growing Latinx population. Likewise, I have a strong interest in points of intersection between black-African Americans and Latinx and how such realities as colorism play out between and among teachers and students in schools.

Ultimately, my effort to detail the contours of my continuing education has been an exercise in personal liberation. Through my reflections, I have gained deeper insights into and appreciation for the complexities inherent in staking claim to the critical multicultural educator/social justice advocate identity. Mine is a story of personal renewal, but I believe it has implications for the evolution of multicultural education as a social justice project. To this end it provokes questions that I believe should be the subject of a larger discourse among the wider community of social justice advocates and critical multicultural education scholars. Foremost among these questions are how do other teacher educators and multicultural education scholars renew, re-orient, and reinvent themselves for deeper, truer, and more authentic commitment to the social justice project that is multicultural education? How do they discern and measure the consistency of their *talk/walk* alignment? It seems to me pursuit of these among other strong questions is an important next step in the evolution of multicultural education. Santos (2014) noted that

> [s]trong questions address not only our specific options for individual and collective life but also the societal and epistemological paradigm that has shaped the current horizon of possibilities within which we fashion our options, the horizon within which certain options are possible while others are excluded or even unimaginable. Such questions are paradigmatic in nature since they confront the very criteria for inclusion and exclusion of specific options. They arouse, therefore, a particular kind of perplexity.
>
> *p. 20*

As I close this essay, the idea of role models is brought to mind. A longstanding precept in equity pedagogy as a dimension of multicultural education emphasizes the importance of tapping into the power of the role model in the teaching-learning process. It holds that seeing someone who *looks like you* engaged in work or activity you hope to do, heightens a sense of possibility. So critical is this concept to some of the more challenging issues in contemporary schooling for black students that one mathematics education scholar put it front and center when he asked, *who will teach mathematics to African American children?* (Martin, 2007). The notion of the role model as a facilitator to learning carries a certain self-evident logic. I have long spoken of this in my own teaching, but its power assumed a raw and palpable realness for me early in my journey toward bilingualism.

It happened one day while I was studying in the university library. An African American male custodian maneuvering a large waste paper receptacle as he made his way through the large study hall apologized as he whispered to me in interruption of my studies. He noted the title of my textbook, and spoke to me in Spanish. The words coming from his mouth were like music to my ears. In the days and weeks that followed, we saw each other often and I learned that he had acquired fluency in Spanish through his work as a missionary in various countries in Central America. Each time I went to the library that semester, I looked for him, often interrupting his work to hear him speak and to contemplate my own possibilities. I had not yet found the language to name what was happening to me, but years later I would describe that fateful day as my first interface with my *referent other-self.*

Unending is my path in pursuit of a fuller embrace of my personal and professional critical multicultural educator identity. It is now unalterably forefronted by my quest for bilingualism, and if the passageway thus far is any indication, I know there will be many challenging twists, turns, and even detours ahead. But, in the words of the late Maya Angelou (1993), I *wouldn't take nothing for my journey now.*

Notes

1 I'm acknowledging several emic concepts inherent to black communities and black families in the U.S. As persons born in Africa and those born throughout its diaspora settle in the U.S. the contemporary black population in the U.S. increasingly has become ethnically diverse. I am a U.S. born *Afrodescendiente.*

2 Here, I seek to distinguish the introspection of the deeply initiated from, say, those "new to the conversation." One scholar characterized the latter as "becoming multicultural educators" (see, for example, Gay, 2003). Instead, I am referring to reflection that comes through direct engagement in directing, studying, analyzing, and even critiquing the growth of *others.* Among the scholars who have taken up the kind of self-introspection challenge I call for here are Cochran-Smith (2000); and Oda (1998).

3 bell hooks makes a similar claim for feminist pedagogy when she notes, "[f]eminist education for critical consciousness is rooted in the assumption that knowledge and critical thought done in the classroom should inform our habits of being and way of living outside the classroom." See hooks (1994, p. 194).

4 With the exception of one very close personal friend and one colleague, I did not share my resolve to study Spanish with anyone else until it had been well underway for several years.

5 I had studied French as a high school student and upon entering the university as an undergraduate, through a placement test I was able to skip four courses and continue my studies through the upper intermediate level. Also, as an undergraduate I completed one basic-level course each in Italian and Spanish. Thus, my interest in languages other than English did not begin with my current journey. Indeed, during the over 30-year interim period between my last formal course of study and the time I began this journey, on occasion I would shamelessly attempt to use my rapidly atrophying knowledge of both French and Spanish whenever I encountered a gracious native speaker who would indulge me. Most efforts were affirming although each invariably concluded with my acknowledging before the friendly stranger that I needed to *practice* more. In 2012, I decided to do just that.

6 The one colleague with whom I shared my plan (see note 4 above) applauded my interest, and recalled his own attempt to learn a second language. Then, as if preparing me for an unavoidable letdown, he noted that for most people beyond early adolescence learning a second language is an exceedingly difficult (if not impossible) task.

7 I later learned that the first three basic courses in Spanish (FLS 101, FLS 102, and FLS 201) were all routinely and exclusively taught as online course experiences. In the latter, all students were required to have a one time, 30-minute face-to-face meeting with the professor for an oral language proficiency assessment.

8 Being allowed to "follow along" in this first course meant I would not enroll formally in the university; rather, I would simply try to keep up with assignments as my schedule permitted. The semester had been underway for about two weeks (I was teaching two graduate courses of my own), when I began following along in FLS 101. I was pleasantly surprised to discover that I was not significantly behind in what had already been covered to that point. My professor/the DUP informed me that a particularly crucial requirement and stipulation of my participation in FLS 101 would be engagement in the oral language activities. To meet this requirement and with his assistance, I contacted via email three different upper-division undergraduate Spanish majors. Two followed up and due to a miscommunication, instead of one I decided to hire them both. They each agreed to come to my campus office one hour per week (one on Wednesdays, the other on Fridays), to serve as my "conversation partners." I logged on weekly to view my professor's online video lectures, and I completed all homework assignments for the course. Although I was not required to do so, I even took the final exam and passed it with a high score.

9 In part this has been owing to advising protocols. For a discussion of these protocols and the resultant resistance to multicultural education that manifested in my workspace, see Marshall (2015).

10 The exception to this would be when I came to school one day each month for departmental, college faculty, or university committee meetings. I teach graduate students exclusively so I schedule my courses and office visitation hours in the late afternoon/evening hours to accommodate the schedules of working professionals.

11 Only one time (the seventh semester of formal course-taking) was my Spanish course held in the same building where my office is located.

12 The university where I teach is a predominantly white institution and so the vast majority of my classmates were also white. I was actually struck by the paucity of

African American students in my Spanish courses and it genuinely surprised me that throughout my formal course-taking period I never had a classmate who was an education major. As a professor of teacher education, I always found the latter especially troubling in light of the fact that the Latinx pre-collegiate student population in our state has been increasing steadily for more than 25 years. When I arrived in North Carolina in 1990, the state's Latinx student population was 8,530 (less than 1%) whereas in 2018–19 it had grown to 274,926 (18%) (source: North Carolina Department of Public Instruction Statistical Profile: www.dpi.nc.gov/districts-schools/district-operations/financial-and-business-services/demographics-and-finances/statistical-profile).

13 Most of the students enrolled in two Spanish courses. Since I had planned to complete other professional work while in Costa Rica, I chose to enroll in just one intermediate-level Spanish course.

14 The couple were parents to two sons and a daughter. One son was high-school age, the other was a university student studying engineering. On occasion their daughter, her husband, and their charming 4-year-old daughter visited on weekends. My oral speaking skills were quite under-developed at that point so conversations were limited. The exception was my interaction with the 4-year-old granddaughter who seemed oblivious to my limitations and happily chatted me up with abandon.

15 Ecuador is a multi-cultural, multi-ethnic, multi-lingual, and pluri-national republic. Many of the disparities that confront African American and Native American children and youth in U.S. schools are present in the schooling of Afro-Ecuadorians and Indigenous Ecuadorian youngsters. This is to say, the lasting impact of historical inequities, coupled with contemporary sociocultural/sociopolitical issues impacting these groups, reveals that not unlike in the U.S., in Ecuador race and class do matter in schooling opportunity and quality. A final similarity is that both Ecuador and the U.S. use the same currency. This has been the situation since 2000 when, to stabilize its national economy, the Ecuadorian government formally adopted *dollarization*.

16 In the aftermath of the worldwide pandemic of Covid-19, President Trump has insisted on referring to the pandemic as "the Chinese virus," and racial violence against Asian Americans has increased. See for example: Rogers, Jakes, & Swanson (2020); and Tavernise & Oppel (2020).

17 There has been a pronounced boldness to attacks on persons speaking Spanish in public spaces. See for example: Levenson (2020); Flores & Stabley (2018); and "Why speaking Spanish is becoming dangerous in America." *The Guardian*. www.theguardian.com/us-news/2018/may/22/speaking-spanish-dangerous-america-aaron-schlossberg-ice

18 The ditty itself was a satiric commentary on the blatant hypocrisy of the very notion of brotherhood as played out against the backdrop of the entrenched racism, ethnocentrism, and religious bigotry throughout U.S. society. As a child I did not understand the satire, but I learned (and sang along with) part of the lyric as I heard it played yearly on WVON, an all-black radio station in Chicago. A performance of the song by its author, Tom Lehrer, can be found at www.pri.org/stories/2018-02-21/whatever-became-national-brotherhood-week.

19 The notion of *el mundo hispano* (the Hispanic world) emphasized in all my coursework was defined as consisting of some 21 different countries across multiple continents including: Africa (Equatorial Guinea); Europe (Spain); North America (México); South America (Argentina, Bolivia, Chile, Colombia, Ecuador, Paraguay, Perú, Uruguay, Venezuela); Central America (Costa Rica, El Salvador, Guatemala, Honduras, Nicaragua, Panamá); and the Caribbean (Cuba, Dominican Republic, Puerto Rico).

Although it is part of the U.S., in Puerto Rico Spanish is the first official language and English is second.

20 For a particularly informative discussion of this concept see Vasconcelos (1948).

21 This is the case despite the fact that anywhere from 5 to 34% of the Venezuelan population could be classified as *Afrodescendientes.* Of course, the broadness of this range reflects the extreme contrasts in how racial classification and racial identity are determined in Venezuela and much of Latin America broadly versus the U.S. For a discussion of the intersections of race, skin-color, and notions of identity and classification, see Telles (2014).

References

Angelou, M. (1993). *Wouldn't take nothing for my journey now.* New York, NY: Random House.

Cho, S., Crenshaw, K. W., & McCall, L. (2013). Toward a field of intersectionality studies: Theory, applications, and praxis. *Journal of Women in Culture and Society, 38*(4), 785–810.

Cochran-Smith, M. (2000). Blind vision: Unlearning racism in teacher education. *Harvard Educational Review, 70*(2), 157–190.

Du Bois, W. E. B. (1989). *The souls of Black folk.* New York, NY: Bantam Books. (Original work published 1903.)

Flores, K., & Stabley, M. (2018, October 19). Woman harasses family for speaking Spanish in Virginia restaurant. *U.S. News & World Reports.* www.nbcwashington.com/news/local/northern-virginia/woman-harasses-family-for-speaking-spanish-in-virginia-restaurant/146333/

Freire, P. (1970). *Pedagogy of the oppressed.* New York, NY: Continuum Press.

Gay, G. (Ed.) (2003). *Becoming multicultural educators: Personal journey toward professional agency.* San Francisco, CA: Jossey Bass.

hooks, b. (1994). *Teaching to transgress: Education as the practice of freedom.* New York, NY: Routledge.

Levenson, M. (2020, February 29). Mother and daughter attacked for speaking Spanish, prosecutor says. *The New York Times.* www.nytimes.com/2020/02/29/us/east-boston-hate-crime-attack.html

Marshall, P. L. (2015). Using my 'you-lie moment' to theorize persistent resistance to critical multicultural education. *International Journal of Multicultural Education, 17*(2), 117–134.

Marshall, P. L. (2018, February). Re-imagining spaces for democratic and critical dialogue in a diversity course. Paper presented at the Annual Meeting of the Association of Teacher Educators, Las Vegas, NV.

Marshall, P. L. (2019, February). Daring to forefront self-talk about our own cross-cultural competence. Research presentation at the Annual Meeting of the Association of Teacher Educators, Atlanta, GA.

Martin, D. B. (2007). Beyond missionaries or cannibals: Who should teach mathematics to African American children? *The High School Journal, 91*(1), 6–28.

Oda, L. K. (1998). Harmony, conflict and respect: An Asian-American educator's self-study. In M. L. Hamilton, et al. (Eds.), *Reconceptualizing teaching practice: Self-study in teacher education* (pp. 113–123). Bristol, PA: Falmer Press/Taylor & Francis Group.

Roediger, D. R. (1994). *Toward the abolition of whiteness.* New York, NY: Verso.

Rogers, K., Jakes, L., & Swanson, A. (2020, March 18). Trump defends using 'Chinese virus" label ignoring growing criticism. *The New York Times.* www.nytimes.com/2020/03/18/us/politics/china-virus.html

Santos, B. D. S. (2014). *Epistemologies of the south: Justice against epistemicide.* New York, NY: Routledge.

Tavernise, S., & Oppel, R. A., Jr. (2020, March 24). Spit on, yelled at, attacked: Chinese-Americans fear for their safety. *The New York Times.* www.nytimes.com/2020/03/23/us/chinese-coronavirus-racist-attacks.html

Telles, E. (2014). *Pigmentocracies: Ethnicity, race, and color in Latin America.* Chapel Hill, NC: University of North Carolina Press.

Vasconcelos, J. (1948). *La raza cósmica: Misión de la raza iberoamericana, Argentina y Brazil.* México: Espasa-Calpe Mexicana.

3

CHALLENGING RACISM AND COLONIALISM THROUGH ETHNIC STUDIES

Christine E. Sleeter

Peoples who are marginalized on the basis of race, ethnicity, and immigration generally experience continued marginalization despite laws or programs that purport equal rights and full integration. In the U.S., this has been the case generally and in education specifically. Due primarily to immigration, minoritized students are no longer a minority in public schools, even though they continue to occupy a subordinate position. By 2018, U.S. public school students were 48% white, 15% African American, 28% Latino, 5% Asian American, 1% American Indian, and 3% other (Institute of Educational Sciences, 2019). But minoritized students continue on the average to experience less success in school than white students, reflected in lower achievement scores, lower rates of graduation, and higher suspension and drop-out rates (Musu-Gillette et al., 2017). After decades of efforts ranging from attempts to prepare teachers to work constructively with minoritized students, to attempts to raise academic expectations through curriculum standardization and testing, gaps remain.

Despite the entrenched racism underlying those gaps, things can be different. This possibility was demonstrated powerfully in Tucson, Arizona, where a Mexican American Studies program flipped the achievement gap (Cabrera et al., 2014). Not only did Mexican American students in the program begin to outperform white students academically, but the program also transformed youth's understanding of themselves. Youth who had not seen themselves as intellectually or politically capable began to graduate from high school, go on to college, and engage in activism in their own communities (Cammarota & Romero, 2009). The program was disbanded by white politicians who viewed its Mexican American-centered curriculum as seditious. They tried (with only temporary success) to outlaw ethnic studies in Arizona. But minoritized youth around the nation had witnessed an alternative to their own stultifying experiences with school. As Cuauhtin and colleagues (2019) write, "a movement has been unleashed in the United States. It is a powerful movement for K–12 Ethnic Studies that has sprung from students, teachers, and community activists seeking to transform curriculum and teaching into tools for social justice in public schools" (p. 1).

This chapter shows how ethnic studies in the U.S. works to reverse the historical amnesia that schooling perpetuates regarding colonialism and racism. After reviewing multicultural education as an earlier movement with a similar aim of challenging historical amnesia and transforming education for social justice, we examine today's ethnic studies movement in the U.S. as a decolonial project, zeroing in on two examples of ethnic studies praxis.

Minoritized Youth and Historical Amnesia

In his incisive examination of colonialism, Quijano (2007) explained that, with the conquest of Latin America, colonizers began to create a new world order. Five hundred years later, that world order culminated "in a global power covering the whole planet. This process implied a violent concentration of the world's resources under the control and for the benefit of a small European minority—and above all, of its ruling classes" (p. 167). This is the system we have now, still intact although "occasionally moderated when faced with the revolt of the dominated" (p. 167).

Colonization is initiated with violence, as colonizers kill people or otherwise force them to acquiesce to theft of their land, labor, and freedom. Quijano (2007) explains that the physical violence of European colonization was followed by "colonization of the imagination of the dominated" (p. 169), where Europeans repressed local memories and replaced them with their own, including a European way of thinking and seeing the world. European and Euro-North American epistemology embodies the Cartesian dualism between mind and body, thinker and worker. Working within such dualisms, Europeans created a "discourse of the Other" (Zavala, 2016) that divided people into invented categories (such as races), ranking them hierarchically, and linking human and cultural hierarchical development with genetics (Kivel, 2013; Mudimbe, 1988). Under this logic, which was tied directly to physical domination and appropriation of land and labor, Europeans defined themselves as most advanced and civilized. By replacing local languages, cultures, identities, and historical memories with European ways of thinking, Europe, and later Euro-North America, sought to convince those who had been colonized or enslaved to accept the social order and their subordinate position within it.

Tejeda, Espinoza, and Gutierrez (2003) characterize minoritized peoples in the U.S. today as occupying a state of internal neocolonialism, although its specific nature differs across groups. What characterizes internal neocolonialism is that those who are colonized are officially integrated with the white colonizers rather than being physically separated. Further, the Civil Rights legislation and court cases that began in the 1950s fundamentally altered how the earlier forms of colonialism worked by making overt racism illegal. Despite changes in laws, however, power relations among groups have changed only piecemeal, and dominant discourses still prevail.

According to Leonardo (2009), a "pedagogy of amnesia" encourages students to consider the nation's "founding fathers" as benign heroes rather than participants in the construction of racist practices (p. 173). Discourses that ignore racism or locate it in the past contribute to collective historical amnesia. Periodically oppressive power relations and attendant historical amnesia are contested vigorously. In the U.S., as a part of the Civil Rights movement of the 1960s and 1970s, minoritized peoples challenged various forms of colonization and racial marginalization, including education's role in producing historical amnesia.

On university campuses, led by coalitions such as the Third World Liberation Front in San Francisco, minoritized students demanded a curriculum relevant to their lives and communities in the form of ethnic studies. At the elementary and secondary levels, African American educators and parents (followed by other minoritized groups) also demanded changes specific to the various forms of racial discrimination minoritized students experienced in desegregated, formerly all-white schools, such as being regarded by teachers as less academically capable than white students, and being taught all-white curricula. This work at the elementary and secondary level came to be known as multiethnic education, then multicultural education "as other groups who considered themselves on the margins of society (particularly women and people with disabilities) began to demand that the school curriculum—and later other aspects of the school—be changed" (Banks, 1996, p. 40).

The U.S. has entered another period in which movements of youth, teachers, and community activists are contesting historical amnesia. Again, students in minoritized communities are taking up leadership demanding change. For example, Carrasco Cardona and Cuauhtin (2019) explain that,

> Youth involvement has been present in districts throughout California, from Oakland where youth catalyzed the push for the Ethnic Studies resolution, to Sacramento, where local youth and a large group from Napa presented to the state Board of Education to advocate for Ethnic Studies.
>
> *p. 311*

One may well ask why young people see the need for a movement now, when just 40 years ago an earlier movement challenging racism in education gave birth to multicultural education. To that question we now turn.

What Happened to Multicultural Education?

By the late 1980s, multicultural education in the U.S. was having some impact. Concerns raised by multicultural education scholars and activists—concerns about curriculum, white teacher attitudes, academic expectations, pedagogy, school–community relationships, and so forth—were becoming recognized. Minoritized groups were being added to curricula, biased grouping of students for instruction (such as tracking) was being reconsidered, and teachers were experiencing professional development for multicultural education (Gorski, 1999). Through a combination of desegregation mandates, the War on Poverty, and multicultural and bilingual education, the academic achievement of minoritized students was improving considerably. On the National Assessment of Education Progress, for example, achievement gaps in reading and math between white students, and African American and Latino students, were narrowing markedly (U.S. Department of Education, 2012).

Then, in the late 1990s, this work stalled due to several factors. First, conservative think tanks orchestrated a public war against multiculturalism. In an opening salvo, Bloom (1987) declared:

> By recognizing and accepting man's natural rights, men found a fundamental basis of unity and sameness. Class, race, religion, national origin or culture all disappear or become dim when bathed in the light of natural rights, which give men common interests and make them truly brothers.
>
> *p. 27*

A barrage of highly publicized books and newspaper articles castigated multiculturalism as divisive to the nation and harmful to African American students (Sleeter, 1995).

Second, neoliberalism, which had taken hold in the U.S. in the late 1970s, drove the school reform agenda by the 2000s, displacing a discourse of equity with one that promoted standardized curriculum and tests, privatization, and market competition among schools. *No Child Left Behind*, passed by Congress and signed into law in 2001, mandated that states receiving federal funding implement statewide accountability systems in all public schools, including regular testing for all students in grades 3–8. Schools failing to meet test score targets received negative publicity and sanctions, and ultimately could be closed. What attention there had been to race and representation in curriculum virtually dissipated (Bohn & Sleeter, 2000).

Third, most white teachers (the majority of the teaching force) had always conceptualized multicultural education in terms of cultural awareness rather than anti-racism. For example, Schoorman and Bogotch (2010) surveyed teachers in a U.S. university lab school to find out how they understood multicultural education. The teachers viewed it as strategies for teaching minoritized students, especially differentiated instruction, and as treating all students fairly and valuing cultural differences, rather than as systemic change for social justice. Vaught and Castagno (2008) interviewed teachers and administrators in two school districts that had undergone training in multicultural education. They concluded that, "awareness did not lead to empathy amongst teachers but resulted instead in a reinvention of meaning that reified existing, culturally constructed, racist frameworks" (p. 110). It is likely that the persistent efforts of multicultural educators to address white teacher attitudes contributed to many people viewing it as having an attitudinal and cultural rather than systemic focus.

So even though the school population was rapidly becoming more racially and ethnically diverse, and despite widespread attention to the racial achievement gap, by the mid-1990s, in dominant discourse multicultural education had been displaced by a framework for addressing these issues through standardization, remediation, and assimilation. Multicultural education, while now a familiar term to most educators, had lost much meaning. For example, while serving as an expert witness for a court case in New Mexico, I was charged with examining how teachers understood and used multicultural education and culturally responsive teaching. The central problem in the court case was that Mexican American and Indigenous students were achieving poorly. Did teachers understand how to teach their students? On a survey to which 1,275 teachers in two large school districts responded, 95% reported familiarity with either multicultural education or culturally responsive teaching. However, on a question about how they interpreted academic struggles of some (or many) of their students, teachers overwhelmingly named the students (for example, apathy or misbehavior) or their families (for example, not supporting education, poverty) as the problem rather than teaching-related factors. Other questions revealed that teachers received much more professional development in Common Core standards and testing than in culturally responsive teaching (Sleeter, 2018). The state's teacher evaluation system added attention to student diversity only here and there. For example, as a part of Demonstrating Knowledge of Students, teachers should attend to student learning styles. Nothing most teachers were offered directly challenged deficit understandings of students, or showed teachers how to teach minoritized students well.

One might characterize how many people today understand multicultural education as "neoliberal multicultural education," which advocates "a 'soft,' palatable approach to community building that is less discomforting for white people" than multiculturalism focused directly on challenging racism (Case & Ngo, 2017). As Gorski (2008) explains, the central challenge is "turning our attention away from the cultural 'other' and toward systems of power and control" (p. 522).

Curriculum: Still through White Points of View

Schools can be understood as part of a larger institutionalized apparatus for maintaining social control (Carmichael, 2012). Apple (2004) argues that curriculum teaches a way of looking at the world: "the common sense interpretations we use" (p. 5), including interpretations of the social system, people like oneself, and people one considers different. His analysis of the relationship between the structure of a capitalist economy, and the formation of a consciousness that accepts capitalism and one's position within the class structure, highlights the mediating role and ideological moorings of the curriculum. Brown and Brown (2015) describe curriculum as "the fabrication of memory, or the way in which a nation imagines and shapes what people come to know about the past and present" (p. 104). They ask whose memory curriculum codifies, pointing out that much of it serves the project of maintaining social cohesion around particular power relationships.

In the United States, textbooks (and other curricular documents to a lesser extent) have been analyzed for decades in order to determine whose perspectives predominate, and how diverse groups are represented. Although I will refer specifically to research in the U.S., one can find similar, though fewer, analyses elsewhere (Chu, 2015; Samper Rosero & Garreta Bochaca, 2011; Weiner, 2018).

One simple method of curriculum analysis consists of counting the people in images, the people mentioned to be studied, or the main characters in literary stories, identifying each by race and gender, and noting how each group is represented (Grant & Sleeter, 2009, pp. 128–134). Although this method does not directly examine a textbook's ideology, it does suggest whose perspective dominates. A more complex method of analysis involves comparing the selection and treatment of ideas and events in the textbooks with scholarship written from minoritized points of view.

Analyses of curricula in the U.S. consistently find that whites dominate. In history texts, white people are still by far the main ones who are studied in the context of an overall storyline that begins in Europe and moves west. In other subject areas, whites are shown in a wider variety of roles and as having made many more accomplishments than members of other groups (Perez, 2014; Sleeter, 2018).

African Americans appear in a more limited range of roles than whites, and less frequently appear within a broader narrative of African American rather than white experiences (Pelligrino, Mann, & Russell, 2013). If texts mention racism, they continue to disconnect racism in the past from racism today; they frame its perpetrators as a few bad individuals rather than a system of oppression, and challenges to racism as actions of heroic individuals rather than organized struggle (Alridge, 2006). For example, Brown and Brown (2010) began their analysis with key time periods and narratives in African American history as written by African American intellectuals, then closely examined how U.S. history textbooks treated those specific time periods. They found that, although the texts included correct information about African American history in each period, "these representations fall short of adequately illustrating how racial violence operated systematically to oppress and curtail African Americans´ opportunities and social mobility in the United States" (p. 150).

Latinos are now slightly more than one-quarter of all public school students in the U.S., but are greatly underrepresented in textbooks. Only about 3% of the space in history texts features Latinos (Noboa, 2005; Sleeter, 2018). While literature texts include some Latino authors and sometimes give more space to Latinos than the history texts do (Sleeter, 2018), they repeat the same few authors, and still draw on stereotypes (Rojas, 2010). The same pattern of under-representation has also been noted in math texts (Piatek-Jimenez, Madison, & Przybyla-Kucheck, 2014).

American Indians continue to be poorly represented, simplified, and located in the past (Sleeter, 2018; Stanton, 2014). Reese (2007) notes that, while American Indian websites recommend excellent children's books featuring Native people, most children's books featuring American Indians either portray them as savages, or as romantic but tragic heroes, disconnected from specific tribes and accurate tribal perspectives. Asian Americans and Arab Americans only make limited appearances and are often stereotyped (Eraqi, 2015; Romanowski, 2009).

How students perceive curriculum depends in part on how they see people like themselves represented. Through a series of interviews, Epstein (2009) found that in elementary school, many African American students noticed discrepancies between what they were taught in school and what they learned at home. As they proceeded through secondary school, these discrepancies became more glaring. She found African American eleventh grade students to bring a fairly sophisticated analysis of racism to their understanding of U.S. history, interpreting its history in terms of systemic racism against which African Americans continue to struggle. But since their textbooks and most of their teachers framed U.S. history as a triumphal march for expansion of individual rights rather than a struggle over systemic racism, Epstein concluded that African American students "learned to distrust the historical knowledge taught in schools and turned to family, community members, and black oriented texts" for their education (p. 115).

Likewise, Mexican American and American Indian students generally feel alienated from the traditional curriculum (Martinez, 2010; Ochoa 2007). For example, in their study of 12 Latino middle school students' perceptions of social studies, Busey and Russell (2017) found that students saw the curriculum as culturally barren. All of them wanted much more attention to cultural diversity—their own backgrounds as well as those of others. As one student put it, "Kids like me, I want to learn about where I came from, how I started, and not only from the United States, but from our culture and every person's culture" (p. 10). The boredom students described was magnified by the fact that their teachers taught mainly through rote memorization. In a three-year ethnographic study, San Pedro (2018b) found that some of the high school Native American students explicitly rejected what their teacher taught about American history because it implicitly denied their existence. One student decided to fail the class rather than swallow a white interpretation of history.

It should not be surprising, then, that minoritized students are on the front lines of those who challenge the danger of a single story (Adichie, 2009) and demand ethnic studies. While curriculum change is usually one of the first things students demand, curriculum is part of a larger project of liberation.

Ethnic Studies as a Decolonial Project

When schools adopt ethnic studies, the motivation of school administrators is usually to raise the academic achievement of their minoritized students, and ethnic studies programs have been found to accomplish that goal (Cabrera et al., 2014; Dee & Penner, 2017; Sleeter, 2011). But the purpose of ethnic studies goes much deeper than that, reflecting an analysis of *why* minoritized students so often disengage from school. Students respond to school based mainly on what happens (or fails to happen) to them while they are there. For example, this Black high school student referred to the history she was being taught as "not like the real history," but rather "what you need to know to graduate," and "what your teacher thinks is important" (Woodson, 2015, p. 62). She went on to say:

> I know that a lot of our history, like Black women and things we did as maybe civil rights leaders in history is missing. It's what you supposed to know to get through this system, you know, to graduate ... just to keep your teachers or the testers happy.
>
> *p. 62*

Her characterization illustrates Carretero's claim that the inability of people to "see their own face in the mirror of the past" of school knowledge (2011, p. 36) calls into question the usefulness or legitimacy of that knowledge.

San Pedro (2018a) argues that traditional schooling "props up Whiteness as a benchmark for what society ought to be" (p. 1210), dehumanizing students who do not acquiesce. Tejeda, Espinoza, and Gutierrez (2003) explain that,

> colonial domination and its ideological frameworks operate and are reproduced in and through the curricular content and design, the instructional practices, the social organization of learning, and the forms of evaluation that inexorably sort and label students into enduring categories of success and failure of schooling.
>
> *p. 20*

From the curriculum, to who teaches, to how learning is constructed, to the relationship between schools and their community contexts—in most schools these reinforce White ways of thinking and being that, while invisible to white students and teachers, impact negatively on minoritized students.

Tejeda, Espinoza, and Gutierrez (2003) call for decolonizing, or dismantling internal neocolonialism of "working class indigenous and nonwhite peoples and their descendants" (p. 13). Decolonization involves a process of delinking consciousness from European and North Euro-American epistemes. According to Mignolo (2007), delinking "brings to the foreground other epistemologies, other principles of knowledge and understanding and, consequently, other economy, other politics, other ethics" (p. 453).

Ethnic studies sits at the nexus of this delinking project. Drawing on Fanon's analysis of decolonization as both the freeing of territory from external control and the freeing of the consciousness of the colonized, Tintiangco-Cubales and colleagues (2015) view decolonization as "a liberatory process that is central to Ethnic Studies pedagogy because it allows for a systematic critique of the traumatic history of colonialism on native and Third World peoples and, subsequently, healing from colonial trauma" (p. 111). Liberating consciousness begins with challenging the worldview normally sanctioned by the school curriculum, and challenging the authority of others to define what is true and worth knowing.

Generally, nation-building projects construct a narrative based on myths of origin and the identity of dominant groups, striving to cultivate people's psychological identification with that narrative (Van Alphen & Carretero, 2015). Ethnic studies interrogates those myths and narratives, drawing on counter-narratives that arise from within marginalized communities. De los Rios (2013) argues that, "Curriculum represents one of the primary instruments for maintaining the legacy of hegemony in U.S. schools," and that "Ethnic Studies works to recover and restore counterhistorical narratives as well as the epistemologies, perspectives, and cultures of those who have been historically marginalized and denied full participation within traditional discourses and institutions" (p. 60; see also Au, Brown, & Calderon, 2016; Diveri & Moreira, 2013). Generally such counter-narratives arise within homes and communities rather than schools.

Ethnic studies classes, while located within schools and universities, subvert the purpose of maintaining social control. In a sense, they operate as fugitive spaces, which Harney and Moten (2013) define as spaces within but not of an institution, where people engage in revolutionary work. Ethnic studies is part of a larger political project to subvert oppressive power relations and the ideologies that support them, including intersections of colonialism, racism, and capitalism (de los Rios, 2013; Tejeda, Espinoza, & Gutierrez, 2003; Tintiangco-Cubales et al., 2015). Buenavista, Stovall, Curammeng, and Valdez (2019) maintain that, "even though Ethnic Studies has been institutionalized, its intent to be critical remains—to encourage acts of subversion that challenge traditional notions of schooling" (p. 228).

Ethnic studies opens space for cross-racial dialog, but dialog that is not dominated by white points of view. Rocco, Berneir, and Bowman (2014) explain that,

> both people of color and Whites experience race; however, for people of color, the experience is typically from the perspective of the oppressed and for Whites, it is from the perspective of oppressor. When a space is made to hear the unique voices of people of color, hope for dialogue and improved racial relations is created.
>
> *p. 461*

Research studies on the impact of university ethnic studies courses on white students support this hope, in fact, finding that even though white students typically find such courses emotionally challenging, gradually they learn to hear minoritized perspectives (Bowman, 2010).

A decolonizing pedagogy builds on Freire's (1970) process for developing critical consciousness. Tejeda, Espinoza, and Gutierrez (2003) propose "an anticolonial and decolonizing pedagogical praxis" that enables students to develop "a critical decolonizing consciousness and activity that work to ameliorate and ultimately end the mutually constitutive forms of violence that characterize our internal neocolonial condition" (pp. 20–21). Decolonizing pedagogy, they explain, is anti-racist, anti-sexist, anti-homophobic. It involves counter-storytelling, healing, and reclaiming (Fernandez, 2019; Zavala, 2016).

Ultimately, San Pedro (2018a) posits that ethnic studies frees space in which students can learn and teach multiple truths about their lives and realities. Ethnic studies "would require that both teachers and students have a chance to face our nation's painful past, to see how we operate within settler colonial states in order to counter that which is within and around us to seek solutions to our intersecting problems" (p. 1223). Ethnic studies would "center pedagogies and curriculum on the rich heritage and cultural practices that students bring with them to school" (San Pedro, 2018b, p. 334). By teaching students to actually hear each other's realities, a radically humanizing ethnic studies curriculum and pedagogy aims to dismantle the gulf between oppressor and oppressed by taking on oppressive relationships themselves.

Ethnic Studies Praxis

Below are two ethnic studies projects that, although different from each other, illustrate commonalities of ethnic studies praxis. *Pinoy Teach* is a small-scale curriculum project developed for the purpose of decolonizing the minds of mainly Filipino American university and middle school students. To assess its impact on students, one of the authors of the curriculum conducted two qualitative follow-up studies. The San Francisco Unified School District's ninth-grade ethnic studies course, which also has the purpose of decolonization and development of activism, grew from a small-scale to a district-wide program. The program's coordinators contracted with researchers at Stanford University to conduct a quantitative study of its academic impact on students. Like most other research studies on the impact of ethnic studies on students (Sleeter, 2011), both found a positive impact.

Pinoy Teach

Patricia Espiritu Halagao co-developed *Pinoy Teach* with a Filipino American activist; the curriculum is based on a decolonizing reading of Filipino American history. She taught the curriculum to university students (most were Filipino American). She described the curriculum as organized from Filipino American points of view around the elementary and secondary school social studies concepts of perspective, revolution, imperialism, immigration, racism, and identity. She explained that, "Learning Filipino content was secondary to understanding how these concepts related to students and their fellow classmates" (2010, p. 500). She led students through a Hawaiian activist decolonization framework that included five stages: (1) rediscovery/recovery, (2) mourning, (3) dreaming, (4) commitment, and (5) action. She used a problem-posing pedagogy that encouraged students to think critically as they grappled with multiple perspectives on history. For example, she taught students to analyze course readings by asking: Who wrote this? "'Whose perspective is privileged?' and 'Whose perspective does it marginalize?'" (Halagao, 2004, p. 464–465). Her aim was not to replace one master narrative with another, but rather to help students grapple with and think their way through diverse and conflicting perspectives, then consider what to do with their new knowledge. As part of the learning process, the university students mentored and taught what they were learning to middle school students in social studies classrooms.

In two studies, Halagao examined the impact of *Pinoy Teach* on the university students. First, through a series of interviews, Halagao (2004) examined the curriculum's impact on six Filipino American college students at the end of the course. Questions focused on students' life histories before the course, their understanding of their ethnic identities, and how they experienced each part of the course. She found that since none of the students had learned about Filipino history in school, they described this curriculum as "filling in the blanks." Students also described collisions between their prior knowledge of Philippine history, learned mainly from their parents, and that in the curriculum, particularly around the experiences of Spanish, then U.S. colonization. The students expressed interest in learning about their own history in relationship to that of other groups. They described shifting from seeing other Filipinos through learned stereotypes to building a shared sense of community, and they developed a sense of confidence and empowerment to stand up to oppression and to work for their own communities.

Several years later, Halagao (2010) reported a follow-up survey of 35 former students who had participated in the course about 10 years earlier; 30 were Filipino American and 5 were Euro-American; all had completed university and were working in various professions. The survey consisted of five open-ended questions about their memory of *Pinoy Teach*, and its impact on them. Respondents reported that what remained with them was a "deeper love and appreciation of ethnic history, culture, identity, and community" (p. 505). The curriculum, through its process of decolonization, had helped them to develop a sense of empowerment and self-efficacy that persisted, as well as a life commitment to diversity and multiculturalism. They also developed ongoing activism in their work as teachers, in other professions, and/or through civic engagement where they lived.

San Francisco's Ninth-Grade Ethnic Studies Program

In 2005, the San Francisco Unified School District school board unanimously passed a resolution to explore the creation of a ninth-grade ethnic studies course, and to authorize resources for a group of teachers to spend a year laying its foundation. During summer 2007, with support from a university ethnic studies faculty member, teachers began to design the course, which they taught a year later. By 2018, the course was being offered in every high school in the district, along with regular professional development for teachers and support staff. Initially, the teachers planned the curriculum around specific racial and ethnic groups' experiences. But as they quickly discovered the impossibility of covering the diverse histories, experiences, and lives of San Francisco's highly diverse population, they shifted toward a framework that enables large, interrelated concepts that center on race and racism to be taught in relationship to local contexts.

The course consists of six units, organized around the following key concepts: (1) identity and narrative, (2) systems and power, (3) hegemony and counterhegemony, (4) humanization and dehumanization, (5) causality and agency, and (6) transformation and change. Essentially, the course is organized around a deep analysis of the institutional structures of racism, and how racism can be systemically challenged. Each unit is elaborated with enduring understandings and essential questions. For example, the curriculum framework defines hegemony (Unit 3) as: "The dominance of one group over another, supported by legitimating norms, ideas and expectations within the existing system(s) in power." Counterhegemony "challenges values, norms, systems and conditions that have been legitimized and promoted as natural and unchanging/unchangeable by the dominant class in society." Concepts that support the analysis of hegemony include stereotypes, mass media, Du Bois' articulation of double consciousness, Freire's conscientization, and Plato's theory of forms. One of the unit's essential questions is: "What are the tools of hegemony used in the United States and how do they empower or disempower groups within society?" To learn to identify and analyze tools of hegemony, students examine media, especially media they consume such as television. A reading preparing students to analyze television begins by asking them to consider how decades of programs, scenes, ads, news stories, and so forth have normalized whiteness. They are also shown examples of the long history of minoritized groups producing television with counterhegemonic messaging. As students analyze media they consume, they are challenged to consider their analysis in relationship to that larger context.

An extensive collection of resources for teachers (including sample syllabi, PowerPoints, readings, films, graphic organizers), organized primarily around the six units of the course, is available on Google Drive. During professional development, teachers learn philosophical and conceptual foundations of ethnic studies, as well as how to use the resources available to them.

Beckham and Concordia (2019) explain that, "There are concerted efforts by conservatives and traditionalists to paint the course as not rigorous, academic, or useful. We believe the best way to neutralize this tendency is to gather as much qualitative and quantitative evidence as possible about the course's efficacy" (p. 333). Toward that end, the program's coordinators contracted with two

Stanford University researchers to evaluate its impact on students. Using a regression discontinuity design, Dee and Penner (2017) evaluated its impact on five cohorts of 1,405 ninth-grade students in three high schools, using data on student grade point average (GPA), attendance, and credits earned toward graduation. After controlling for several variables (such as students' entering GPA and measures of teacher effectiveness), their "results indicate that assignment to this course increased ninth-grade student attendance by 21 percentage points, GPA by 1.4 grade points, and credits earned by 23" (p. 18). In other words, the course content, rather than weakening students academically, actually strengthened their academic performance even on traditional measures.

Ethnic Studies Praxis

As these two examples illustrate, ethnic studies reframes academic knowledge from the points of view of historically marginalized racial and ethnic groups. Both projects intentionally reframed history—*Pinoy Teach* from Filipino American perspectives, and the San Francisco course from multiple marginalized groups' points of view.

The two examples also illustrate decoloniality. First, both offered minoritized students frameworks for critically examining the subordinate position their communities occupy, and their legacies of resistance to subordination, so that students learn to identify systemic structures that can be changed, rather than locating the roots of their subordination within themselves and their culture. The studies by Halagao (2004, 2010) revealed the impact of these frameworks on students' development of a sense of community with each other, a sense of personal empowerment, and ongoing activism. The study by Dee and Penner (2017) revealed the power of such framing to engage minoritized students in school, including attending class and taking classwork seriously.

Second, both treated minoritized students as intellectuals who are capable of complex critical thinking. A persistent problem minoritized students encounter is being treated as needing remediation rather than as intellectuals. *Pinoy Teach* specifically challenged students to grapple with multiple and conflicting historical narratives, and to think through their own understanding based on doing so. Beckham and Concordia (2019) explain that central to San Francisco's ethnic studies course is engaging students in critical analysis as well as reading, writing, and conducting research. Ultimately, they "want our students to apply their skills and knowledge in the service of the creation and maintenance of a just society" (p. 331).

The examples show potential for dialog across groups. While most of the students in the *Pinoy Teach* course were Filipino American, some were white. All of the students learned an alternative history discourse than they had learned previously, one rooted in a critical analysis of racism and colonization. San Francisco's ethnic studies course, which explicitly makes space for the voices and perspectives of people marginalized by racism, is open to all students, including white students.

The two examples also suggest areas for further development. While both of these examples illustrate social studies curriculum for older students, the entire elementary and secondary experience can be designed and taught through ethnic studies. For example, while it is possible to teach math through ethnic studies (e.g., Gutstein & Peterson, 2006; Lipka, et al., 2005), much more has been written about doing so in social studies than in other disciplines. And while similar work can be done with younger students (e.g., Valdez, 2019), so far most of what is written addresses the secondary level.

Implications

Schools generally produce historical amnesia, framing the social order as natural by teaching knowledge that reflects dominant perspectives (Apple, 2004). When considered from the vantage point of how colonization works, we can understand much of school knowledge as a continuation of European and Euro-North American attempts to replace knowledge held by subordinate groups with their own. While up to a point, students from subordinate communities learn to see school knowledge as of value, if for no other reason than its serving as a gatekeeper. But many students also question its truth, and from time to time, rebel. Rebellion can take the form of dropping out of school, but it can also take the form of organized demands for an alternative. Such is the case of ethnic studies in the U.S.

Over the past few years in the U.S., ethnic studies has experienced considerable success in becoming instantiated in schools largely through the strength of its advocacy and its demonstrated positive impact on minoritized students academically and on white students attitudinally (Sleeter, 2011). Buenavista and colleagues (2019) explain that, "Ethnic Studies is the only academic discipline to be conceptualized for People of Color and by People of Color" (p. 228). White people can participate, but not at the expense of its central framing of issues, its commitments, and its purpose. Because of its direct challenge to deeply entrenched power relationships and the processes legitimizing them, we can anticipate efforts to either dismantle or domesticate ethnic studies, as those in power seek to marginalize "dangerous" discourse.

The applicability of this U.S.-based work to other contexts will need to be judged by members of minoritized groups themselves. When I talk about this work outside the U.S., I am usually met with skepticism, especially by members of dominant social groups. I may be told that there are too few minorities for ethnic studies to be relevant, or that ethnic studies seems to separate people rather than integrating them. And yet, on more than one occasion, someone from a minoritized group has privately expressed to me great interest in this work because it names the forms of racism that they experience. Ultimately, as a liberating project that draws insights and energy from fugitive spaces, it will not be the dominant society that takes up ethnic studies, but rather those who experience racial injustice everyday and see ethnic studies as a constructive way forward.

References

Adichie, C. N. (2009). El peligro la historia única—español. TED talk. www.youtube.com/watch?v=sYItZ3bTosU

Alridge, D. P. (2006). The limits of master narratives in history textbooks. *Teachers College Record 108*(4), 662–686.

Apple, M. W. (2004). *Ideology and curriculum*, 3rd ed. New York: Routledge Falmer.

Au, W., Brown, A. L., & Calderón, D. (2016). *Reclaiming the multicultural roots of U.S. curriculum*. New York: Teachers College Press.

Banks, J. A. (1996). The African American roots of multicultural education. In J. A. Banks (Ed.), *Multicultural education, transformative knowledge, and action* (pp. 30–45). New York: Teachers College Press.

Beckham, K., & Concordia, A. (2019). We don't want to just study the world, we want to change it. In R. T. Cuauhtin, M. Zavala, C. Sleeter, & W. Au (Eds.), *Rethinking ethnic studies* (pp. 327–335). Milwaukee, WI: Rethinking Schools Ltd.

Bloom, A. (1987). *The closing of the American mind*. New York: Simon & Schuster.

Bohn, A. P., & Sleeter, C. E. (2000). Multicultural education and the standards movement: A report from the field. *Phi Delta Kappan 82*(2), 156–159.

Bowman, N. A. (2010). Disequilibrium and resolution: The non-linear effects of diversity courses on well-being and orientations towards diversity. *The Review of Higher Education 33*(4), 543–568.

Brown, A. L., & Brown, K. D. (2015). The more things change, the more they stay the same: Excavating race and the enduring racisms in U.S. curriculum. *Teachers College Record, 117*(14), 103–130.

Brown, K. D., & Brown, A. L. (2010). Silenced memories: An examination of the sociocultural knowledge on race and racial violence in official school curriculum. *Equity & Excellence in Education 43*(2), 139–154. DOI: 10.1080/10665681003719590

Buenavista, T. A., Stovall, D., Curammeng, E. R., & Valdez, C. (2019). Ethnic studies educators as enemies of the state and the fugitive space of the classroom. In R. T. Cuauhtin, M. Zavala, C. Sleeter, & W. Au (Eds.), *Rethinking ethnic studies* (pp. 228–233). Milwaukee, WI: Rethinking Schools Ltd.

Busey, C. L., & Russell, W. B. (2017). "We want to learn": Middle school Latino/a students discuss social studies curriculum and pedagogy. *RMLE Online*, 39(4), 1–20. DOI: 10.1080/19404476.2016.1155921

Cabrera, N. L., Milam, J. F., Jaquette, O., & Marx, R. W. (2014). Missing the (student achievement) forest for all the (political) trees: Empiricism and the Mexican American student controversy in Tucson. *American Educational Research Journal 51*(6), 1084–1118.

Cammarota, J., & Romero, A. (2009). The Social Justice Education Project: A critically compassionate intellectualism for Chicana/o students. In W. Ayers, T. Quinn, & D. Stovall (Eds.), *Handbook for social justice education* (pp. 465–476). New York: Routledge.

Carmichael, J. (2012). Social control. *Oxford Bibliographies*. DOI: 10.1093/OBO/9780199756384-0048

Carrasco Cardona, G., & Cuauhtin, R. T. (2019). The emergence of the Ethnic Studies Now coalition in Yanga and beyond. In R. T. Cuauhtin, M. Zavala, C. Sleeter, &

W. Au (Eds.), *Rethinking ethnic studies* (pp. 310–315). Milwaukee, WI: Rethinking Schools Ltd.

Carretero, M. (2011). *Constructing patriotism*. Charlotte, NC: Information Age Publishing.

Case, A., & Ngo, B. (2017). "Do we have to call it that?" The response of neoliberal multiculturalism to college antiracism efforts. *Multicultural Perspectives 19*(4), 215–224.

Chu, Y. (2015). The power of knowledge: A critical analysis of the depiction of ethnic minorities in China's elementary textbooks. *Race Ethnicity and Education, 18*(4), 469–487. DOI: 10.1080/13613324.2015.1013460

Cuauhtin, R. T., Zavala, M., Sleeter, C., & Au. W. (2019). Introduction. In R. T. Cuauhtin, M. Zavala, C. Sleeter, & W. Au (Eds.), *Rethinking ethnic studies* (pp. 11–15). Milwaukee, WI: Rethinking Schools Ltd.

Dee, T., & Penner, E. (2017). The causal effects of cultural relevance: Evidence from an ethnic studies curriculum. *American Educational Research Journal 54*(1), 127–166. DOI: 10.3102/0002831216677002

de los Rios, C. V. (2013). A curriculum of the borderlands: High school Chicana/o-Latina/o studies as sitios y lengua. *The Urban Review 45*, 58–73.

Diveri, M., & Moreira, C. (2013). Real world: Classrooms as decolonizing sites against neoliberal narratives of the other. *Cultural Studies Critical Methodologies 13*(6), 469–473.

Epstein, T. (2009). *Interpreting national history*. New York: Routledge.

Eraqi, M. M. (2015). Inclusion of Arab-Americans and Muslim-Americans within secondary U.S. history textbooks. *Journal of International Social Studies 5*(1), 64–80.

Fernandez, A. E. (2019). Counter-storytelling and decolonial pedagogy. In R. T. Cuauhtin, M. Zavala, C. Sleeter, & W. Au (Eds.), *Rethinking ethnic studies* (pp. 43–47). Milwaukee, WI: Rethinking Schools Ltd.

Freire, P. (1970). *Pedagogy of the oppressed*. New York: Continuum.

Gorski, P. (1999). *A brief history of multicultural education*. Critical Multicultural Pavilion. www.edchange.org/multicultural/papers/edchange_history.html

Gorski, P. C. (2008). Good intentions are not enough: A decolonizing intercultural education. *Intercultural Education, 19*(6), 515–525.

Grant, C. A., & Sleeter, C. E. (2009). *Turning on learning*, 5th ed. New York: Wiley.

Gutstein, E., & Peterson, B. (2006). *Rethinking mathematics*. Milwaukee, WI: Rethinking Schools Ltd.

Halagao, P. E. (2004). Holding up the mirror: The complexity of seeing your ethnic self in history. *Theory and Research in Social Education 32*(4), 459–483.

Halagao, P. E. (2010). Liberating Filipino Americans by decolonizing curriculum. *Race Ethnicity and Education 13*(4), 495–512.

Harney, S., & Moten, F. (2013). The undercommons: Fugitive planning and Black study. 1–165. Research Collection Lee Kong Chian School of Business. https://ink.library.smu.edu.sg/cgi/viewcontent.cgi?article=6024&context=lkcsb_research

Institute of Educational Sciences. National Center for Education Statistics (2019). *Fast Facts*. https://nces.ed.gov/fastfacts/display.asp?id=372

Kivel, P. (2013). *Living in the shadow of the cross*. Gabriola Island, BC: New Society Publishers.

Leonardo, Z. (2009). *Race, whiteness and education*. New York: Routledge.

Lipka, J., Hogan, M. P., Webster, J. P., Yanez, E., Adams, B., Clark, S., & Lacy, D. (2005). Math in a cultural context: Two case studies of a successful culturally-based math project. *Anthropology & Education Quarterly 36*(4), 367–385.

Martinez, G. (2010). *Native pride*. Cresskill, NJ: Hampton Press, Inc.

Mignolo, W. D. (2007). Delinking: The rhetoric of modernity, the logic of coloniality and the grammar of de-coloniality. *Cultural Studies, 21*(2–3), 449–514.

Mudimbe, V. Y. (1988). *The invention of Africa: Gnosis, philosophy, and the order of knowledge.* Bloomington: Indiana University Press.

Musu-Gillette, L., de Brey, C., McFarland, J., Hussar, W., Sonnenberg, W., & Wilkinson-Flicker, S. (2017). *Status and trends in the education of racial and ethnic groups 2017 (NCES 2017–051).* U.S. Department of Education, National Center for Education Statistics. Washington, DC. Retrieved from http://nces.ed.gov/pubsearch.

Noboa, J. (2005). *Leaving Latinos out of history: Teaching US history in Texas.* New York: Routledge.

Ochoa, G. L. (2007). *Learning from Latino teachers.* San Francisco: Jossey Bass.

Pelligrino, A., Mann, L., & Russell, W. B., III (2013). Lift as we climb: A textbook analysis of the segregated school experience. *The High School Journal 96*, 209–231.

Perez, D. R. (2014, December 9). Characters in children's books are almost always white, and it's a big problem. *The Washington Post.* www.washingtonpost.com/posteverything/wp/2014/12/08/characters-in-childrens-books-are-almost-always-white-and-its-a-big-problem/?noredirect=on&utm_term=.50bb947b004c

Piatek-Jimenez, K., Madison, M., & Przybyla-Kucheck, J. (2014). Equity in mathematics textbooks: A new look at an old issue. *Journal of Women and Minorities in Science and Engineering 20*(1), 55–74.

Quijano, A. (2007). Coloniality and modernity/rationality. *Cultural Studies, 21* (2–3), 168–178.

Reese, D. (2007). Proceed with caution: Using Native American folktales in the classroom. *Language Arts 84*(3), 245–256.

Rocco, T. S., Bernier, J. D., & Bowman, L. (2014). Critical race theory and HRD: Moving race front and center. *Advances in Developing Human Resources 16*(4), 457–470.

Rojas, M. A. (2010). (Re)visioning U.S. Latino literatures in high school English classrooms. *English Education 42*(3), 263–277.

Romanowski, M. H. (2009). Excluding ethical issues from U.S. history textbooks. *American Secondary Education 37*(2), 26–48.

Samper Rosero L., & Garreta Bochaca, J. (2011). Muslims in Catalonian textbooks. *Journal of Educational Media, Memory, and Society 3*(1), 81–96.

San Pedro, T. (2018a). Abby as ally: An argument for culturally disruptive pedagogy. *American Educational Research Journal 55*(6), 1193–1232.

San Pedro, T. (2018b). Sustaining ourselves in unsustainable places: Revitalizing sacred landscapes within schools. *Journal of Adolescent and Adult Literacy 62*(3), 333–336.

Schoorman, D., & Bogotch, I. (2010). Moving beyond 'diversity' to 'social justice': The challenge to reconceptualize multicultural education. *Intercultural Education 21*(1), 79–85.

Sleeter, C. E. (1995). An analysis of the critiques of multicultural education. In J. A. Banks & C. M. Banks (Eds.), *Handbook of research on multicultural education* (pp. 81–94). New York: Macmillan.

Sleeter C. (2011). *The academic and social value of ethnic studies.* Washington, DC: National Education Association.

Sleeter, C. E. (2018). Multicultural programming in New Mexico. Unpublished report prepared for Martinez v. New Mexico, D-101-CV-2014-00793.

Stanton, C. R. (2014). The curricular Indian agent: Discursive colonization and Indigenous (dys)agency in U.S. history textbooks. *Curriculum Inquiry 44*(5), 649–676.

Tejeda, C., Espinoza, M., & Gutierrez, K. (2003). Toward a decolonizing pedagogy: Social justice reconsidered. In P. P. Trifonas (Ed.), *Pedagogies of difference* (pp. 10–40). New York: Routledge Falmer.

Tintiangco-Cubales, A., Kohli, R., Sacramento, J., Henning, N., Agarwal-Rangnath, R., & Sleeter, C. (2015). Toward an ethnic studies pedagogy: Implications for K-12 schools from the research. *Urban Review* 47(1), 204–225. DOI: 10.1007/s11256-014-0280-y

U.S. Department of Education (2012). Top stories in NAEP long-term trend assessments 2012. *The Nation's Report Card*. www.nationsreportcard.gov/ltt_2012/

Valdez, C. (2019). Challenging colonialism: Ethnic studies in elementary social studies. In R. T. Cuauhtin, M. Zavala, C. Sleeter, & W. Au (Eds.), *Rethinking ethnic studies* (pp. 161–164). Milwaukee, WI: Rethinking Schools Ltd.

Van Alphen, F., & Carretero, M. (2015). The construction of the relation between national past and present in the appropriation of historical master narratives. *Integrative Psychology and Behavioral Sciences* 49, 512–530. DOI: 10.1007/s12124-015-9302-x

Vaught, S. E., & Castagno, A. E. (2008). "I don't think I'm a racist": Critical race theory, teacher attitudes, and structural racism. *Race Ethnicity and Education 11*(2), 95–113.

Weiner, M. (2018). Curricular alienation: Multiculturalism, tolerance, and immigrants in Dutch primary school history textbooks. *Humanity & Society 42*(2), 147–170.

Woodson, A. N. (2015). "What you supposed to know:" Urban Black students' perspectives on history textbooks. *Journal of Urban Learning, Teaching, and Research, 11*, 57–65.

Zavala, M. (2016). Decolonial methodologies in education. In M.A. Peters (Ed.), *Encyclopedia of educational philosophy and theory*. Singapore: Springer Science. DOI: 10.1007/978-981-287-532-7_498-1

4

IMAGINING: "A LETTER ON RACIAL PROGRESS"—JAMES BALDWIN'S KEYNOTE AT THE 30TH ANNUAL NAME CONFERENCE—EVOLUTION OF MULTICULTURAL EDUCATION

Twenty-First Century

Carl A. Grant

James Baldwin was not a multiculturalist, per se, but, he marched in protest, wrote, spoke, and delivered interviews in support of the foundational concepts of multicultural education before there was multicultural education. Baldwin's purpose and duty in life was arguing for the humanity of Black, Brown, Asian American, and Native American people; all poor people; and people who were gay and lesbian; and interrogating the evils of white supremacy, privilege, and willful ignorance. To those of us who conceptualized and advocated for multicultural education during the last half of the twentieth century and first two decades of the twenty-first century, James Baldwin's conceptualizing, theorizing, framing, articulating, and practicing of education discourses have been invaluable. But this, you all know. Your copy of *The Fire Next Time* (1963), *Notes of a Native Son* (1955), and my favorite, *Baldwin: Collected Essays* (1998) edited by Toni Morrison, is filled with scribbled notes on race, democracy, poverty, being Black, life as a gay Black woman or man that you wrote to yourself on the margins of the pages.

Thus, when I received the request from Drs. H. Prentice Baptiste and Jeanette Haynes Writer to write a chapter on "social justice and neoliberalism" for this collection: *Visioning Multicultural Education: Past, Present, Future*, I would be lying if I said I was overjoyed; quite the contrary, I had just completed a manuscript for a new book, *"Bearing Witness": James Baldwin and the American School House* (Grant, forthcoming), and wanted a breather. Besides, for the time, I had said all I wanted to say about social justice and neoliberalism. Prentice, however, is a good friend and colleague; we go way-back. Saying, "No" to his request, just isn't something you do.

I wondered how I could satisfy Prentice and Jeanette's request and make writing a chapter an engaging and joyous undertaking. My wondering led to imagining, based upon the Baldwin manuscript that I had just completed, what James Baldwin would say as a keynote speaker to the annual NAME conference in Montgomery, Alabama on October 7–11, 2020 when the book would be released and especially at this time of public resurgence of white supremacy. Baldwin, as I thought about keynote speakers, for such a special contemplation, at such a historical place (Montgomery, Alabama) in the deep confederated South, was PERFECT! I recalled Baldwin's friend Maya Angelou's (n.d.) statement, "I have great respect for the past. If you don't know where you've come from, you don't know where you're going" (p. 1).

Selecting speech topic(s), I must admit, was a bit challenging, as there is so much Baldwin could say about the racialized sexualized violence we are living in as well as the "Visioning of Multicultural Education." He could speak for days and days about racism and Trump and other isms and Trump. I asked myself, could I pull this off? Here, the grad class on Baldwin I teach was very helpful. They, especially Kyle and Rosette, my grad students, encouraged me in Baldwin speak, "to go for broke." Use my study of Baldwin's life, and work, and let it rip. Provide readers with background knowledge to give historical and contemporary context—*I do this in italics*—make Baldwin spontaneous and brilliant; be respectful, in your deed, but "go for broke!"

Background: Jimmy Preparing for NAME

Baldwin is aware of the heightened significance of NAME being in Montgomery. He knows the racial history of Montgomery; the legacy of Black blood spilled and Black bodies violently beaten, and killed to bring about the Voting Rights Act of 1965. Baldwin knows of the people seated before him—their roles, responsibilities and efforts in advocating social justice and multicultural education policies and practices for children of color. NAME, since its birth in 1990, has not only warmly welcomed, but sought out social justice educators. NAME members are Jimmy's kind of people. No phoniness, no pretense; local community members, teachers, scholars, deans, school superintendents, chancellors, elected officials, and media personalities all leave their egos and CV's [curriculum vitae] at the conference door and become humble people, seeking to heighten their consciousness at NAME. Geneva Gay, Christine Sleeter, Jim and Cherry Banks, Sonia Nieto, and other notable rock stars at AERA and other conferences are everyday people at NAME, for they know as Robert Kennedy learned when meeting with Baldwin and other civil right activists (like Harry Belafonte, Lena Horne, Kenneth Clark, Lorraine Hansberry) in 1963 that they are there for Black children. If not rushing between engagements, Jimmy would have attended sessions at the conference before he spoke; joined a table of NAME members having breakfast or lunch on the day before his talk. Jimmy is congenial and friendly. He likes people and shows it. If Jimmy had arrived early enough the night before he was to speak, he would have joined NAME members dancing and/or engaged in discussion with them late into the night; with flowing drink, food, cigarettes, and politically engaged minds, Jimmy will talk and listen all night. Jimmy wants democracy to work and he believes dialogue, communication between and among people, is important and necessary. The essay—personal essay, his choice of engagement—allows him to bend his artistic and political expression. That said, he "holds court" with the best of them. Baldwin, as Bernstein and Mooney (2019) observe,

> *believes that real freedom is built out of small, intimate encounters, moments where we examine ourselves and others and do our best to see one another clearly and completely. And it is only as we build that sort of freedom individually that we will have a chance at true democracy together.*
>
> *p. 2*

The NAME membership finds Baldwin not only charming and one of them, but brilliant. Again and again throughout the late evening, they hear him providing a full reckoning of the difficulty of attaining home, love, or democracy in America let alone all three (Bernstein & Mooney, 2019). They come to understand that his criticism of America is because he loves America and knows America is cheating herself in not "going for broke" to fulfill her constitutional mandate. They hear his beliefs about love reclaiming the lost promise of American democracy and they contemplate the psychological and embodied demands of love that Jimmy argues are necessary to transform the consciousness of Black and White Americans (Butorac, 2018). They nod in agreement and offer one another high-fives as Jimmy's critique of property links self-transformation to the need for structural transformation (Butorac, 2018).

Throughout the evening, individually to Jimmy or as small groups, they welcome him and compliment his avocation of each and everyone's life as miraculous; and they give tribute to his remarks on the need to preserve the miraculousness of human individuality; and they snap their fingers when Jimmy gives voice to his prose from No Name in the Street *(1972), that people—each individual, woman, man, and child, Black or white—must treat each other "as the miracles they are, while trying to protect oneself against the disasters they've become"* (p. 4). *Some speak to Jimmy about* The Fire Next Time (1963) *and* Giovanni's Room *(1956), explaining how it influenced their life. Some graduate students ask him to comment on the slogan "Make America Great Again" and its implications for a loss of America's European identity, especially after the election of a two-term Black president. These graduate students invite him to put into context Trump's slogan with his statement in "A letter to My Nephew" (Baldwin, 1962),*

> *the danger in the minds of most white Americans is the loss of their identity ... those innocents who believe that your imprisonment made them safe are losing their grip on reality ... If integration means anything, this is what it means: that we, with love, shall force our [white] brothers to see themselves as they are.*
>
> *p. 2*

Jimmy responds to the grad students, sincerely and with patience and respect—the way he always responds to young people, acknowledging to them they are the hope and future. Jimmy argues, he was attempting to expose the monster(s) that lives within the dark corners of our mind that inspires micro and macro aggressions that resist democracy from becoming a reality.

The final question of the evening comes from graduate students, who ask him to respond to Ta-Nehisi Coates' (2015) book Between the World and Me, *where Coates write to his son, Samori, "the police departments of [this] country have been endowed with the authority to destroy your body," and "In America, it is traditional to destroy the black body—it is heritage" (p. 103). These graduate students tell Jimmy that Michelle Alexander (2015) argues that a major difference between your "Letter" and Coates' book is a difference in how the two of you view the future of Black people. Alexander (2015) writes that you [Jimmy] "repeatedly emphasize [James'] power and potential and you urge him to believe that revolutionary change is possible against all odds. You [Jimmy] have hope, not 'specious hope' (Coates, 2015, p. 10); you believe, and argue, 'we must believe that it [change and growth] is possible' … that people can be better than they are" (Baldwin, 1963, p. 47). Coates' emphasis, one grad student says, referencing Ferriter (2016), is "fear and stasis"—"the permanence of racial injustice in America, the foolishness of believing that one person can make a change, and the dangers of believing in the American Dream" (p. 128). Coates (2015) focuses on "the world and certainly democracy in the United States seems fixed, unwilling to acknowledge the possibility for societal change or even the capacity for individuals to change and evolve over time" (p. 2), and your emphasis is on "love and growth" (p. 3), and you see American democracy as experiential, it is evolving, with the ability to change, and that both people and society have the capacity to change. In other words, you [Jimmy] argue that "as our country and its people progress and evolve, we move toward love, openness, and a more inclusive democracy" (Ferriter, 2016, p. 129). Additionally, you [Jimmy] argue that it is because I am aware of the horrific evil done to Black bodies that I bear witness and report on the racial attention that plagues the nation. I speak of hope and offer guidance for the future in this time of activism that NAME advocates and despair that NAME rallies against because I am not pessimistic, nor fearful, and I believe that democracy must be realized, race must be understood, otherwise there are serious consequences for all. I understand that there is "no possibility of a real change in the Negro's situation without the most radical and far-reaching changes in the American political and social structure" (Baldwin, 1963, p. 85). Concluding, Jimmy says, "The person who distrusts himself has no touchstone for reality … whatever white people do not know about Negroes reveals, precisely and inexorably, what they do not know about themselves" (Baldwin, 1963, p. 85).*

Welcome to NAME, Jimmy, His Friends Call Him Jimmy, You May if You …

I imagine Jimmy beginning his remarks to the over-flowing, standing-room-only NAME audience, after a glowing introduction by Dr. Prentice Baptiste. Seated on the stage, not far from Jimmy, is the Founder of NAME, Rose Duhon-Sells, and founding members: Drs. Cherry Gooden, Marjorie Kyle, and Pritchy Smith. Prentice would tell the NAME audience that Jimmy Baldwin, according to Amiri Baraka (2009), is an "elegant griot of our oppressed African-American nation," who gave his people the "black warm truth" (p. 242).

His novels, plays, and essays alike, explore the psychological implications of racism for both the oppressed and the oppressor (Poetry Foundation, 2020, p. 1). Henry Gates describes his meeting with Baldwin as the determining factor in his decision to become a literary critic. Prentice would remind NAME that in 1963, at the height of the Civil Rights Movement, Jimmy was on the cover of Time Magazine, and was a feature story in Life Magazine (May 24, 1963). For many, Prentice would say, "James Baldwin is the 'Pulitzer prize writer on the Civil Rights Movement.' Baldwin achieved prominent spaces on the covers of magazines and celebrity recognition throughout the media because of the 'poignancy and abrasiveness' he brings to America's dark realities. He shines a light on the systemic and personal racial subjugation and argues that racism is not a series of discrete issues—schools, employment, confederate statues and so forth." Baldwin, Prentice argues, believes America spends too much time avoiding race and bathing in willful ignorance. An honest examination will show how far the country has fallen from the standard of freedom we profess and our Constitution ascribes. "Baldwin," Prentice says, "argues that, 'The recovery of this standard—of human freedom—demands of everyone who loves this country a hard look at himself and herself, for the greatest achievements must begin somewhere, and they always begin with the person' (Baldwin, 1961, p. 2)."

Continuing, Prentice posits, "Baldwin's writings are quintessential, his speeches and interviews are eloquent and straightforward. His unique personal perspective and style set him apart from other writers; and, while his words are important, it is his emotional testimony and iconic persona that made the biggest impact on the (Civil Rights) Movement." Closing the introduction, Prentice concludes, "Today, 2020, James Baldwin has returned to the center stage of America's discussion of systemic racism, white privilege and democracy. His insistence as a writer and speaker on removing, layer by layer, the hardened skin with which Americans shield themselves from the racism in the country is exceptional (Coombs, 1976). Baldwin is center stage because people want someone who can describe, frame, analyze, and critically discuss the increase of racially charged politics, the killings of unarmed Black men by police, with an apathetic public in a way that wakes them up." Finally, Prentice says, "I believe that Baldwin is the person who has articulated what it means to be an American and what it means to be Black, with more eloquence than anybody in the last century and Baldwin's words speak passionately and urgently about the renewed, energized systemic racism that is currently overflowing in America today. They speak to white anxiety about demographic change that encapsulates, 'Make America Great Again.'"

JIMMY!

After a rousing ovation from the audience, Baldwin asks, as he often does, when he begins a speech in a large crowded room: "Can you hear me? Can you hear me?" Hearing, "Yes, we can hear you" from Bette Tate-Beaver, Executive Director, Donna Gollnick, a past president, and others seated throughout the room, Baldwin launches into his unscripted, conscious remarks.

"Let's begin by saying the times we are living in are a major threat to American democracy, particularly the welfare of Black people and poor and oppressed people. These are very dangerous times; times when racist, sexist, homophobic vitriol is increasing in America. Children see other children living in cages; they are confused as their textbook tells them that the U.S. is founded on principles of equality for all. But, what I am saying: you already know. You fight against it. I will speak for a few minutes. I want to tell you what I think about racial progress in America and then I would like to hear from you."

"Know from Whence You Came"

Jimmy, as he does in many of his speeches, gives the audience a historical context. Using 1990, the year of the founding of NAME, as a significant moment in the history of multi-cultural education, Jimmy salutes the Founder and the founding members, telling them that he too, like NAME, is committed to a philosophy of inclusion that embraces the basic tenets of democracy and cultural pluralism.

"I witnessed the attacks on the civil rights and women's rights advances of the 1950s and 1960s by a counter-movement, 'the New Right,' that developed to take back the gains of the past two decades after World War II. The counter-movement advocated a different kind of freedom. Instead of equality for people of color, women, people who were gay and lesbian, and people with disabilities, it sought freedom for American businesses (Barrett, 2018). The New Right was guided by a philosophy called 'neoliberalism,' and had four goals that continue to loom large today: '(1) To have complete freedom to make money through businesses. This included the freedom to exploit their workers and pollute the environment; (2) To get rid of public property, such as public parks and schools; (3) To cut taxes for the richest Americans; and (4) To cut funding for public services, like education, housing, and food stamps. Neoliberal policies move the federal government away from helping the poor and protecting the environment to help the richest Americans get even richer' (Barrett, 2018, p. 2)."

Applauding the title and purpose of the conference, "Living Multicultural Education Peace & Justice thru the Ballot Box & Activism" and the get-out-the-vote effort of the NAME members, Jimmy reminds his audience of the brutal deed to impede that work that took place only a short stroll from here. "Remember," bellows Jimmy, with one hand pointing outwardly,

"We are only 166.37 miles away from Philadelphia, Mississippi where James Chaney (21), Andrew Goodman (20), and Michael Schwerner (24) were brutally murdered in 1964 for their work with the Freedom Summer voter registration project. Goodman, Schwerner, and Chaney had driven to see a Black church, recently destroyed by fire in Longdale, Mississippi, when their car was stopped and they were arrested for a traffic violation. Two months later their bodies were discovered in an earthen dam. Then as now, American democracy is in a fight against racism. NAME, and other social justice organizations must 'go for broke' against white supremacy."

Jimmy then paraphrases what he wrote in the closing of The Fire Next Time*:*

"Everything now, we must assume, it is in our hands ... We, conscious whites and conscious Blacks must insist on, or create the consciousness of others. If we do ... we may be able, handful that we are, to end the racial nightmare ..." (Baldwin 1963, p. 141). *Jimmy continues,* "In one of the darker moments of the civil right struggle when Chaney, Goodman, and Schwerner were killed, civil right activists rose up against white supremacy. NAME coming to Montgomery reminds me of that time."

Baldwin then addresses Ronald Reagan and the New Right's influence on the birth of NAME. "Reagan in 1980, took advantage of the New Right and promoted neo-liberalism when he began his presidential campaign with a speech for state rights seven miles from the lynching of Chaney, Goodman, and Schwerner. Reagan asked southern Democrats to join him (Crespino, 2007)."

Looking over at Rose and founding members seated only a few feet away, Jimmy states, "You saw America was becoming increasingly filled with racial and religious hypocrisies. You saw a world that denigrates Black people, denies them opportunities, sequesters them in ghettoes, hoping and believing they will fight and kill one another; and/or turn to drugs or alcohol over despair and self-denigration." *Recalling what he said to his nephew, James, Jimmy states*: "The root of my dispute with [this] country is that we [Black people] were born where we were born and faced the future that we faced because we are Black and for no other reason" (Baldwin, 1962, p. 7).

Turning to religious hypocrisies, Jimmy argues in the 1980s, he witnessed what the founding members observed and knew something needed to be done about it. A mass-mediated, predominantly white, born-again Christian movement connected to politics and capitalism (Vogel, 2018). Jimmy states: "The people who call themselves 'born again' had simply become members of the richest, most exclusive private club in the world, a club that the man from Galilee could not possibly hope –or wish—to enter (quoted in Vogel, 2018, p. 30). This movement: the 'religious right' or 'Moral Majority' initiated cultural wars with people of color. In addition, the 1980s was when Ronald Reagan argued for a return to traditional values, a pre-civil rights time when men were men, main streets were safe and white, and no one questioned America's strength and power. 'It was morning in America.'" (Vogel, 2018, p. 33).

Jimmy continues, "You and I could not let the 'Right' and Reagan perpetuate such mythology. You took action and pushed back as argued in NAME's (2020) second objective: 'To proactively reframe public debate and impact current and emerging policies in ways that advance social, political, economic and educational equity through advocacy, position papers, policy statements and other strategies.'"

An Illusion of *Progress*

Pausing for a moment, looking out beyond the audience, Jimmy says,
"Today if you cross the Mason and Dixon line between Maryland and Pennsylvania traveling from the north, you have much less fear about returning to your home in the north or west. There is much less a chance you will leave your blood on southern soil or your Black body will hang from a southern tree. I am not inferring progress, I am discussing the fantasy and the illusion of progress that Du Bois (1903) describes in one of my favorite essays: 'Of the Meaning of Progress' in the *Souls of Black Folks*; Martin Luther King (1963) details in his 'I Have a Dream' speech; and we—Black people—hear explicitly and implicitly about progress in the contemporary political and social rhetoric."

"I will start my discussion on progress with Du Bois, because Willie argued, correctly, years ago that the violence and suffering African Americans experience are the consequences of white supremacist policies and practices and have nothing to do with Blacks' capacity (e.g., knowledge, skills, and dispositions). Du Bois' (1903) 'Of the Meaning of Progress' is an essay that challenges the racial status quo of the twentieth century and tells of his personal journey as a teacher in Tennessee, for two summers when he was a student at Fisk University from 1885 to 1888 and his return to the school community 10 years later. The essay describes Du Bois' continuous discovery of the evils of racism and how institutionalized racist policies and whites' attitude impedes, almost to a standstill, the progress of Black Americans, including viciously attacking their personal worth. Perhaps not since a new student, a white girl, refused his card when he attended Searles High School, in Great Barrington Massachusetts, had Du Bois suffered such racial humiliation and learned that Emancipation and his Fisk college education, notwithstanding, he was still a Negro. And because he was Black, and for no other reason, his humanity was rebuked. Du Bois tells how he was not allowed to eat with another white teacher and the white commissioner of education at the home of the commissioner."

> Come in, said the commissioner .... Have a seat [Du Bois]. Stay to dinner ... Oh [said Du Bois to himself]—this is lucky. But then fell the awful shadow of the Veil, for they ate first, then I—alone.
>
> *Du Bois, 1903, p. 98*

"In the essay, Du Bois centers the education of a young Black woman, 'Josie,' and her desire and pursuit of progress, and describes the daily struggles and hardships of several members of Black families, particularly his students as they pursue progress. Du Bois describes how, thanks to 'Josie,' he located a Black community in rural Tennessee desirous of a school; and how he turned a dilapidated shack, with rented chairs, and an old chalkboard, into an instructional and learning place and taught the children of the local Black sharecroppers."

Jimmy gesturing with his hand, as he often does when making a point, says to the audience: "As educators, you know about the authentic energy, desire and purpose that Black and Brown students come to school with—when the opportunity is presented to them to learn—to be taught by teachers who genuinely love and care for their humanity. When Willie first saw that energy and purpose—a hunger for racial progress and education in living form: young Black beautiful humanity; it caused him to tremble. Willie (1903) states: 'It was a hot morning late in July when the school opened. I trembled when I heard the patter of little feet down the dusty road, and saw the growing row of dark solemn faces and bright eager eyes facing me' (p. 101). Progress, real true honest progress, these children and Willie believed was in their future; it was theirs to earn, to achieve. They did not shun or resent the hard work necessary to achieve it; they looked forward to it. They welcomed the opportunity!" *Jimmy argued.* Du Bois explains,

> There they sat, nearly thirty of them, on the rough benches, their faces shading from a pale cream to a deep brown, the little feet bare and swinging, the eyes full of expectation, with here and there a twinkle of mischief, and the hands grasping Webster's blue–black spelling-book. I loved my school, and the fine faith the children had in the wisdom of their teacher was truly marvelous.
>
> *from "Of the Meaning of Progress," Du Bois, 1903, p. 101*

"But progress, Willie learned and King reported, is an illusion for Black people. It gaslights damage done to self and family; and keeps buried or destroyed that which was taken by force."

"Ten years after he had said goodbye to his students and their families, Willie returned for a class reunion at Fisk University and went to see his old school and the students he taught. He discovered that his students and their families had made little progress. They were in a daily struggle to survive. Josie had died from overwork. Jim, Josie's younger brother, had been charged by white farmer Durham with stealing wheat, and instead of leaving town as his family urged, Jim protested the charge, stood his ground, but was jailed."

Taking a half step back from the podium, Jimmy tilts his head upward and says:

"Willie summarizes Black progress, ten years removed from his last visit as follows: 'My log schoolhouse was gone. In its place stood Progress; and Progress, I understand, is necessarily ugly' (Du Bois, 1903, p. 103). The ugliness of progress, or the illusion of progress, Willie defines, when he describes the new school for Black students as a 'jaunty board house' with broken windows, a chalkboard larger than before by two feet, students' seats without backs, and school policy: that every year there is one session of school. Willie (1903) asks: 'How should progress be measured that also results in the tragic death of a young Black woman (Josie) and a young Black man being sent to prison for taking a bushel of wheat because he had not financially compensated for his labor? Do we say the measuring glass is half empty or half full? Are we making strides or are we a long ways off and need plenty work, prayer, etc.?' (p. 104)."

To that question of progress, Jimmy states,

"Willie concludes his exemplary tale, with its fantasy opening line 'Once upon a time …' by doubling down on the progress of Black people since they were freed: Willie writes: 'Thus sadly musing, I rode to Nashville in the Jim Crow car' (Du Bois, 1903, p. 104)."

"The progress narrative, described by Du Bois in 'Of the Meaning of Progress,' is not yesterday. The past persists, here and now. During Willie's day progress for Black people was an illusion—two steps forward, one and one-half steps back—as it collided with white supremacy. Today the illusion of progress still exists, two steps forward with the election of a Black president and one and one-half steps back with the election of Donald Trump as President of the United States."

"A Searing Indictment of American Racism That Still Exists" in 16 Minutes (Younge, 2013, p. 1)

"Let me say one more thing about *progress* then I will take your questions. I want to hear from you. Martin, I want you to know, explicitly addresses the progress of Black people in America on August 28, 1963 in the 'I Have a Dream' speech and in a speech, 'America's Chief Moral Dilemma' (1967), published in *The Atlantic*. The speech published in *The Atlantic* is a must-read for NAME membership as it attends to post-civil right issues."

"Martin's (1963) speech at the 'March on Washington for Jobs and Freedom' is a progress report to the nation about how well the American democratic project is working for Black people. It is a report card on the progress for racial equality assessed according to American democratic ideals. Martin starts his report on racial progress from the day Black people were freed, January 1, 1863, when the Emancipation Proclamation was signed, and argues one hundred years later, Black people don't have their freedom as defined by the U.S. Constitution. Martin (1963) states:

> One hundred years later, the Negro still is not free … One hundred years later, the Negro lives on a lonely island of poverty in the midst of a vast ocean of material prosperity. One hundred years later, the Negro is still languished in the corners of American society and finds himself an exile in his own land.
>
> *p. 1*

"Martin believed racial injustice was Black people's burden and America's shame; and that many white people would like to have a nation which is a democracy for white Americans but simultaneously a dictatorship over Black Americans (King, 1967). Calling attention to the Declaration of Independence that declares 'all men are created equal,' Martin argues, White people willfully ignore the fundamental principles of democracy. The right to equality in the Constitution was 'a bad cheque' marked with 'insufficient funds,' Martin told the audience."

"In an address in Atlanta on May 10, 1967, to The Hungry Club Forum, Martin answered a question continually raised by many in America and throughout the world: Has the Civil Rights Movement made Racial Progress? Martin begins his response, declaring there has been some progress, particularly in the South. The greatest progress has been the breakdown of legal segregation; the Civil Right Movement in the South profoundly shook the entire edifice of segregation. However, Martin (1967) says, 'The plant of freedom has grown only a bud and not yet a flower' (p. 1); there is no place in the U.S. that can boast of excellent race relations."

"'The new phase,' after our twelve years of struggle to end legal segregation Martin says, 'is a struggle for genuine equality; not merely a struggle for decency or to get rid of the brutality of a Bull Connor and a Jim Clark. Phase 2 is a struggle for genuine equality on all levels, and thus it will be a much more difficult struggle. The gains in period 1 were obtained from the power structure at bargain rates; the nation paid little to integrate lunch counters, hotels, and motels and it didn't cost the nation a penny to guarantee the right to vote. But in Phase 2, it will cost the nation billions … to get rid of poverty, urban slums, to make quality integrated education a reality. This is where we are now' (King, 1967, p. 2)."

"In Phase 2," *Jimmy says,* "Martin posits 'we're going to lose some friends; allies who were with us … will not stay …. We will feel a white backlash, but … there has never been any …. determined commitment on the part of the majority of white Americans to genuine equality for Negroes. In 1863 African Americans were granted freedom from physical slavery but they were not given land to make that freedom meaningful. However, the Federal government was giving away millions of acres of land, in the Midwest and the West to white peasants from Europe while refusing to do it for its Black peasants from Africa who were held in slavery.' Such racial inequality caused Frederick Douglass to say:

> [E]mancipation for the Negro was freedom to hunger, freedom to the winds and rains of heaven, freedom without roofs to cover their heads. It was freedom without bread to eat, without land to cultivate. It was freedom and famine at the same time. And it is a miracle that the Negro has survived.
>
> *as quoted in King, 1967 p. 27*

Finally, Jimmy says, "I have given you some of Willie's and Martin's thoughts on racial progress, let me share my observations and give attention to multicultural education in the twenty-first century. NAME is in Montgomery, both the birthplace of the Confederacy and the Civil Rights Movement to celebrate 2020 as the landmark anniversary of women in the United States going to the ballot box to vote. However, there is—today—voter suppression in many areas across the country and racial progress in general for Black people and other people of color remains slow or is going backward. Since the 2013 ruling that gutted the

Voting Rights Act, more than half of the states have acted to restrict the right to vote. Many Black people feel as Willie felt having to ride in the Jim Crow car. Birmingham, Alabama, as a center of civil rights activity during the 1950s and 1960s, and populated by 75% people of color, maintains a wide racial economic gap—paying $20 an hour to white people and $14 an hour to people of color (E Pluribus Unum, 2019). According to Black people who live in Birmingham, institutionalized racism controls who owns businesses and controls the purse strings of development and the who-you-know economy that prevents Black residents from accessing information about opportunities. White people in Birmingham claim they do not see racism. They insist you can do well if you work hard and are kind (E Pluribus Unum, 2019, p. 40)."

Pausing, lowering his head and then quickly looking up, along with taking a deep breath, Jimmy says:

"I still remember my first trip south. I was afraid. I had terrifying nightmares about the journey. I thought, my blood too, would become a part of southern soil. Nevertheless, I had to come south and see for myself, bear witness to the heroic efforts of Martin, Medgar, Dorothy, and all the civil right marchers and protesters. In 1957, at the age of 33, I came south on assignment, for the Partisan Review to report on the Civil Rights Movement. The assignment took me from New York to Washington on to Charlotte, Atlanta, Montgomery, Tuskegee, Birmingham, Nashville, Little Rock, and Arlington, Virginia. I have reported my observations and discoveries in an article: 'Nobody Knows My Name: Letter from the South' (Baldwin, 1961). What struck me and I wonder, especially if you are Black and this is your first time in the south, if you witnessed what I observed and felt:

> Everywhere you turn you see yourself. Being here is like looking in a mirror …
>
> I saw my "inescapable identity" within the context of what America is—inequality, white supremacy, strange fruit hanging on a tree; white police beating black youth—and is not—"liberty and justice for all," unadulterated citizenship for people of color, and education equal and excellence for Black and White children …
>
> *p. 109*

"The first Southern city I visited was Charlotte, North Carolina. Charlotte became a 'city,' because it became a central hub for the plantation economy of enslaved Black people. I discovered Black people there were not even licensed to become electricians or plumbers … although white people said race relations were excellent (Baldwin, 1961, p. 200). Today, real progress in Charlotte remains a fantasy: Black unemployment is more than 2.5 times the rate for white workers. There are also wide gaps in earnings by race. White workers earn $27 per hour compared to just $16 for Black workers and $12 for Latino workers (E Pluribus Unum, 2019, p. 64)."

"I have been here in Montgomery, Alabama before. The reasons were much the same as today; civil rights with an emphasis on the right to vote. I marched the fifty-four miles, starting-off with approximately three thousand, two hundred others in civil protest from Selma to Montgomery, Alabama on March 21–March 25, 1965, and I stood on the steps of the capitol building here in Montgomery, with an enlarged crowd of approximately 25,000 as Martin Luther King, Jr. (1965) spoke at the completion of the five-day march from Selma. The march was a 'heroic effort' and 'The Selma [to Montgomery] experience is one which I shall never forget' (Baldwin, 1961, p. 30). We walked twelve miles a day and would sleep in the fields at night. We were told by some that we would not get here; or that we would get here only over their dead bodies. We faced deadly violence from local authorities and white vigilante groups. A recent article in *The Atlantic* by Vann R. Newkirk II, December 7, 2017, argues that much needs to be done and re-done in order for Black and Brown people to be able to exercise their constitutional right. Newkirk argues: the Voting Right Act of 1965 was not ironclad; the state of Alabama has served and continues to serve as the headquarters of resistance to voting rights, and the 2013 Supreme Court case decision for Shelby County v. Holder, which released Alabama from federal VRA oversight, is making it difficult for people of color to vote. Add to this, since the *Shelby County* case, voter suppression has become a norm: strict ID laws, and closures of 31 Department of Motor Vehicles offices across the state mostly in areas where Black people live, thereby causing voters of color to travel long distances to other counties to get licenses or visit special registrar's offices in order to vote (Newkirk,, 2017). In addition, since the turn of the century there has been a one hundred per cent increase in hate groups, including neo-Nazis, anti-Muslim, and anti-LGBTQ groups."

"My final observation on racial progress comes from the Brennan Center at New York University. The Center reports since 2000, states have imposed obstacles to voting: strict voter ID laws, reduced voting times, registration constraints, and voter rolls have been purged. Further, these efforts were strengthened with the invalidation of a pivotal section of the Voting Rights Act by the Supreme Court in 2013, allowing states—nine states, mostly in the South—to change their election laws without prior federal approval. Such voting restrictions have affected all Americans, but they have especially burdened people of color, poor people, and young and old voters (Rao, Dillon, Kelly, & Bennett, 2019)."

Glancing toward Prentice and Rose seated on the stage with him, and then looking out into the audience, pursing his lips, solemn, Jimmy cogently says,

"The nation's present social and political apparatus cannot and does not serve the human need of all of its people (Baldwin, 1985). Whereas multicultural education has continued to evolve because of organizations like NAME and the social justice-dedicated people who make up the organization, the persistence of white supremacy exercised by those who hold the nation's highest and most powerful office makes the evolution exceedingly tough. That said, 'I am not a pessimist because I am alive. To be a pessimist, it means that you have agreed that human life is an academic matter. So I am forced to be an optimist. I'm forced to believe that we can survive whatever we must survive' (p. 145). Multicultural education—the future of Black people and other people of color—is 'precisely as bright or as dark as the future of the country … It is entirely up to the American people and our representatives […] whether or not they will deal with and embrace the stranger they have maligned for so long.'"

"Thanks for the invitation to speak, and where is my first question? Make it a tough one!"

Quickly rising from her seat, and looking at Jimmy, Dr. Jeanette Haynes Writer says: "What would you tell White people they need to do to save this country, because Black people have been doing …."

Measuring his words, fingers outward, eyes sweeping the audience, Jimmy says,

"What white people have to do is try to find out in their hearts why it was necessary for them to have a nigger in the first place. Because I am not a nigger. Rose, Prentice, Bette, Cherry, Ann and the NAME membership are not the nigger. I'm a man, they are men and women. If we are not the nigger here and white people invented him, then they have to find out why. And the future of the country depends on that. Whether or not they are able to ask that question."

With that statement, Jimmy moves to shake Rose's and Prentice's hand, smiles at Jeanette, says hello to Drs. Alexandra (Alex) Allweiss and Anthony and Kefferlyn Brown and heads off stage to a thundering ovation.

References

Alexander, M. (2015, August 17). "Ta-Nehisi Coates's 'Between the World and Me.'" *The New York Times*, Sunday Book Review. Retrieved from https://nytines.com

Angelou, M. (n.d.). BrainyQuote.com. Retrieved from www.brainyquote.com/quotes/maya_angelou_634505

Baldwin, J. (1955). *Notes of a native son*. Boston, MA: Beacon Press.

Baldwin, J. (1956). *Giovanni's room*. New York, NY: Dial.

Baldwin, J. (1961). "Nobody knows my name: A letter from the South." In *Nobody knows my name*. New York, NY: Dial.

Baldwin, J. (1962). A letter to my nephew. *The Progressive*. Retrieved from https://progressive.org/magazine/letter-nephew/

Baldwin, J. (1963). *The fire next time*. New York, NY: Vintage International.

Baldwin, J. (1972). *No name in the street*. New York, NY: Dial.

Baldwin J. (1985). *Price of the ticket*. New York, NY: St. Martin's Press.

Baldwin, J. (1998). *Baldwin: Collected essays*. New York, NY: Literary Classics of the U.S.

Baraka, A. (2009). "Jimmy!" *Black Renaissance/Renaissance Noire, 9*(2–3), 242–248.

Barrett, D. (2018). *The defiant: Protest movements in post liberal America*. New York, NY: University Press.

Bernstein, I., & Mooney, K. C. (2019, September). James Baldwin's quest for democratic union, and ours. *The Common Reader: A Journal of Essays*. Retrieved from https://commonreader.wustl.edu/c/introduction/

Butorac, S. K. (2018, March 21). Hannah Arendt, James Baldwin, and the politics of love. *Political Research Quarterly*. Retrieved from https://journals.sagepub.com/doi/abs/10.1177/1065912918760730. 2/9/2020.

Coates, T. (2015). *Between the world and me*. New York, NY: Spiegel and Grau.

Coombs, O. (1976). The devil finds work. *The New York Times*. Retrieved from https://archive.nytimes.com/www.nytimes.com/books/98/03/29/specials/baldwin-devil.html.

Crespino, J. (2007). *In search of another country: Mississippi and the conservative counterrevolution*. Princeton, NJ: Princeton University Press.

Du Bois, W. E. B. (1903). *The soul of Black folk*. Chicago, IL: A.C. McClurg & Co.

E Pluribus Unum (2019). Divided by design. Retrieved from www.dividedbydesign.org/static/report-09da5f2905801cb7265cb94c5eee7ee7.pdf

Ferriter, C. D. (2016). The uses of race and religion: James Baldwin's pragmatic politics in *The Fire Next Time*. *James Baldwin Review, 2*(1), 126–139. Retrieved from www.manchesteropenhive.com/view/journals/jbr/2/1/article-p126.xml

Grant, C. A. (forthcoming). *"Bearing witness": James Baldwin and the American school house.*

King, M. L., Jr. (1963). I Have A Dream Speech. Retrieved from www.archives.gov/files/press/exhibits/dream-speech.pdf

King, M. L., Jr. (1965, March 25). Address at the conclusion of the Selma to Montgomery March. The Martin Luther King, Jr. Research and Educational Institute, Stanford. Retrieved from https://kinginstitute.stanford.edu/king-papers/documents/address-conclusion-selma-montgomery-march. 2/8/2020.

King, M. L., Jr. (1967). Martin Luther King Jr. saw three evils in the world: Racism was only the first. *The Atlantic*. Retrieved from www.theatlantic.com/magazine/archive/2018/02/martin-luther-king-hungry-club-forum/552533/

National Association for Multicultural Education (NAME) (2020). About NAME, NAME's Mission: Objectives. Retrieved from www.nameorg.org/mission_goals_objectives.php

Newkirk, V. R., II (2017, December 12). What's missing from reports on Alabama's Black turnout. *The Atlantic*. Retrieved from www.theatlantic.com/politics/archive/2017/12/can-doug-jones-get-enough-black-voters-to-win/547574/

Poetry Foundation (2020). James Baldwin. Retrieved from www.poetryfoundation.org/poets/james-baldwin.

Rao, A., Dillon, P., Kelly K., & Bennett, Z. (2019, November 7). Is America a democracy? If so, why does it deny millions the vote? *The Guardian*. Retrieved from www.theguardian.com/us-news/2019/nov/07/is-america-a-democracy-if-so-why-does-it-deny-millions-the-vote. 2/9/2020.

Vogel, J. (2018). The forgotten Baldwin. *Boston Review*. Retrieved from http://bostonreview.net/race/joseph-vogel-forgotten-baldwin

Younge, G. (2013, August 14). The misremembering of 'I Have a Dream.' *The Nation*. Retrieved from www.thenation.com/article/archive/misremembering-i-have-dream/

5

TRUTH, LAND, AND SOVEREIGNTY

Native American Intellectual Activists, Their Critique of Settler Colonialism, and the Unsettling of Multicultural Education

Jeanette Haynes Writer and Kristen B. French

Introduction

In this chapter we bring forth the words and work of three Native intellectual activists of the early twentieth century, Gertrude Simmons Bonnin, Charles Eastman, and Luther Standing Bear, as Native Multicultural Education (MCE) antecedents and foundational scholars. Unsettling MCE must address issues of colonization, specifically in the areas of Western Christianity, white supremacy, and capitalism, as illustrated by Grande (2015), drawing from Bonnin, Eastman, and Standing Bear. After grounding the chapter in a discussion of settler colonialism and employing it as our lens of analysis, we then present the biographical sketches of the Native MCE antecedents highlighting their positions and critiques of settler colonialism. Finally, we grapple with the complexity of Indigenous futurities, or the possibilities of Indigenous futures (Richardson, 2011) within MCE, and what must be brought into the vision and work of MCE: truth-telling, Land,[1] and sovereignty.

The roots of Multicultural Education (MCE) are often located in the civil rights movement, but the origins are much earlier. According to Banks (2004), "a historical perspective is necessary to provide a context for understanding the contemporary developments and discourse in multicultural education" (p. 7). He identified the early ethnic studies movement, with leaders such as Carter G. Woodson, W. E. B. Du Bois, and others, as foundational. Banks concluded that "further investigations are needed to determine the fate of various early ethnic studies and intergroup education movements" (p. 7). Therefore, we bring forth Gertrude Simmons Bonnin (1876–1938), Charles Eastman (1858–1939), and Luther Standing Bear (1868–1939) as Native[2] early ethnic studies and intergroup contemporaries of Woodson (1875–1950) and Du Bois (1868–1963).

In the decades since MCE has come into its own as a scholarly field and catalyst of educational equity and culturally-based practice, Native Peoples have found some entrance into the discourse. However, Indigenous scholars have maintained that the "entrance" has not been enough or has been problematic (Grande & Anderson, 2017; Haynes Writer, 2008; Richardson, 2012). Nieto (Nieto & Bode, 2018) urges teachers and scholars "not to develop just one way to understand MCE but instead to encourage … interplay of societal and school structures and contexts and how they influence learning" (p. 31). We offer the interplay of anti-settler colonialism as a way to understand MCE and advocate for early Native historical foundations of MCE. As we consider a vision for its future, we are emphatic that MCE must address settler colonialism to envision, create space for, and support Indigenous futurities (Tuck & Gaztambide-Fernández, 2013).

Settler Colonialism: An Analysis for Unsettling Multicultural Education

Including historical Native scholars and activists as antecedents to MCE alone does not offer the structural unsettling of MCE for a renewed vision of the field. Settler colonial studies provide promising understandings, discussions, and a lens of analysis for unsettling MCE. In settler colonial studies (Coulthard, 2014; Rifkin, 2017; Tuck & Gaztambide-Fernandez, 2013; Veracini, 2015; Wolfe, 1999), defining colonialism, colonization, and settler colonialism is an enormous task, too large for this chapter. However, to ground MCE in anti-settler colonialism, or what we understand as unsettling multicultural erasures (Grande, 2017), we provide essential understandings and characteristics of settler colonialism, as well as teachings from our Native antecedents as an initial means to unsettle MCE.

In researching "place," Tuck and McKenzie (2015) define settler colonialism as "a form of colonization in which outsiders come to land inhabited by Indigenous Peoples and claim it as their own new home" (p. 59). Wolfe (1999) asserts that settler colonialism is ultimately structural. He argues that settler colonization is not an event, but an invasion and the primary object to claim "is the land itself" (p. 163). Engaging with Nieto's (Nieto & Bode, 2018) call to interplay, we are situating our analysis of unsettling MCE in Grande's (2015) definition of *colonialization* as "a multidimensional force underwritten by Western Christianity [i.e., Papal Bull and Doctrine of Discovery], defined by White supremacy, and fueled by global capitalism" (p. 18).

Our intention is to identify the complexity of settler colonialism, settler colonial characteristics (Tuck & McKenzie, 2015), and the need for MCE to address the impact of colonization in the U.S. and the field of MCE. To do this we coded our antecedents research by examining their words and work in connection to colonization, specifically to the topics they addressed concerning Christianity, white supremacy, and capitalism. From there we identified themes—their teachings—consistent across the antecedents that formed our recommendations for MCE.

Unsettling MCE is a call to action informed by our Native antecedents. The following biographical sketches situate our antecedents as contributors to the early ethnic studies movement, yet their experience is differentiated based on colonization. That is, colonization is "endemic to society" (Brayboy, 2005, p. 429).

Introducing Native Intellectual Activists as Multicultural Antecedents

Gertrude Simmons Bonnin (Zitkala-Ša), Yankton Dakota

Born in 1876, to the Yankton Dakota people, Gertrude Simmons Bonnin emerged into life in reservation confinement (Welch, 2001). Her "civilizing" process commenced fully at a Quaker boarding school, continuing through to graduating from Earlham College; she went on to attend the New England Conservatory of Music. She developed and honed her writing and oratory skills; however, her academic merits did not insulate her from racism (Chiarello, 2005). Held as an emblem of the success of assimilation (Spack, 2001; Welch, 2001), Bonnin's experiences in the Westernized boarding schools did not assimilate her mind, but rather steeled her will and provided her tools to wield a resistance against the colonizer's agenda as she fully embraced and advocated for cultural maintenance.

While working briefly at Carlisle Indian School (Chiarello, 2005), she began writing as Zitkala-Ša—Red Bird. Although a talented author of short stories (Zitkala-Ša, 1921/1987), her essays in *Atlantic Monthly*[3] first garnered her attention. Her essays strategically weaved praises of Westernized civilization with the painful and mournful experiences of leaving her mother, her culture, and facing the bitter reality of off-reservation schools, where Native children were stripped of their identities. Adams (1995) states her truth-based essays contained "[t]he most devastating attack" (p. 311) on the boarding schools, leading to substantial policy changes. Zitkala-Ša's other essays summoned plaintive, yet strong constructions of the cultural and spiritual realm, waging rhetorical resistance to the enforcement of assimilation and Christianity onto Native Peoples. In her essay, "Why I Am a Pagan" (Zitkala-Ša, 1902), she names the settlers' foreign religion as "the new superstition" (p. 803) taken up by some of the People due to the conversion work of missionaries. In the essay, standing resolute in her belief while questioned about her absence in church by a Native clergyman, she paints a portrait of Native spirituality that gives reverence to the natural world as evidence of the Creator,

> A wee child toddling in a wonder world, I prefer to their dogma my excursions into the natural gardens where the voice of the Great Spirit is heard in the twittering of birds, the rippling of mighty waters, and the sweet breathing of flowers. If this is Paganism, then at present, at least, I am a Pagan.
>
> *p. 803*

Bonnin resisted not only issues of racial oppression, but also gender oppression as a result of patriarchy embedded within white supremacy. Holding to the status of women among the Dakota people, she would not embrace the subjugation that was the experience of White women. Bonnin pushed forward to assume positions of national leadership (Spack, 2001; Welch, 2001). She worked with the American Indian Defense Association and Indian Rights Association through her collaboration with the General Federation of Women's Clubs (Hoxie, 2001) to investigate and report on the Indian probate scandal in eastern Oklahoma (Fabens & Sniffen, 1924, p. 5). The probate scandal was a state-sanctioned method to steal land and oil rights of tribal people—many being orphaned children—through a court-mandated White guardian system (Debo, 1940/1991).

Occupying key positions for the Society of American Indians (SAI), including as the SAI journal editor, Bonnin advocated for Native citizenship, self-determination, and justice (Hoxie, 2001). She and her husband, Raymond T. Bonnin, later co-founded the National Council of American Indians in 1926 to protect Native rights and privileges and recoup historical losses. Elected as president and serving as its Washington D.C. lobbyist until her death in 1938, Bonnin provided testimony at U.S. governmental hearings (Hafen, 2013; Willard, 1985). The Bonnins' organization laid the foundation for the National Congress of American Indians (NCAI), established in 1944. Native right to nation, culture, land, and resources was a focus of Bonnin's writing and political advocacy throughout her career (Hafen, 2013; Willard, 1985).

Charles Eastman (Ohiyesa), Santee Dakota Sioux

Born in 1858, in a northern Minnesota Dakota village, White settler encroachment resulted in the "Sioux Uprising," forcing Ohiyesa and family members into Canada. Ohiyesa's father was missing; Many Lightnings was one of over 300 Dakota patriots to hang for participation in the uprising. In Ohiyesa's fifteenth year, his father made a surprising return—his sentence had been commuted. Many Lightnings came as Jacob Eastman, having converted to Christianity while in prison. Ohiyesa left with his father for Dakota Territory and enrolled in a mission school, where he became Charles Alexander Eastman (Eastman, 1911/2003; Fitzgerald, 2007).

After years of the colonizer's education and Christian influence, Eastman was a successful student but remained a Dakota at his core. Seeing the vocation of medicine as a way to serve the People, he graduated from Boston University's School of Medicine in 1890. He secured the physician's position at Pine Ridge in South Dakota, arriving in conjunction with the rise of the Ghost Dance religion. An event transpired that shook Eastman to his core and brought him to clarity and purpose: Wounded Knee Massacre. In late December, 500 men of the Seventh Cavalry raided a camp of 350 Lakota in the onset of a snowstorm. Soldiers hunted down fleeing victims, mostly women and children; 200 people were killed or badly wounded. Eastman witnessed the ravaged bodies of the fallen and attended to survivors (Eastman, 1911/2003).

Wounded Knee prompted a confrontation of Eastman's previous thoughts regarding assimilation into White settler society and settler power over Native Peoples. As the "supreme ruler on the reservation" (Eastman, 1915, p. 42), white supremacy supplied the Indian agent with "almost autocratic power … the conditions of life on an agency are such as to make every resident largely dependent upon his good will" (Eastman, 1916/2003, p. 76). Challenging corrupt Indian agents and others resulted in personal and professional consequences (Eastman, 1915).

In an expression of insurgence and resurgence, Eastman began making speeches, writing essays, and eventually produced ten books. His writing and activism positioned him as one of the prominent Native voices in the Progressive era (Hoxie, 2001). Eastman (1911/2003) asserted that the settlers' behavior illustrated a lack of civility. Naming it as "[s]piritual arrogance" (Eastman, 1911/2003, p. 23), he critiqued Christianity as weapon of assimilation and control. Eastman maintained that the Dakota people did not accept Christianity because it was an improvement on the Dakota faith, but rather, after the 1862 "uprising" and resultant oppression, "subjection, starvation, and imprisonment turned our brokenhearted people to accept Christianity, which seemed to offer them the only gleam of kindness or hope" (Eastman, 1911/2003, p. 17).

Connected to capitalism, Eastman (1911/2003) found hypocrisy and inconsistency in Christians, saying that the settlers,

> spoke of much spiritual things, while seeking only the material. They bought and sold everything: time, labor, personal independence, the love of woman, and even the ministrations of their holy faith! The lust for money, power, and conquest so characteristic of the Anglo-Saxon race did not escape moral condemnation …
>
> *p. 6*

Values within Dakota culture aligned with justice, whereas the greed of White settlers for material culture and power did not. Visiting "slums and dives … which gave another shock to my ideals of 'Christian civilization,'" Eastman asserted that as a Dakota "[w]e could not conceive of the extremes of luxury and misery existing side by side" (Eastman, 2003/1916, p. 83). Civilized precepts of the Dakota people would have taken care of those in need.

Eastman was a founding member of the Society of American Indians (SAI), the first pan-Indian organization which supported the cultural assimilation into White society and termination of the reservation system and the Bureau of Indian Affairs (Hoxie, 2001; Misiarz, 2016). SAI influenced federal Indian policy such as U.S. citizenship extended to Indians and the protection of Native rights. Reflecting upon the international discourse on rights following World War I and the Versailles Paris

Peace Conference, Eastman asserted that as international relationships were being formed, "new must also begin at home" (as cited in Hoxie, 2001, p. 132).

Eastman's writings reflected an embrace of White culture and religion, while simultaneously upholding the value of his Santee culture. Viewed as a "role model for all Indians" (Hagan, 1997, p. 26), Ellinghaus (2006) described him as a person "struggling to find freedom and happiness" (p. 78). The work of Eastman's life centered on Native rights and justice. He turned the workings of assimilation to his own purpose:

> [W]hile I have learned much from civilization, for which I am grateful, I have never lost my Indian sense of right and justice. I am for development and progress along social and spiritual lines, rather than those of commerce, nationalism, or material efficiency. Nevertheless, so long as I live, I am an American.
>
> *Eastman, 1916/2003, p. 109*

Luther Standing Bear (Ota K'Te), Oglala Lakota

Ota K'Te (Plenty Kill), an Oglala Lakota, was born in 1868 in what is now South Dakota. Recognizing the invasion of White settlers would not cease, his father impressed upon him the need to learn White ways for the survival of his people (Standing Bear, 1928/1975). At 11 years old, he left his homelands and became Luther Standing Bear, a student at Carlisle Indian Boarding School. After Carlisle, Standing Bear returned home, but struggled to fit his education to his lived contextual reality. His learned vocation as a tin smith was not applicable on the reservation. He found work as an educator, shopkeeper, rancher, and Episcopal lay minister. His job as an interpreter and performer in Buffalo Bill's Wild West Show (Burt, 2010; Hale, 1993) broadened his perspectives on racism and rights, which "inaugurated a career in cultural production that would ultimately position him as one of the harshest critics of America's mythologized frontier past and the arrogance of progressive reformers" (Burt, 2010, p. 627).

Selected as the chief of the Oglala people in 1905 (Hale, 1993), Standing Bear left South Dakota for California in 1912 after continued clashes with controlling agency officials and lack of employment opportunity. He became a Hollywood consultant and actor for "Indian movies" (Burt, 2010; Hale, 1993). Using the academic skills acquired in the boarding school to share his experiences and express his perspectives, he penned several books. Returning to the Pine Ridge and Rosebud reservations in 1931, he was appalled at the conditions he witnessed—situations of food-insecurity and starvation—under the purview of corrupt Indian agents (Standing Bear, 1931). The disturbing visit generated an anger that began Standing Bear's criticism, critique of, and response to White worldviews, settler colonialism, and U.S. governmental entities.

In *Land of the Spotted Eagle* (Standing Bear, 1933/1978), considered perhaps his most important book, he performed a critique of White settlers' efforts to "make over" the Indian into the likeness of the White race, yet denying him the recognition as a human being with inherent rights gifted from the Creator, instead making him "a hostage on a reservation" (p. 191). Questioning the superior station reserved for White settlers, Standing Bear (1933/1978) stood firm: "*The white man claims the right to guide and supervise the Indian!* Yet, from whence emanated the *right?*" (p. 246, emphasis his). Seeing an overlap of oppression between African Americans and Native Peoples, Standing Bear (1933/1978) asserted that the extension of U.S. citizenship to Native Peoples, what he referred to as "the greatest hoax" (p. 229) because the power dynamic did not shift, "disclosed the fact that a bonded and enslaved people lived in the 'land of the free and the home of the brave,' even though it was then more than half a century since slavery was supposed to have been wiped from the land" (p. 245).

Standing Bear's criticism and critique of the oppression imposed by a settler colonialist worldview speaks to Native Peoples' spiritual relationship to the land, inherent sovereignty, inalienable rights, and perspective of justice. Spiritual traditions and philosophy facilitated that the Native person was "kin to all living things and he gave to all creatures equal rights with himself" (Standing Bear, 1933/1978, p. 166). "But the white man has put distance between himself and nature; and assuming a lofty place in the scheme of order of things has lost for him both reverence and understanding" (Standing Bear, 1933/1978, p. 196). "The white man considered natural animal life just as he did the natural man life upon this continent as 'pests'" proclaimed Standing Bear (1933/1978, p. 165), justifying the control over and destruction of animals, plants, and Native Peoples through the enactment of white supremacy. He concluded that "White men seem to have difficulty in realizing that people who live differently from themselves still might be traveling the upward and progressive road of life" (1933/1978, p. xv). Questioning the Eurocentric notion of progress and the means to move toward it, Standing Bear (1933/1978, p. 249) asked, "And if it be the part of civilization to maim, rob, and thwart, then what is progress?" Standing Bear (1933/1978) recognized the effect of settler colonialism on Lakota women—but also White women. Because of the intrusion of the white system of patriarchy the power of mothers had "been willed away and practically annulled" (p. 109).

Standing Bear clearly assessed that the "Indian Problem" was not caused by Native Peoples themselves, but was created through colonialist takeover. Coveting the lands of the Lakota and what were viewed as resources[4] upon and within those lands was at the heart of settler colonial capitalism and greed. The "contaminating influence of the white man's dollar" (Standing Bear, 1933/1978, p. 184) was a threat to the Lakota way of life. Greed was not understandable to his people,

> It was no Indian custom for individuals to lay up stores for revenue, to fence land, to capture and hold animals for sale, to fight kith and kin, or to lay by any goods for the sake of mere possession.
>
> *Standing Bear, 1933/1978, p. 168*

Standing Bear (1933/1978) addressed the concept of "going back to the blanket" (p. 190) as Native Peoples' rescue from disappearance; arguing that Native continuance resulted from the Native individual "clinging to Indian ways, Indian thought, and tradition, that has kept him and is keeping him today" (p. 190). In the last paragraph of *Land of the Spotted Eagle*, Standing Bear provides testimony to the importance of, and valuable teachings embedded in, his Lakota culture. After all he had done and experienced as an educator, author, philosopher, and actor and after all that he and his people endured in childhood and adulthood as Indians in America, he was tenacious in voicing his right to a Lakota existence. He concluded that had he a child to raise, "I would, for its welfare, unhesitatingly set that child's feet in the path of my forefathers. I would raise him to be an Indian!" (Standing Bear, 1933/1978, p. 259).

Recommendations for Multicultural Education: Truth-Telling, Land, and Sovereignty

MCE challenges white supremacy, critiques historical inaccuracies, and advocates for school reform. As MCE honors great Black intellectuals Du Bois, Woodson, and others in their historical truth-telling, resistance to injustice, and advocacy for meaningful and quality education of Black children, in a parallel journey, MCE must unsettle the histories of U.S. boarding schools and settler-controlled education, as expressed by Bonnin, Eastman, and Standing Bear. The historical legacies of scholars of color are central to the present and future of MCE. For Native Peoples, recommendations for Indigenous futurities involve truth-telling about purposes, practices, and legacies of settler colonialist education, the understanding of relationships and responsibilities to Land, and the centrality of sovereignty to Native Peoples.

Truth-Telling

Throughout the process of unsettling MCE, our antecedents, Bonnin, Eastman, and Standing Bear, all identified characteristics of settler colonialism pertaining to truth-telling. Tuck and McKenzie (2015) suggest that we are complicit in settler colonialism when we support "the disavowal of history … and how settler colonialism is indeed ongoing" (p. 60). Our antecedents all identified the lack of truth-telling about colonization, settler colonialism, and experiences and histories of Native Peoples. Luther Standing Bear (1933/1978) wrote, "the mothers and fathers of this land do their children an injustice by not seeing that their offspring are taught the true history of this continent and its people" (pp. 228–229). Therefore, we urge the field of MCE to extend theories of critical pedagogy to unsettle Indigenous erasures. As Stein (2020) suggests, "we cannot address our colonial present without a clear account of our colonial past" (p. 164). From the writings of Bonnin, Eastman, and Standing Bear, we identified multiple opportunities for MCE to focus on truth-telling, including: *1. Understanding the detrimental impact and colonial history of boarding schools and residential schools*; and, *2. Interrupting the misrepresentations of Native Americans, particularly in "books, schools, and libraries"* (Standing Bear, 1933/1978, p. 228), and *teaching the accurate history of Native Peoples.*

The detrimental impact of U.S. boarding schools was the personal experience of each antecedent. Bonnin, Eastman, and Standing Bear each wrote about the challenges they faced and critiqued the U.S. system of American Indian education. In *Education for Extinction*, Adams (1995) claims that the criticisms and truths concealed within Bonnin's essays, reflective of her boarding school experience, influenced policy makers and educators into the action of "reassessing the ideological underpinnings of Indian education" (p. 314). Although the U.S. has not officially addressed this atrocity of boarding schools, Canada offered a national apology for residential schools in 2008. In response, the Canadian government began the *Truth and Reconciliation Commission* (TRC) to address reparations. Although TRCs are complicated and often serve to "legitimize and reinforce colonial relationships, thus maintaining the status quo … strategies for Indigenous restorying offer alternatives for resisting contemporary colonial realities and legacies of residential schools" (Corntassel, Chaw-win-is, & T'lakwadzi, 2009, p. 155).

While all three antecedents advocated for *Interrupting the misrepresentations of Native Peoples and teaching accurate history*, Luther Standing Bear (1933/1978) proclaimed,

> Books, paintings, and pictures have all joined in glorifying the pioneer—the hunter, trapper, woodsman, cowboy, and soldiery—in their course of conquest across the country, a conquest that could only have been realized by committing untold offenses against the aboriginal people.
>
> *p. 227*

Charles Eastman in his 1903 essay, "The Indian's View of the Indian in Literature," also critiqued the ways Native Peoples were portrayed in mainstream literature; he was resolute in his displeasure of the "frightful and repulsive" depictions (Emery, 2017, p. 227), which upheld the construction of the "savage," Eastman stressed, "The effect is altogether bad, for the general reader is fortified in a heartless prejudice, and it is really a gross injustice, though it may be without intention" (Emery, 2017, p. 227).

Aligned with our antecedents, contemporary Indigenous and educational researchers are responding to "data that proves hegemonic curriculum across the nation in standards and implementation" still exists when teaching about American Indians (Shear, Knowles, Soden, & Castro, 2015, p. 90). One effort to use and gather data, that mirrors goals of MCE, is the *Reclaiming Native Truth Project* (First Nations Development Institute, 2018). This collaboration with NCAI and IllumiNative is a "national effort to achieve equity, inclusion and policy changes that will improve the lives of Native families and communities" (p. 4). A primary goal of the project is to "ensure the respectful inclusion and accuracy of Native American history and cultures in educational curricula" (p. 3). The results are strikingly clear for education, revealing that inaccuracy and underrepresentation of Native Peoples in curricular content leaves educators and the general public feeling "disappointment or anger" for being misled, creating an overwhelming desire to "make significant changes" (p. 13). In summary, they conclude that "across the research, people call for more accurate education about Native Americans" (p. 13). Together, Indigenous and multicultural scholars have critiqued settler colonial curriculum (Au, Brown, & Calderon, 2016; Grande & Anderson, 2017; Tuck & Gaztambide-Fernández, 2013) and advocated for the unsettling of multicultural erasures. Grande and Anderson (2017) call on teachers and schools,

> who will take interruptive aim at the settler colonial logics that pervade the spaces where they live and work, most especially schools where liberalism conceals 'inconvenient truths' that would otherwise unsettle, productively, the lie that is 'America.' Without such teachers, our schools will continue to enlist young people into that lie and, thus, into the work of defending and perpetuating American exceptionalism.
>
> *pp. 139–140*

Land

Throughout their writings, Bonnin, Eastman, and Standing Bear honored "Land" as central to their ways of being in the world. Highlighting the scholarship of Styres (2019), we also use "L" (capital L) to define Land as a "physical geographic space," as well as "underlying conceptual principles, philosophies, and ontologies of that space" (p. 27). Styres (2019) describes Land as, "spiritual, emotional, and relational; Land *is* experiential, (re)membered, and storied; Land *is* consciousness—Land *is* sentient ... [Styres has] come to know Land both as a fundamental sentient being and as a philosophical construct" (p. 27). Therefore, Land creates dynamic opportunities for "interpretation and meaning-making" (p. 28). The ways that our Native antecedents understood Land fundamentally differed from the characteristics of settler colonialism. Their teachings created "storied landscapes" which now offer opportunities to unsettle MCE's absence of Land as a foundational conceptual framework of the field (p. 28).

In our review of the literature, three Land-based themes emerged from Bonnin, Eastman, and Standing Bear's scholarship addressing relationships to Land, which include: *1. Land as relational*; *2. Land as "settler colonial property"*; and *3. Land as sovereignty.* Standing Bear (1933/1978) asserted that "nature makes the man to fit his surroundings. If that be the case, then a description of the land partly, at least, describes the people" (p. 42). This notion has been expanded by many Indigenous scholars (Bang et al., 2014; Deloria & Wildcat, 2001; Tuck &

Yang, 2012), as described by Tuck and McKenzie (2015). Like, Styres (2019), these scholars emphasize the importance of being from place rather than arriving or coming to a place. Tuck argues that, "Indigenous peoples have creation stories, not colonization stories about how Indigenous people came to (be) a place" (quoted in Tuck & McKenzie, 2015, p. 56). To further the notion *of land as relational*, Eastman (1911/2003) described the relationship of more-than-human "peoples" (p. 33) who held equal authority to human beings. He wrote that, "we believed that the spirit pervades all creation and that every creature possesses a soul in some degree, though not necessarily a soul conscious of itself" (Eastman, 1911/2003, p. 4). Eastman continued by stating that, "the Spirit of God is not breathed into man alone, but that the whole created universe is a sharer in the immortal perfection of its Maker" (Eastman, 1911/2003, pp. 31–32). Each antecedent maintained a powerful relationship to Land throughout their lives and in their scholarship.

In contrast to *Land as relational*, Standing Bear (1933/1978) identified the dichotomy between Indigenous and settler colonial concepts of Land. He wrote, "but the white man has put distance between himself and nature; and assuming a lofty place in the scheme of order of things has lost for him both reverence and understanding" (p. 196). Standing Bear identified another characteristic of settler colonialism which disassociates Land as sentient to *Land as settler colonial property*. In the process and structuring of colonization (Grande, 2015), land (lower-case "l") becomes an object of capitalism, Western Christianity, and white supremacy. Standing Bear identified this form of colonization when he wrote,

> It was not hard to see that the white people coveted every inch of land on which we lived. Greed, human greed, wanted the last bit of ground which supported Indian feet. It was land—it has ever been land—for which the white man oppresses the Indian and to gain possession of which he commits any crime.
>
> *p. 244*

During the turn of the twentieth century, Bonnin, Eastman, and Standing Bear each spoke out against federal policy that was actively dispossessing Native Peoples of Land. Our antecedents used their positions and writing to courageously speak out against *Land as settler colonial property*. At the turn of the twenty-first century, Land is still essential to any conversations or actions toward decolonization (Tuck & Yang, 2012). This is most recently illustrated in the Indigenous fight for environmental justice at Standing Rock (Gilio-Whitaker, 2019). As Simpson (2017) states, "Everyday acts of resurgence sound romantic, but they are not. Put aside visions of 'back to the land,' and just think land– some of it is wild, some of it is urban, a lot of it is ecologically devastated" (p. 195). Therefore, this call to action for MCE must also be understood through *Land as Sovereignty*. Simpson reminds us that "every piece of North America is Indigenous land regardless of whether it has a city on top of it, or it is under threat, or it is coping with industrial development" (Simpson, 2017, p. 195).

Although we will discuss sovereignty in more detail shortly, *Land as Sovereignty* highlights Indigenous relations to Land, which include identity, culture, governance, and history connected to place since time immemorial (Gilio-Whitaker, 2019). Throughout Bonnin's career, her writing and political advocacy focused on inherent Native rights to Land and resources (Willard, 1985). In a "Letter to the Chiefs and Headmen of the Tribes" (Bonnin, 1919), she asked that care be taken to preserve what "inherited lands" were left, "For the sake of our children's children we must hold on to a few acres that they may enjoy it as we have" (p. 197). Similarly, Standing Bear (1933/1978) argued that, "The white man excused his presence here by saying that he had been guided by the will of his God; and in so saying absolved himself of all responsibility for his appearance in a land occupied by other men" (p. 249). Our antecedents unearthed additional settler colonial characteristics in which settlers do not consider "themselves to be implicated in the continued settlement and occupation of unceded Indigenous lands" and see themselves "simultaneously most superior and most normal" (Tuck & McKenzie, 2015, p. 60). As we discuss further, Indigenous Peoples of North America have an inherent right to their ancestral homelands. Understanding and unsettling colonization (Grande, 2015) illuminates "settler moves to innocence" (Tuck & Yang, 2012) that challenge MCE to take anti-colonial action, with Land as a central principle.

Land, like the many characteristics of MCE, must be considered "basic education" and be "pervasive" throughout learning experiences (Nieto & Bode, 2018, p. 32). Our antecedents and Native scholars share urgency for our children to learn from the Land as teacher, philosophy, and developing ways of being in the world for Indigenous and all futurities. In Eastman's (1921) suggestions for Land-based education, he wrote, "if you give him into the hand of God in the wilderness he will find philosophy, and with these teachings we are sure of a sound civilization" (p. 605). Multicultural education calls for transformative action through sociopolitical and historical awareness. In *The Revolution Has Begun* (2018), Native scholar and artivist, Christi Belcourt, brings that awareness back to the land and responsibilities of educators, recognizing that, "the only education that our children need is from the land. [Educators] must have the courage to disrupt the system … rebuild so schools cease being institutions … providing mentorship so children can develop their gifts to be free thinkers" (p. 120). She concludes that, "children will be able to find the solutions that we are not capable of due to our conditioning through colonization" (p. 120).

Sovereignty

Unsettling MCE requires Land-based pedagogy, Indigenous nation building, and activism. Just as our antecedents held Land and sovereignty[5] as inextricably interconnected, they were also keenly aware of the imperial gaze. As a contemporary Indigenous scholar, Simpson (2017), writes, "Being engaged in land as pedagogy as a life practice inevitably means coming face-to-face with settler colonial authority, surveillance, and violence because this practice places Indigenous between settlers and their money" (p. 166). As discussed in our definition of settler colonization (Grande, 2015), Bonnin, Eastman, and Standing Bear clearly experienced the ways colonization was subsidized by capitalism (as well as white supremacy, and Western Christianity). The magnitude of their accomplishments can be understood by the settler colonial challenges they faced while advocating for sovereignty, including the following characteristics (Tuck & McKenzie, 2015): 1. Settler dysconsciousness to "Indigenous Peoples' resistance to settlement" and "claims to stolen land … ceded by broken treaties" (p. 60); and 2. "Settler colonial attempt (and failure) to contain Indigenous agency and resistance" (p. 61). As survivors of U.S. boarding schools and the usurping of their ancestral homelands, our antecedents fought for their sovereign rights.

Bonnin, Eastman, and Standing Bear resisted containment within the structures of settler colonialism by speaking out and writing for change during the *Allotment and Assimilation (1887–1934)* and the *Indian Reorganization (1934–1945)* periods of Native American and U.S. history (NCAI, 2020). Although it would be over two decades before the *Self-Determination (1968–2000)* period, our antecedents were advocating for: *1. The right to self-determination*; *2. Sovereignty over democracy*; and *3. Refusal of settler colonial containment.*

During the era of the Dawes Act (1887–1934), marked by forced assimilation and dispossession of Native lands from communal to private property, the U.S. government sanctioned settler taking of Native allotments. While the focus of the U.S. government was on assimilation and abstraction, Gertrude Simmons Bonnin fearlessly advocated, nationally and internationally, for Indigenous *rights to self-determination*. In 1919, in her position as SAI editor, she addressed the Paris Peace Conference and overlaid the international discourse on self-determination for small nations (the "little peoples") to govern themselves as sovereign (as cited in Hoxie, 2001, p. 132).

After founding the National Council of American Indians with her husband in 1926 (Hoxie, 2001), and her election as the organization's president, Bonnin provided testimony at U.S. governmental hearings (Hafen, 2013; Willard, 1985). One such instance involved tribal members having to sign away power of attorney to reservation superintendents. Taking away power from Native Peoples over their own lands, this Bureau of Indian Affairs policy authorized superintendents to negotiate land leases with companies or individuals without approval of the Native landowner (Willard, 1985). Bonnin's testimony to the U.S. Senate Indian Committee regarding the practice spoke to the negation of tribal self-determination.

Sovereignty has always been understood by Native Nations as an inherent right from the Creator, rather than an accepted formality of the U.S. settler government. There are currently 574 sovereign tribal nations "that have a formal nation-to-nation relationship with the U.S. government" (National Congress of American Indians (NCAI), 2020, p. 11). This tribal nationhood (Haynes Writer, 2010) was affirmed by Supreme Court Justice John Marshall, in Worcester v. Georgia (1832), stating that, "Indian Nations had always been considered as distinct, independent political communities, retaining their original natural rights, as the undisputed possessors of the soil … the very term 'nation' so generally applied to them means 'a people distinct from other'" (as cited in NCAI, 2020, p. 9). Our antecedents understood sovereignty beyond treaty rights and recognition by the U.S. constitution. They valued Indigenous *sovereignty over democracy*. Eastman recognized Native Peoples as the "original American" (Emery, 2017, p. 230) and the "first American" when he spoke of his People teaching "national traditions and belief" to the young (1911/2003, pp. 23 and 8). He asserted that for the Dakota, the "government is a pure democracy, based solidly upon intrinsic right and justice" (Eastman, 1915, p. 5). Standing Bear argued that no word existed for democracy in Lakota society, however, the phrase "Oyate ta woecun" implied "done by the people" or Nation (Standing Bear, 1933/1978, p. 129). As is commonly understood, settler politician Benjamin Franklin's vision of U.S. democracy was heavily influenced by the Iroquois constitution (Grinde, 1992). Indigenous scholar Sandy Grande (2015) suggests that "Indigenous sovereignty does not oppose U.S. democracy" (p. 50). In fact, she argues that "sovereignty is democracy's only lifeline" (p. 50). Grande illuminates the denial and manipulations of U.S. mainstream (whitestream) narratives that obscure truthful articulations that the birth of this nation began "by denying the existence of Native peoples, weaving a tale of 'discovery' and 'democracy'" (p. 54). Our antecedents were not denying the U.S. mainstream society their right to democracy. On the contrary, as Grande concludes, "imposed democracy significantly depreciated Indian sovereignty" (p. 62).

In significant *refusal of settler colonial containment,* Bonnin, Eastman, and Standing Bear used the tools of their time, particularly writing, public speaking, and community organizing, to disrupt the policies and practices of settler colonialism. For example, Eastman was highly critical of the corruption and graft that flowed from controlling Native Peoples and their capacity of self-sufficiency. In 1919, Eastman published "The Indian's Plea for Freedom," in the SAI journal. In wearing the mantle of Native rights advocate, he reflected upon the international discourse on rights following World War I and the Versailles Paris Peace Conference. He commented that as international relationships were being formed, "new order must also begin at home" (as cited in Hoxie, 2001, p. 132). Standing Bear, offered a tribally specific critique of the limitations of U.S. policy articulating that the timeless rights for the Lakota people emerged from "a great tribal consciousness" of self-governing (p. 124). In fact, he critiqued the need for enforcement of written laws on Lakota people, saying "[s]uch laws are written to be, in time, rewritten or unwritten, and that means to be kept and broken" (p. 125). The urgency for justice in the writings and actions of Bonnin, Eastman, and Standing Bear was courageous in the active *Allotment and Assimilation* era under the Dawes Act, "which within half a century reduced treaty-reserved lands by two-thirds in what Indians consider to be blatant treaty violations" (Gilio-Whitaker, 2019, p. 131). Within their lifetime they saw the lands of their specific Nations seized and diminished by acts of Congress that were never ratified. It is in this unceded territory that the Dakota Access Pipeline threatens Standing Rock's water source and sacred lands (Gilio-Whitaker, 2019). Although they could not have predicted the specificities of our current political moment and the continued struggle for the protection of Native Land and people, Bonnin, Eastman, and Standing Bear fought for the sovereign rights of Indigenous Peoples to determine their own governance, history, culture, identity, relationships to Land, and education without interference of other nations.

The activism, leadership, and scholarship of Bonnin, Eastman, and Standing Bear largely remain hidden, as do the everyday lived realities of Native Americans in U.S. society. In 2019, NCAI published the report, *Becoming Visible: A Landscape Analysis of State Efforts to Provide Native American Education for All.* As alluded to in the title, Native visibility within the U.S. mainstream is still "absent from the classroom or relegated to brief mentions, negative information, or inaccurate stereotypes" (p. 6). The goal of this report is to provide "an analysis of the landscape of current state efforts to bring high-quality educational content about Native peoples and communities into all kindergarten to 12th grade (K-12) classrooms across the United States" (p. 6). In an analysis of the research in the 35 states with federally recognized Nations, although most states had Native American curriculum and content standards few required the curriculum in public schools. In addition to a lack of tribally specific curriculum within local communities, additional barriers included a lack of access to curricula, inadequate funding, and absence of policies to expand Native American curriculum. The report advocates for "advancing adoption of Native American curricula" by including "state legislation mandating collaboration between state education agencies and tribal nations, state legislation empowering or requiring state education agencies to develop curriculum, and state education agency policy to develop culturally responsive guidelines for local districts" (NCAI, 2019, p. 7).

In the twenty-first century, Bonnin, Eastman, and Standing Bear's urgency to understand tribal sovereignty remains. As a recommendation for unsettling MCE, Native education and social justice scholars "have offered a critique of multiculturalism for ignoring the significance of Indigenous (struggles for) sovereignty" (Tuck & Gaztambide-Fernández, 2013). In the critical study of representations of Indigenous Peoples in K–12 U.S. history standards, Shear et al. (2015) recommend that social justice education "must also advance sovereignty and treaty rights as central to the larger discourse or else we face a reification of colonial thinking" (p. 90).

Conclusion

For MCE to remain viable and dynamic, it must continue to evolve as scholars and educators contemplate the temporal context and cultivate new knowledge and ideas to address issues of the lived realities and experiences of children, families, and communities. We contend that MCE also needs to discover, uncover, and recover voices from the past that provide historical rootedness and wisdom to assist the field in addressing the present, while visioning the future.

We presented Native scholars Bonnin, Eastman, and Standing Bear, contemporaries of Du Bois and Woodson, whose work and legacy must be considered foundational to the origins of MCE. Our Native antecedents' experiences with settler colonialism drove their intellectual writing, speeches, and actions toward justice, providing understandings of present-day settler colonialism—that must be taken up and unsettled by coalitions of MCE and Native scholars and educators. The antecedents deserve historical recognition and MCE must address the ways settler colonialism continues to impact Native Peoples (as well as all historically marginalized peoples within the United States), which is typically overlooked because of an incommensurable MCE focus on democracy. Engaging in an "ethic of incommensurability" between Indigenous futurities and the future of MCE can create "an alternate mode of holding and imagining solidarity" (Tuck & Yang, 2018, p. 2).

For Indigenous futurities, Bonnin, Eastman, and Standing Bear call us to engage in truth-telling, already a grounding principle within MCE. The antecedents call also for the recognition of Land and the advancement of tribal sovereignty, two concepts that present conceptualizations and practices MCE does not adequately or consistently include. As Tuck and Gaztambide-Fernández (2013) proclaim, "Indigenous futurity does not require the erasure of now-settlers in the ways that settler futurity requires of Indigenous peoples" (p. 80). What is at stake for Indigenous futurities, and what must be brought into the vision and work of MCE, is truth-telling, Land, and sovereignty. We remain emphatic that MCE must address settler colonialism to envision, support, and create space for Indigenous futurities as we participate in a future visioning of Multicultural Education.

Notes

1 Drawing on McCoy, Tuck, and McKenzie (2017), the term "Land" is used but stands for land, below and above, water, and air. Reflective of the centrality of Land to Indigenous Peoples, we capitalize the word.

2 The terms *Native Peoples*, *Native American*, *Native*, *Indigenous*, and *Indigenous Peoples* are preferred and used interchangeably; most Native people prefer to use their specific Pueblo, tribal, group or homeland name. Each nation/tribe/band is distinct, having a defined worldview with a specific language or language referents and a specialized knowledge system (epistemology), a named and structured reality (ontology), and established values (axiology). Additionally, Native Peoples differ from each other in their time and type of

emergence into their revered place of storied origin and their dispossession from place, land, and territory. Each also differs in their historical, legal, economic, cultural, spiritual, political, social, and educational realities based on their interactions with settlers and the settler colonialist governments.

3 Zitkala-Ša's essays included: "Impressions of an Indian Childhood" (January, 1900, *Atlantic Monthly, 85*, 37–45); "The School Days of an Indian Girl" (February, 1900, *Atlantic Monthly, 85*, 185–193); and "An Indian Teacher among Indians" (March, 1900, *Atlantic Monthly, 85*, 381–386).

4 We say "what were viewed as resources" to distinguish between a capitalistic view of Nature as an inanimate profit generator, that is, exploitable products or materials to be harvested, obtained, or extracted for monetary production. Indigenous relationship to Land, thus Nature, is one of interdependence, set upon values of respect, reciprocity, and responsibility, because most Native worldviews convey that "the world in which we live is alive" (Deloria, 1997, p. 40). That is, "Everything is viewed as having energy and its own unique intelligence and creative process, not only obviously animate entities, such as plants, animals, and microorganisms, but also rocks, mountains, rivers, and places large and small" (Cajete, 2000, p. 21). Carroll (2015) discussed the former as a resource-based approach and the latter as a relationship-based approach. He maintained that operating within a settler colonial context, "In speaking the language of 'resources' indigenous nations are able to assert some form of sovereignty over them" (p. xvii).

5 *Sovereignty* is a legal word for an ordinary concept—the authority to self-govern. Hundreds of treaties, along with the Supreme Court, the President, and Congress, have repeatedly affirmed that tribal nations retain their inherent powers of self-government. These treaties, executive orders, and laws have created a fundamental contract between tribes and the United States. Tribal nations are located within the geographic borders of the United States, while each tribal nation exercises its own sovereignty (NCAI, 2019, p. 16). As Peoples being on the Land since time immemorial, and since sovereign nation status is a political identity, rather than a racial or ethnic identity, *Native Americans are not "minorities."*

References

Adams, D. W. (1995). *Education for extinction: American Indians and the boarding school experience, 1875–1928.* Lawrence, KS: University of Kansas Press.

Au, W., Brown, A. L., & Calderon, D. (2016). *Reclaiming the multicultural roots of U.S. curriculum: Communities of color and official knowledge in education.* New York, NY: Teachers College Press.

Bang, M., Curley, L., Kessel, A., Marin, A., Suzukovich, III, E. S., & Strack, G. (2014). Muskrat theories, tobacco in the streets, and living Chicago as Indigenous land. *Environmental Education Research, 20*(1), 37–55. DOI: 10.1080/13504622.2013.865113

Belcourt, C. (2018). The revolution has begun. In E. Tuck & K. W. Yang (Eds.), *Toward what justice? Describing diverse dreams of justice in education* (pp. 113–121). New York: NY: Routledge.

Bonnin, G. (1919, Winter). Letter to the chiefs and headmen of the tribes. *The American Indian Magazine, 5*(4), 196–197.

Brayboy, B. M. J. (2005). Toward a tribal critical race theory in education. *Urban Review, 37*(5), 425–446.

Burt, R. E. (2010). "Sioux yells" in the Dawes era: Lakota "Indian play," the wild west, and the literature of Luther Standing Bear. *American Quarterly, 62*(3), 617–637.

Cajete, G. (2000). *Native science: Natural laws of interdependence.* Santa Fe, NM: Clear Light Publishers.

Carroll, C. (2015). *Roots of our renewal: Ethnobotany and Cherokee environmental governance.* Minneapolis, MN: University of Minnesota Press.

Chiarello, B. (2005). Deflected missives: Zitkala-Ša's resistance and its (un)containment. *Studies in American Indian Literatures, 17*(3), 1–26.

Corntassel, J., Chaw-win-is, & T'lakwadzi (2009). Indigenous storytelling, truth-telling, and community approaches to reconciliation. *English Studies in Canada, 35*, 137–159. Retrieved from www.corntassel.net/IndigenousStorytelling%202009.pdf

Coulthard, G. S. (2014). *Red skin, white masks: Rejecting the colonial politics of recognition.* Minneapolis, MN: University of Minnesota Press.

Debo, A. (1991). *And still the waters run: The betrayal of the Five Civilized Tribes.* Princeton, NJ: Princeton University Press. (Original work published 1940)

Deloria, V., Jr. (1997). *Red earth, white lies: Native Americans and the myth of scientific fact.* Golden, CO: Fulcrum Publishing.

Deloria, V., Jr., & Wildcat, D. R. (2001). *Power and place: Indian education in America.* Golden, CO: Fulcrum Resources.

Eastman, C. A. (1915). *The Indian to-day: The past and future of the first American.* Retrieved from www.gutenberg.org/files/27448/27448-h/27448-h.htm

Eastman, C. A. (1921). What can the out-of-doors do for our children? *Education, 41*(9), 599–605.

Eastman, C. A. (2003). *From deep woods to civilization.* Mineola, NY: Dover Publications, Inc. (Original work published 1916)

Eastman, C. A. (2003). *The soul of the Indian.* Mineola, NY: Dover Publications, Inc. (Original work published 1911)

Ellinghaus, K. (2006). *Taking assimilation to heart: Marriages of white women and Indigenous men in the United States and Australia, 1887–1937.* Lincoln, NE: University of Nebraska Press.

Emery, J. (2017). *Recovering Native American writings in the boarding school press.* Lincoln, NE: University of Nebraska Press.

Fabens, C. H., & Sniffen, M. K. (1924). *Oklahoma's poor rich Indians: An orgy of graft and exploitation of the Five Civilized Tribes, legalized robbery.* (No. 127). Philadelphia, PA: Office of the Indian Rights Association.

First Nations Development Institute (2018, June). *Reclaiming Native Truth. Research findings: Compilation of all research.* Retrieved from https://rnt.firstnations.org/wp-content/uploads/2018/06/FullFindingsReport-screen.pdf

Fitzgerald, M. O. (Ed.) (2007). *The essential Charles Eastman (Ohiyesa): Light on the Indian world.* Bloomington, IN: World Wisdom, Inc.

Gilio-Whitaker, D. (2019). *As long as grass grows: The Indigenous fight for environmental justice, from colonization to Standing Rock.* Boston, MA: Beacon Press.

Grande, S. (2015). *Red pedagogy: Native American social and political thought* (10th anniversary ed.). Lanham, MD: Rowman & Littlefield.

Grande, S., & Anderson, L. (2017). Un-settling multicultural erasures. *Multicultural Perspectives, 19*(3), 139–142. DOI: 10.1080/15210960.2017.1331742

Grinde, D. A., Jr. (1992). Iroquois political theory and the roots of American democracy. In O. Lyons, J. Mohawk, V. Deloria Jr., L. Hauptman, H. Berman, D. Grinde Jr., et al. (Eds.), *Exiled in the land of the free: Democracy, Indian nations, and the U.S. constitution* (pp. 227–280). Santa Fe, NM: Clear Light Publishers.

Hafen, J. P. (2013). "Help Indians help themselves": Gertrude Bonnin, the SAI, and the NCAI. *American Indian Quarterly, 37*(3), 199–218.

Hagan, W. T. (1997). *Theodore Roosevelt and six friends of the Indian.* Norman, OK: University of Oklahoma.

Hale, F. (1993). Acceptance and rejection of assimilation in the works of Luther Standing Bear. *Studies in American Indian Literatures, 5*(4), 25–41.

Haynes Writer, J. (2008). Unmasking, exposing, and confronting: Critical race theory, tribal critical race theory and multicultural education. *International Journal of Multicultural Education, 10*(2), 1–15.

Haynes Writer, J. (2010). Broadening the meaning of citizenship education: Native Americans and tribal nationhood. *Action in Teacher Education, 32*(2), 70–81.

Hoxie, F. E. (2001). *Talking back to civilization: Indian voices in the Progressive Era.* Boston, MA: Bedford/St. Martin's Press.

McCoy, K., Tuck, E., & McKenzie, M. (Eds.) (2017). *Land education: Rethinking pedagogies of place from Indigenous, postcolonial, and decolonizing perspectives.* New York, NY: Routledge.

Misiarz, R. (2016). The Society of American Indians and the "Indian question," 1911–1923. *Białostockie Teki Historyczne, 14,* 91–109.

National Congress of American Indians (NCAI) (2019). *Becoming visible: A landscape analysis of state efforts to provide Native American education for all.* Retrieved from www.ncai.org/policy-research-center/research-data/prc-publications/NCAI-Becoming_Visible_Report-Digital_FINAL_10_2019.pdf

National Congress of American Indians (NCAI) (2020). Tribal nations and the United States: An introduction. Retrieved from www.ncai.org/tribalnations/introduction/Indian_Country_ 101_Updated_February_2019.pdf

Nieto, S., & Bode, P. (2018). *Affirming diversity: The sociopolitical context of multicultural education* (7th ed.). New York, NY: Pearson.

Richardson, T. A. (2011). Navigating the problem of inclusion as enclosure in Native culture-based education: Theorizing shadow curriculum. *Curriculum Inquiry, 41*(3), 332–349.

Richardson, T. A. (2012). Indigenous political difference, colonial perspectives and the challenge of diplomatic relations: Toward a decolonial diplomacy in multicultural educational theory. *Educational Studies, 48,* 465–484.

Rifkin, M. (2017). *Beyond settler time: Temporal sovereignty and Indigenous self-determination.* Durham, NC: Duke University Press.

Shear, S, Knowles, R. T., Soden, G. J., & Castro, A. J. (2015). Manifesting destiny: Re/presentations of Indigenous Peoples in K–12 U.S. history standards. *Theory & Research in Social Education, 43*(1), 68–101. DOI: 10.1080/00933104.2014.999849

Simpson, L. B. (2017). *As we have always done: Indigenous freedom through radical resistance.* Minneapolis, MN: University of Minnesota Press.

Spack, R. (2001). Dis/engagement: Zitkala-Sa's letters to Carlos Montezuma, 1901–1902. *MELUS, 26*(1), 173–203.

Standing Bear, L. (1931, November). The tragedy of the Sioux. *The American Mercury.* Retrieved from https://gutenberg.ca/ebooks/standingbearl-tragedyofthesioux/standingbearl-tragedyofthesioux-00-h.html

Standing Bear, L. (1975). *My people the Sioux.* Lincoln, NE: University of Nebraska Press. (Original work published 1928)

Standing Bear, L. (1978). *Land of the spotted eagle.* Lincoln, NE: University of Nebraska. (Original work published 1933)

Stein, S. (2020). 'Truth before reconciliation': The difficulties of transforming higher education in settler colonial contexts. *Higher Education Research & Development, 39*(1), 156–170. DOI: 10.1080/07294360.2019.1666255

Styres, S. (2019). Literacies of land: Decolonizing narratives, storying, and literature. In L. T. Smith, E. Tuck, & K. W. Yang (Eds.), *Indigenous and decolonizing studies in education: Mapping the long view* (pp. 24–37). New York: NY: Routledge.

Tuck, E., & Gaztambide-Fernandez, R. A. (2013). Curriculum, replacement, and settler futurity. *Journal of Curriculum Theorizing, 29*(1), 72–89.

Tuck, E., & McKenzie, M. (2015). *Place in research: Theory, methodology, and methods.* New York, NY: Routledge.

Tuck, E., & Yang, K. W. (2012). Decolonization is not a metaphor. *Decolonization: Indigeneity, Education & Society, 1*(1), 1–40.

Tuck, E., & Yang, K. W. (2018). *Toward what justice? Describing diverse dreams of justice in education.* New York, NY: Routledge.

Veracini, L. (2015). *The settler colonial present.* New York: NY: Palgrave Macmillan.

Welch, D. (2001). Gertrude Simmons Bonnin (Zitkala-Ša)/Dakota. In R. D. Edmunds (Ed.), *The new warriors: Native American leaders since 1900* (pp. 35–53). Lincoln, NE: University of Nebraska Press.

Willard, W. (1985). Zitkala Sa: A woman who would be heard!. *Wicazo Sa Review, 1*(1), 11–16.

Wolfe, P. (1999). *Settler colonialism and the transformation of Anthropology: The politics and poetics of an ethnographic event.* New York: NY: Cassell.

Worcester v. Georgia, 31 U.S. (6 Pet.) 515, 561 (United States Supreme Court 1832).

Zitkala-Ša (1902, December). "Why I am a Pagan" *Atlantic Monthly, 90,* 801–803. Retrieved from http://xtf.lib.virginia.edu/xtf/view?docId=modern_english/uvaGenText/tei/ZitPaga.xml&query=Zitkala-Sa

Zitkala-Ša (1987). *American Indian stories.* Lincoln, NE: University of Nebraska. (Original work published 1921)

SECTION II
Limits and Transformation

The four chapters composing this section present themes, relevant to their topics, that inform us on issues, laws or policies that limit individuals or specific constituent groups. The authors, in visioning a Multicultural Education future, also alert us to possibilities of transformation. The topics of standardized testing, myth of free speech, immigration status, and reforming citizenship education are invoked in unique passionate messages that will definitely engage the reader.

Leading off the section, Wayne Au's chapter, "Testing for Whiteness? How High-Stakes, Standardized Tests Promote Racism, Undercut Diversity, and Undermine Multicultural Education," speaks definitively to the limits placed on particular groups through the use of standardized tests. Revealing the origins and purposes of the tests in the eugenics movement and examining the present oppression and inequities caused by the tests, Au presents a cogent argument that the United States' embrace of standardized testing and its progeny, high-stakes testing, have simultaneously served the interests of Whiteness and homogenization while actively working against the interests of diversity and Multicultural Education.

In his chapter titled, "Inclusive Diversity and Robust Speech: Examining a Contested Intersection," Carlos Cortés raises salient points regarding the dilemmas resulting from the interaction of free speech and inclusive diversity. He also assesses the influence of the Internet and neuroscientific research on the evolving diversity-speech dialogue. As a transformative move, Cortés shares two questions he often poses to multicultural educators to assist them in interrogating the intersection of robust speech and inclusive diversity.

In "Education in Times of Mass Migration," legal scholar, Angela Banks, presents a compelling case for educators understanding immigration statuses. She points out that immigration status itself is a significant form of difference that shapes an individual's right to remain in the United States, access to employment and education, and opportunities for political participation. She also describes the difference that immigration status makes in the lives of school-age children and their families. Banks makes the point that multicultural education scholars and practitioners can prompt change by helping students to understand the history and laws involving immigration status and citizenship, and assisting students to think critically about broader conceptions of membership and belonging in their society.

James Banks' chapter, "Transforming Citizenship Education in Global Societies," is timely and timeless considering the global challenges presented by mass migration and the Covid-19 pandemic. He challenges the historical liberal nation-state concept of citizenship and citizenship education. Citizenship education, he argues, should be reformed to reflect the home cultures and languages of students from diverse groups. He convincingly explains why transformative citizenship education needs to be implemented in order to reflect and respond to the citizenship needs and aspirations of diverse groups.

6

TESTING FOR WHITENESS?

How High-Stakes, Standardized Tests Promote Racism, Undercut Diversity, and Undermine Multicultural Education

Wayne Au

Introduction

While standardized testing has gained different levels of traction in education policy in the United States at various times since the early 1900s, it was not until the late 1980s that such testing began its evolution into the central form of measuring educational outcomes and effectiveness in K–12 education policy. The evolutionary dominance of standardized testing in the ecology of U.S. education policy eventually took firm hold with the passing of the No Child Left Behind Act of 2002, which federally mandated these tests and attached various punishments to test scores. This shift functionally and officially turned "standardized testing" into "high-stakes, standardized testing," and it was done under the guise of promoting race, economic class, and individual equality (Au, 2009b). The idea that standardized tests, and later high-stakes, standardized tests, serve in the interests of racial, economic, and individual equality and justice is where we see the critical juncture of testing and the principles of multicultural education.

Historically, the core principles of multicultural education in the United States have revolved around a constellation of issues that build on each other. The first is that the concept of "culture" is broad and encompassing, such that it includes more than just race or ethnicity, and instead recognizes that "culture" also includes communities built around other aspects of identity including economic class, religion, sexuality, nationality, gender identity, disability, and age, among a myriad of possibilities. Multicultural education, then, argues that we have always been a culturally diverse society and that the cultural diversity of our student and general populations only continues to increase. Building from this base, multicultural education further suggests that there is a need for our populations, in all their diversity, to better understand themselves and each other as historical and cultural beings, because this can serve to strengthen our democracy and our commitment to our shared and deeply connected futures. Further, and consequently, multicultural education posits that, because they are places where most of us gather and are collected together, schools are crucial sites in advancing the multicultural needs of society (Banks et al., 2005; Orfield & Frankenberg, 2011). In this way, multicultural education is not simply a matter of including diverse content in curriculum and diverse forms of pedagogy. Rather, multicultural education also implicates the ways that our diverse, multicultural student bodies experience schooling.

The juncture of high-stakes, standardized testing and equality is extended to argue that such testing not only serves the principles of multicultural education, but also the needs of a multicultural and just society. In this chapter I argue that, not only are these presumptive logics false, but that they are damaging to both the core principles of multicultural education and our children. More sharply, I argue that, in the United States, standardized testing and its progeny, high-stakes testing, have simultaneously served the interests of Whiteness and homogenization while actively working against the interests of diversity and multicultural education. This chapter begins by detailing the ways that standardized testing has been used historically to undermine multiculturalism and diversity in the United States, including its role in supporting White supremacy and the eugenics movement. I continue with a discussion of modern-day high-stakes, standardized testing and how through test design itself, such assessments work against diversity and multicultural education while promoting race and class inequality. I end this chapter by recounting how high-stakes testing materially supports Whiteness through the racial resegregation and the propagation of the schools-to-prisons pipeline. All of which, I argue, serve to undercut multicultural education for our diverse democracy.

Standardized Testing, Whiteness, and Schooling

Considering how widespread the use of high-stakes, standardized testing is today in the United States, and given how often such tests are wielded in arguments about diversity, equality, and schooling, it is surprising how few people know that the lineage of high-stakes, standardized testing can be traced directly back to intelligence (or IQ) testing and the racism, classism, and sexism of the eugenics movement of the early 1900s. Essentially, during this period U.S. psychologists crassly distorted French psychologist Alfred Binet's original conception of IQ by using their own underlying presumptions about humans and human ability to interpret test results (Au, 2009b; Blanton, 2003; Gould, 1996).

As one example, in 1917, Robert Yerkes, an Army Colonel and psychologist in charge of the mental testing of 1.75 million recruits during World War I, worked with Henry Goddard, Lewis Terman and others to develop the Alpha and Beta Army standardized tests to sort incoming soldiers according to what they deemed as "mental fitness." These psychologists used this large pool of army recruit data to draw several conclusions they thought the tests had "scientifically" proven. Their test scores led them to argue that the intelligence of European immigrants was based according to their country of origin: The lighter-skinned peoples of western and northern Europe were, genetically, more intelligent than darker-skinned peoples of eastern and southern Europe. Using their test data, these psychologists also argued that the poor were less intelligent than the wealthy and that African Americans were the least intelligent of all peoples (Gould, 1996). In Terman's own words, certain races inherited "deficient" IQs, and "No amount of school instruction will ever make them intelligent voters or capable citizens." He also remarked that, "feeblemindedness" was "very, very common among Spanish-Indian and Mexican families of the Southwest and also among negroes [sic]," that, "Children of this group should be segregated in special classes and be given instruction that is practical," and that, "[These children] cannot master abstractions, but they can often be made efficient workers" (as quoted in Blanton, 2003, p. 43).

Eugenicists of the time believed in the genetic basis for behavioral and character traits they associated with gender, race, immigration, and class difference. Armed with the "scientific" findings of psychologists like Terman, these eugenicists rallied around the idea that race mixing was spreading the alleged inferior intelligence genes of African Americans, other non-White peoples, and immigrants (Gould, 1996). In this context, it is important to note that concepts of racial purity and impurity were also combined with notions of human ability and disability such that non-White races were constructed as "disabled" and as departures from the White, able-bodied norm (Annamma, Connor, & Ferri, 2013; Mitchell & Snyder, 2003). As such, standardized IQ tests provided supposedly "scientific" evidence to claims of White racial superiority and were used as a weapon against the multicultural diversity of the U.S.

In this way, early standardized testing in the U.S. was an articulation of a particularly sharp contradiction regarding individual inequality and structural discrimination in society, and this contradiction has been and is currently expressed in the view that such testing provides an objective measurement of individual effort, capability, or merit. So, on the one hand, in addition to the inherent efficiency of standardized tests to sort humans, early advocates of such testing also saw them as powerful tools to challenge class privilege and hierarchies because, to their minds, any individual could work hard, pass the test, and gain access to educational opportunities and socio-economic advancement regardless of social status. On the other hand, all prevailing evidence demonstrated that these tests were clearly sorting human populations along the structural lines of race, economic class, cultural norms, facility with English language, and immigrant experience. Thus, under the guise of meritocratic notions of individual effort and under the cover of "naturally" occurring aptitude amongst individuals, standardized testing came to be used to simultaneously laud individual achievement and mask structural discrimination embedded both in the tests themselves and in the lives of the test-takers (Au, 2009b, 2016).

Scholars of color during this time period were well aware of the ways such testing was racially and culturally biased, including how these tests worked to oppress the multicultural population of the United States. For instance, Horace Mann Bond—the Director of the School of Education at Langston University in Oklahoma—was one of the earliest African American educators to publicly challenge the findings of prominent psychologists involved in the IQ testing and eugenics movements. In 1924 Bond critiqued IQ testing and eugenics in *Crisis*, the magazine of the National Association for the Advancement of Colored People (Stoskopf, 2007). Similarly, writing in 1940, the professor and eminent scholar W. E. B. Du Bois (2007/1940) recalled:

> It was not until I was long out of school and indeed after the (first) World War that there came the hurried use of the new techniques of psychological tests, which were quickly adjusted so as to put black folk absolutely beyond the possibility of civilization.
>
> *p. 51*

He went on to comment on how these psychologists embedded their racism in their "science":

> I had too often seen science made the slave of caste and race hate .... [I]t was interesting to see Odum, McDougall and Brigham eventually turn somersaults from absolute proof of Negro inferiority to repudiation of the limited and questionable application of any test which pretended to measure innate human intelligence.
>
> *Du Bois, 2007/1940, p. 51*

In 1934 George I. Sanchez, a prominent Latinx scholar who at the time served as the Director of the New Mexico Department of Education and later was a professor at the University of Texas, observed the following with regard to the ways IQ testing was being used to the detriment of Latinx peoples in the Southwestern United States:

> Who would champion the thesis that half or more of Spanish-speaking, or any other such ... group is dull, borderline, and feeble-minded when it is generally accepted that only 7 per cent of 'normal' groups may be so classified? ... [S]uch a champion would find test-results to support his cause.
>
> *Quoted in Blanton, 2003, p. 58*

As these scholars and leaders of color recognized, the lower test scores of African Americans and Latinx students were regularly used to track Black students into vocational education or for White teachers to simply explain away any difficulties they might be having with non-White students in their classrooms (Blanton, 2003).

Regardless of the discriminatory aspects of early standardized tests, they became powerful within education in the U.S. in the first quarter of the twentieth century due to a confluence of factors. Not only was the science of mental measurement and the racist eugenics movement gaining momentum at the time, but the country also was in the throes of the establishment of mass, public schooling. This growth in schooling meant two things. First, it meant the country was trying to figure out a relatively efficient and standardized system for educating large numbers of school-aged children. Second, it also meant the establishment of local governance for education systems, which at the time came to be dominated by businessmen (Au, 2009b). Because standardized testing was so useful for sorting people efficiently, and because it matched a model of schooling-as-production, it quickly became a popular technology for use in public education in the United States. Lewis Terman, then a Stanford University professor of psychology, and under the sponsorship of the National Academy of Sciences, was central to adapting the army tests into the National Intelligence Tests for school children in 1919. By 1920 he had sold over 400,000 copies of these tests nationwide. Terman was also involved in the creation of the original Stanford Achievement Test in 1922, and by late 1925, he reported nearly 1.5 million test copies sold. In subsequent years, surveys of cities in the U.S. with populations over 10,000 people in 1925, 1926, and 1932 found that the majority of their schools were using these tests to classify and sort students into ability groups (Chapman, 1988; Haney, 1984).

Modern-Day High-Stakes Testing and Racist, Classist Inequality

While standardized testing went on to be used regularly throughout the U.S. public school system in ensuing decades, it wasn't until the 1980s and 1990s that these tests began to gain the prominence in education policy that they have today. The 1983 publication of *A Nation at Risk* is really the touchpoint for modern high-stakes tests. This Cold War era report decried U.S. education as failing and likened this failure as akin to a foreign attack on the nation. It triggered a wave of test-based education reform: Within three years of the publication of *A Nation at Risk*, 26 U.S. states raised graduation requirements and 35 instituted comprehensive education reforms that revolved around testing and increased course loads for students. Forty-three U.S. states implemented state-wide assessments for K–5 by 1994, and by the year 2000 every U.S. state but Iowa administered a state mandated test. Within the first week of taking office in 2001, President George W. Bush pushed for federal Title I funding to be tied to student test scores, and in 2002 the U.S. government passed the No Child Left Behind Act (NCLB) into law with overwhelming bipartisan support. NCLB mandated that subgroups of students based on race, economic class, special education, and English language proficiency, among others, show consistent growth on standardized tests or schools would be subject to punishments such as a loss of federal funding, conversion of public schools to charter schools, or face possible state takeover (Au, 2009b).

Despite the utter failure of NCLB and its focus on high-stakes testing to improve educational outcomes, despite growing public criticism of many aspects of NCLB, and despite then presidential candidate Obama's campaign rhetoric about the need for multiple measures of student learning and teacher evaluation in education (Au, 2009a), the change of presidential administrations only intensified the use of high-stakes, standardized testing. Upon taking office, President Obama launched the federal Race to the Top program, which promoted the use of tests to evaluate teachers, attacks on teachers' unions' right to collective bargaining, and the proliferation of charter schools. Race to the Top also provided the framework of support for national standards connected to high-stakes, standardized tests, which manifested as Common Core State Standards and subsequent standardized assessments (Karp, 2014). The U.S. federal government replaced NCLB with the Every Student Succeeds Act (ESSA) in 2015. While ESSA gave individual states more autonomy and minimally acknowledged parents' rights to refuse testing for their children as a gesture to the growing movement to opt out of testing, ultimately ESSA further entrenched high-stakes, standardized tests as the core of education reform (Karp, 2016).

Importantly, we can see key alignments between the use of high-stakes, standardized tests now and how standardized IQ tests were used 100 years ago, as well as the broader entanglement of diversity and the multiculturalism goals of education, both discussed above. For instance, in almost exactly the same way that early architects of standardized tests saw their assessments as a means of challenging social inequities through what they thought were objective measures of individual merit, the arc of high-stakes, standardized testing in education policy since the implementation of NCLB in 2002 right through ESSA has similarly been built upon a narrative of challenging social and educational inequities related to race and economic class. Most notably, regardless of political party, every president—or their educational leadership—has linked their test-based education reforms to the aspirational race equality associated with the U.S. Civil Rights movement for racial justice and equality. In 2002, then President George W. Bush asserted that, "Education is the great civil rights issue of our time" (CNN, 2002, para. 1). Two years later, in a speech delivered at Harvard University, Bush's then Secretary of Education, Rod Paige, suggested that closing race-based achievement gaps in test scores was "the civil rights issue of our time" (Feinberg, 2004, para. 11). Bush's successor, President Barack Obama, in 2011 also said that education is the "civil rights issue of our time" (Cooper, 2011, para. 1), and in the same year his Secretary of Education, Arne Duncan, also asserted that, "Education is the Civil Rights movement of our generation" (Ballasy, 2011, para. 1). Not to be outdone, in 2017, President Donald Trump also said that education is "the Civil Rights issue of our time" (Halper, 2017, para. 1).

Beyond the framing around equality and justice, there is another key alignment between the current use of high-stakes testing and that of 100 years ago: *They are not effective at improving achievement, and they still produce unequal, discriminatory outcomes.* A 2011 report found that, despite almost a decade NCLB's high-stakes, standardized testing, the reforms proved to be inadequate to accurately measure student learning, and they were not working to increase student achievement (National Research Council, 2011). Additionally, when we look at modern-day high-stakes test scores generally, it appears that the 100-year-old ghosts of IQ testing and the eugenics movement still haunt them. Essentially, the "achievement gaps" in test scores of today seem to mirror the results of a century ago, with poor kids of all races, Black and Latinx students, English language learners, and many immigrant populations getting consistently lower scores than their Whiter, more affluent counterparts (Au, 2016; Contreras, 2010; Reardon, 2011; Thompson & Allen, 2012). Further still, other research has highlighted that, despite an overall relative increase in test scores over the last 15 years based on the National Assessment of Education Progress (a standardized test given to a random sample of students in the U.S.), the gap in test scores between White and Black students has actually increased over this time (Ravitch, 2014). Based on these entrenched inequalities and consistent outcomes across the last 100 years it raises the possibility that the tests themselves have racist, classist, and other forms of discrimination hardwired into their very structure (Au, 2009b, 2015).

High-Stakes Testing Against Multicultural Education

In addition to the racist, inequitable origins and disparate outcomes of the tests, it is critical to understand that when it comes to effect on curriculum and instruction, policy implementation in schools, and direct impact on students, high-stakes testing works directly against multicultural education and the educational experiences of our diverse student population. For instance, research has consistently found that, since high-stakes testing became the central tool used for accountability for education policy, teachers have been compelled to "teach to the test," resulting in both pedagogy and curriculum being limited due to test pressures (Au, 2007; Bacon, Rood, & Ferri, 2016; Giambo, 2017; Gunn, Al-Bataineh, & Al-Rub, 2016; Hikida & Taylor, 2020; Martin, 2016). This teaching to the test has been detrimental to all teaching and learning, but it has been specifically bad for multicultural education and the diversity of our students. For instance, research has found that high-stakes testing has promoted predominantly White, Eurocentric, and Western views through world history, geography, and U.S. history tests (Grant, 2001). Toussaint (2000) tells the story of how, as an employee of a test scoring company, he was told to give higher scores to students who provided Eurocentric answers to test questions about Manifest Destiny and the colonization of the Americas. Other research has found that teachers who enter into the teaching profession with the stated goal of using multicultural, anti-racist content as a means to effectively teach the diverse students in their classrooms are giving up this goal in response to the curriculum pressures created by the tests (Agee, 2004).

Overall, this curricular and pedagogic squeezing of multicultural education out of high-stakes impacted classrooms creates less welcoming and supportive environments that can lead to essentially locking some student identities out of the classroom and contributing to more apathy amongst students of color (Au, 2009b; Thompson & Allen, 2012). Since multicultural, anti-racist perspectives and content are not deemed legitimate by the tests, the end result is that, within the high-stakes testing environment, multicultural, diverse, and non-White perspectives and content are more likely to be excluded from the classroom, thereby centering Whiteness and promoting a colorblind norm (Au, 2015). This subtraction of multicultural education curriculum and pedagogy from classrooms due to high-stakes testing also works to the detriment of students. Research has consistently shown how standardized testing environments contribute directly to the disengagement of students of color and bilingual students (Knoester & Meshulam, 2020; McNeil, 2000, 2005; Thompson & Allen, 2012; Valenzuela, 1999). Of equal importance is that research also indicates that multicultural and anti-racist education leads to higher engagement and academic achievement for students of color (Cabrera, Milem, & Marx, 2012; de los Rios, Lopez, & Morrell, 2015; Dee & Penner, 2017; Luna, Evans, & Davis, 2015; Romero, Arce, & Cammarota, 2009), while also benefiting White students' awareness of social, cultural, and political relations in communities (Okoye-Johnson, 2011; Sleeter, 2011; Ware, 2017).

Additionally, it is important to note that high-stakes testing has disparate material impacts across the diversity of our student populations. For instance, more diverse student populations and students of color feel the curricular and pedagogic squeeze of high-stakes testing more than their Whiter peer groups. At the level of state analysis, the pressures of high-stakes, standardized testing are experienced with greatest intensity in states with large, diverse populations of non-White students (Nichols & Berliner, 2007). Classroom-level analyses similarly find that test-based narrowing of the curriculum and teaching is most drastic in schools with large populations of non-White students. For instance, the Center for Education Policy (Renter et al., 2006, p. 214) found that 97% of high-poverty school districts, which are largely populated by diverse groups of non-White students, have instituted policies specifically aimed at increasing time spent on reading. This is compared to only 55 to 59% of wealthier, Whiter districts.

As another example, research has found that high-stakes testing contributes to the segregation of schools and communities (Knoester & Au, 2015). This happens through a mix of Whiteness, affluence, and what gets defined as a "good" school. Essentially, schools are defined as a "good" school if they produce high test scores. White, affluent parents, in their search for ever-increasing opportunities for their children to maintain upward mobility and success (Ball, 2003), only look to enroll their children in "good" schools with high test scores. In the U.S. this even influences where these parents choose to purchase their homes, in hopes of placing themselves in a neighborhood where their child will automatically be assigned to a "good" school. Consequently, even though these parents may talk about and make their decisions without using race or class as an explicit factor in their decision-making process, they ultimately use their definition of "good" schools and high test scores as a proxy for having their children attend Whiter and wealthier schools. In this way high-stakes test scores end up propagating segregation and undercutting the democratic aims of multicultural education (Knoester & Au, 2015).

High-Stakes Testing and Disciplining Multicultural Student Populations

High-stakes, standardized testing is also being used to disproportionately discipline our increasingly diverse, multicultural student body. For instance, because of testing, working-class Black and Brown students are far more likely to feel the impact of school closures. Schools are often labeled as "failing" for producing low test scores, and schools that are labeled as failing are regularly targeted by policy-makers for closure as punishment for low performance (Aggarwal & Mayorga, 2012). For example, in 2013 Chicago planned to close 54 low-scoring public schools, New York City planned to close 26 low-scoring public schools, and Philadelphia planned to close 23 low-scoring public schools. In Chicago, the population of these schools slated for closure was African American and 94% low income; in New York City it was 97% African American and Latino and 82% low income; and in Philadelphia it was 96% African American and Latino and 93% low income (National Opportunity to Learn Campaign, 2013).

Students of color are also being disciplined through testing in another fashion: increased suspensions and expulsions as an extension of the mistreatment of students labeled with disabilities. Using the framework of Dis/ability Critical Race Studies (DisCrit), a conceptual area of analysis which focuses on the intersection of critical race theory and disability studies, Annamma et al. (2013) highlight how students with disabilities sit at a particular nexus with regard to racism, testing, and discipline. Not only do they use DisCrit to consider how standardized testing and concepts of IQ are central to the construction of a White, able-bodied norm, and its conceptual counterpart, the disabled abnormal, they also go on to explain that, in addition to Latinx and Native American populations being disproportionately diagnosed as having a disability based on standardized IQ tests,

> African American students continue to be three times as likely to be labeled mentally retarded, two times as likely to be labeled as emotionally disturbed,

> and one and a half times as likely to be labeled as learning disabled, compared to their white peers.
>
> *p. 3*

The over-identification of Black and Brown students as "disabled" through standardized testing becomes particularly important to the arguments here in light of the research surrounding the discipline of students with disabilities. For instance, a UCLA Civil Rights Project report (Losen, Hodson, Keith, Morrison, & Belway, 2015) found that elementary-aged children with disabilities were suspended at twice the rate of their peers, and that 18% of high school students with disabilities were suspended, compared to 10% overall. Other research at the confluence of race and disability highlights further disparity with the use of these tests in the over-identification of students of color as having a disability: 20% of Black girls and 25% of Black boys labeled as having a disability will be suspended at least once during the school year (Lewis, 2015). In this way we see how the test-based over-identification of Black students as having a disability contributes to those same students being disproportionately disciplined by their teachers and schools.

This intersection of high-stakes testing, race, and discipline also manifests in the schools-to-prisons pipeline. This happens in two very concrete ways. First, the tests contribute to the kind of school culture experienced by students who are being educated in spaces where high-stakes, standardized tests are being used to evaluate teachers, students, and schools. When school communities are required to raise test scores or face consequences, this functionally promotes a school culture of discipline and punishment (Foucault, 1995). In these spaces, students and teachers are placed within the disciplinary gaze of the tests, in essence being surveilled through test scores. When test scores are not raised, they are identified as being out of line by not performing well and are subsequently punished. In a very real sense, the high-stakes testing environment promotes teaching and learning under constant threat and fear. Not only are threats and fear not conducive to learning, these conditions also serve to acculturate students to accepting a more prison-like school culture.

Additionally, and linked to the DisCrit analyses of high-stakes testing discussed above (Annamma et al., 2013), the use of tests to define success and failure ultimately pathologizes those who fail. In turn, because working-class students of color have had persistently lower test scores historically, those students and their communities are thus pathologized (Au, 2015, 2019). As Ekoh (2012) explains, this pathologizing of students and failure relates directly to the systematic functioning of institutions:

> If unable to thrive within the confines of the system, they [students] are pathologized and condemned as incompetent and lazy, for it's not the system that fails them, but they, that fail the system. As such they must be re-made "healthy" and "reintegrated" into the oppressive status quo. Healthy, in this

> context referring to the state of mind that results when one has been successfully disciplined and "indoctrinated" into the dominant and oppressive system in such a way as to lose one's critical consciousness ....
>
> *pp. 70–71*

Ekoh's point is important for the point being made here, because it highlights the fact that high-stakes testing equates to a zero-sum game: In order for one or some groups to be labeled as successful by the tests, other groups must be labeled as unsuccessful. Or, in Ekoh's above terms, the pathologizing of some groups within a system of education simultaneously requires other groups to be deemed healthy within that same system. As damning as it sounds, viewed within this frame, high-stakes standardized tests provide a pathway to success for affluence and Whiteness *at the cost* of the failure of low-income students of color.

The second way that high-stakes testing contributes to the schools-to-prisons pipeline is even more direct: They literally push students out of schools, onto the streets, and make them much more likely to end up in the criminal justice system (The Advancement Project, 2010). For instance, an empirical study by the National Bureau of Economic Research (Baker & Lang, 2013) found that if a state has a standards-based high school exit exam in order to graduate, it increased the rate of incarceration of their student population by 12.5%. Essentially, kids who fail high school exit exams have their options in life greatly limited, and one of the end results is a 12.5% increase in the likelihood they might end up in the criminal justice system. This grim reality is particularly damaging to the African American and Latinx communities given the disproportionate levels of test-defined failure for African American and Latinx students and the disproportionate number of African American and Latinx students who choose to leave school as "drop outs" (Contreras, 2010; Thompson & Allen, 2012).

Conclusion

In this chapter I have argued that high-stakes, standardized testing and multicultural education simply do not mix. For over 100 years, standardized tests have consistently produced and maintained racial, class, and cultural inequalities, and these test-produced inequalities have, in turn, been weaponized in their use against working-class and non-White communities in the U.S. In their modern iteration as high-stakes tests, despite claims as being essential for racial equity in education, they ultimately reproduce the same inequitable results as in the past. Further, our modern-day tests squeeze multicultural curriculum and pedagogies out of classrooms since teachers and administrators are so compelled to teach to the tests within high-stakes environments. Moreover, this curricular and pedagogic squeeze has been implemented with disproportionate veracity on schools and classrooms populated by low-income students of color. This in turn has contributed to the over-identification of students of color as having a disability, while also exposing students of color to disproportionate levels of discipline, punishment, and even incarceration.

The fact of the matter is, if we truly cared about multicultural curriculum and pedagogy and the educational experiences of all of our students—but especially students who have been marginalized from schools because of the diversity of their identities—and if we truly were committed to the equitable and democratic promise of schooling in the U.S., then we would heed the mountain of evidence that high-stakes testing is in fact harmful to both multicultural education and the multicultural diversity of our students. Ultimately, such care and commitment would mean the outright abolition of high-stakes, standardized testing as an affront to the cultural humanity of our students, teachers, and parents, and it would mean that we embrace forms of assessment that are culturally affirming, that challenge racism, and that can work towards healing our cultural selves (Au, 2019).

References

The Advancement Project (2010). *Test, punish, and push out: How "zero tolerance" and high-stakes testing funnel youth into the school-to-prison pipeline.* Washington, DC: The Advancement Project.

Agee, J. (2004). Negotiating a teaching identity: An African American teacher's struggle to teach in test-driven contexts. *Teachers College Record, 106*(4), 747–774.

Aggarwal, U., & Mayorga, E. (2012). Slow violence and neoliberal education reform: Reflections on a school closure. *Peace and Conflict: Journal of Peace Psychology, 18*(2), 156–164. https://doi.org/10.1037/a0028099

Annamma, S. A., Connor, D., & Ferri, B. (2013). Dis/ability critical race studies (DisCrit): Theorizing at the intersections of race and dis/ability. *Race Ethnicity and Education, 16*(1), 1–31. https://doi.org/10.1080/13613324.2012.730511

Au, W. (2007). High-stakes testing and curricular control: A qualitative metasynthesis. *Educational Researcher, 36*(5), 258–267.

Au, W. (2009a). Obama, where art thou? Hoping for change in U.S. education policy. *Harvard Educational Review, 79*(2), 309–320.

Au, W. (2009b). *Unequal by design: High-stakes testing and the standardization of inequality.* New York, NY: Routledge.

Au, W. (2015). High-stakes testing: A tool for White supremacy for 100 years. In B. Picower & E. Mayorga (Eds.), *What's race got to do with it? How current school reform policy maintains racial and economic inequality* (pp. 21–44). New York, NY: Peter Lang.

Au, W. (2016). Meritocracy 2.0: High-stakes, standardized testing as a racial project of neoliberal multiculturalism. *Educational Policy, 30*(1), 39–62. https://doi.org/10.1177/0895904815614916

Au, W. (2019). Racial justice is not a choice: White supremacy, high-stakes testing, and the punishment of Black and Brown students. *Rethinking Schools, 33*(4). Retrieved from www.rethinkingschools.org/articles/racial-justice-is-not-a-choice

Bacon, J., Rood, C., & Ferri, B. (2016). Promoting access through segregation: The emergence of the "prioritized curriculum" class. *Teachers College Record, 118*(140304), 1–22.

Baker, O., & Lang, K. (2013). The effect of high school exit exams on graduation, employment, wages and incarceration (Working Paper). National Bureau of Economic Research. www.nber.org/papers/w19182.pdf

Ball, S. J. (2003). *Class strategies and the education market: The middle classes and social advantage.* New York, NY: Routledge.

Ballasy, N. (2011, January 17). *U.S. Secretary of Education: Education is "the civil rights issue of our generation."* Retrieved from Cnsnews.Com. http://cnsnews.com/news/article/us-secretary-education-education-civil-rights-issue-our-generation

Banks, J. A., Banks, C. A. M., Cortes, C., Hahn, C. L., Merryfield, M. M., Moodley, K. A., Murphy-Shigematsu, S., Osler, A., Park, C., & Parker, W. C. (2005). *Democracy and diversity: Principles and concepts for educating citizens in a global age.* Center for Multicultural Education, College of Education, University of Washington. Retrieved from https://education.uw.edu/sites/default/files/cme/docs/pdf/_notes/DEMOCRACY%20AND%20DIVERSITY%20pdf.pdf

Blanton, C. K. (2003). From intellectual deficiency to cultural deficiency: Mexican Americans, testing, and public school policy in the American Southwest, 1920–1940. *Pacific Historical Review, 72*(1), 39–62.

Cabrera, N. L., Milem, J. F., & Marx, R. W. (2012). An empirical analysis of the effects of Mexican American Studies participation on student achievement within Tucson Unified School District. Report to Special Master Dr. Willis D. Hawley on the Tucson Unified School District Desegregation Case. Retrieved from http://works.bepress.com/nolan_l_cabrera/17/

Chapman, P. D. (1988). *Schools as sorters: Lewis M. Terman, applied psychology, and the intelligence testing movement, 1890–1930.* New York, NY: New York University Press.

CNN (2002, January 19). Bush calls education "civil rights issue of our time." CNN.Com/Insidepolitics. Retrieved from http://edition.cnn.com/2002/ALLPOLITICS/01/19/bush.democrats.radio/

Contreras, F. E. (2010). The role of high-stakes testing and accountability in educating Latinos. In E. G. Murillo Jr., S. Villenas, R. T. Galvan, J. S. Munoz, C. Martinez, & M. Machado-Casas (Eds.), *Handbook of Latinos and education: Theory, research, and practice* (pp. 194–209). New York, NY: Taylor & Francis.

Cooper, H. (2011, April 6). Obama takes aim at inequality in education. *The New York Times.* Retrieved from www.nytimes.com/2011/04/07/us/politics/07obama.html

Dee, T. S., & Penner, E. K. (2017). The causal effects of cultural relevance: Evidence from an Ethnic Studies curriculum. *American Educational Research Journal, 54*(1), 127–166. https://doi.org/10.3102/0002831216677002

de los Rios, C. V., Lopez, J., & Morrell, E. (2015). Toward a critical pedagogy of race: Ethnic studies and literacies of power in high school classrooms. *Race and Social Problems,* 7(1), 84–96. https://doi.org/10.1007/s12552-014-9142-1

Du Bois, W. E. B. (2007). *Dusk of dawn: An essay toward an autobiography of a race concept* (The Oxford W.E.B. Du Bois). New York, NY: Oxford University Press. (Original work published 1940)

Ekoh, I. (2012). *High-stakes standardized testing in Nigeria and the erosion of a critical African worldview.* Toronto: University of Toronto.

Feinberg, C. (2004, April 29). Rod Paige offers high praise for No Child Left Behind: Education secretary marks 50th anniversary of Brown decision with Kennedy School keynote address. *Harvard University Gazette.* Retrieved from https://news.harvard.edu/gazette/story/2004/04/rod-paige-offers-high-praise-for-no-child-left-behind/

Foucault, M. (1995). *Discipline and punish: The birth of the prison* (A. Sheridan, Trans.). New York, NY: Vintage Books.

Giambo, D. A. (2017). "I will study more … and pray": Metacognition about high-stakes test preparation among culturally and linguistically diverse students. *Multicultural Education, 24*(3–4), 26–34.

Gould, S. J. (1996). *The mismeasure of man* (Rev. and expanded). New York, NY: Norton.

Gunn, J., Al-Bataineh, A., & Al-Rub, M. A. (2016). Teachers' perceptions of high-stakes testing. *International Journal of Teaching and Education*, *4*(2), 49–62. https://doi.org/10.20472/TE.2016.4.2.003

Halper, D. (2017, March 3). Trump calls education "civil rights issue of our time" during school visit. *New York Post*. Retrieved from http://nypost.com/2017/03/03/trump-calls-education-civil-rights-issue-of-our-time-during-school-visit/

Haney, W. (1984). Testing reasoning and reasoning about testing. *Review of Educational Research*, *54*(4), 597–654.

Hikida, M., & Taylor, L. A. (2020). "As the test collapses in": Teaching and learning amid high-stakes testing in two urban elementary classrooms. *Urban Education*, 1–29. https://doi.org/org/10.1177/0042085920902263

Karp, S. (2014). The problems with the Common Core. *Rethinking Schools*, *28*(2). Retrieved from www.rethinkingschools.org/archive/28_02/28_02_karp.shtml

Karp, S. (2016). ESSA: NCLB repackaged. *Rethinking Schools*, *30*(3). Retrieved from www.rethinkingschools.org/archive/30_03/30-3_karp.shtml

Knoester, M., & Au, W. (2015). Standardized testing and school segregation: Like tinder to fire? *Race Ethnicity and Education*, *20*(1), 1–14. https://doi.org/10.1080/13613324.2015.1121474

Knoester, M., & Meshulam, A. (2020). Beyond deficit assessment in bilingual primary schools. *International Journal of Bilingual Education and Bilingualism*, 1–14. https://doi.org/10.1080/13670050.2020.1742652

Lewis, K. L. (2015, July 24). Why schools over-discipline children with disabilities. *The Atlantic*. Retrieved from www.theatlantic.com/education/archive/2015/07/school-discipline-children-disabilities/399563/

Losen, D., Hodson, C., Keith II, M. A., Morrison, K., & Belway, S. (2015). Are we closing the school discipline gap? UCLA Civil Rights Project, Center for Civil Rights Remedies. Retrieved from www.civilrightsproject.ucla.edu/resources/projects/center-for-civil-rights-remedies/school-to-prison-folder/federal-reports/are-we-closing-the-school-discipline-gap/AreWeClosingTheSchoolDisciplineGap_FINAL221.pdf

Luna, N., Evans, W. P., & Davis, B. (2015). Indigenous Mexican culture, identity and academic aspirations: Results from a community-based curriculum project for Latina/Latino students. *Race Ethnicity and Education*, *18*(3), 341–362. https://doi.org/10.1080/13613324.2012.759922

Martin, P. C. (2016). Test-based education for students with disabilities and English language learners: The impact of assessment pressures on educational planning. *Teachers College Record*, *118*(140310), 1–24.

McNeil, L. M. (2000). *Contradictions of school reform: Educational costs of standardized testing*. New York, NY: Routledge.

McNeil, L. M. (2005). Faking equity: High-stakes testing and the education of Latino youth. In A. Valenzuela (Ed.), *Leaving children behind: How "Texas-style" accountability fails Latino youth* (pp. 57–112). Albany, NY: State University of New York.

Mitchell, D., & Snyder, S. (2003). The eugenic Atlantic: Race, disability, and the making of an international eugenic science, 1800–1945. *Disability & Society*, *18*(7), 843–864. https://doi.org/10.1080/0968759032000127281

National Opportunity to Learn Campaign (2013). The color of school closures. Retrieved from www.otlcampaign.org/blog/2013/04/05/color-school-closures

National Research Council (2011). *Incentives and test-based accountability in education*. Committee on Incentives and Test-Based Accountability in Public Education, M. Hout

& S.W. Elliott (Eds.). Board on Testing and Assessment, Division of Behavioral and Social Sciences and Education. Washington, DC: The National Academies Press.

Nichols, S. L., & Berliner, D. C. (2007). *Collateral damage: How high-stakes testing corrupts America's schools*. Cambridge, MA: Harvard Education Press.

Okoye-Johnson, O. (2011). Does multicultural education improve students' racial attitudes? Implications for closing the achievement gap. *Journal of Black Studies*, *42*(8), 1252–1274. https://doi.org/10.1177/0021934711408901

Orfield, G., & Frankenberg, E. (2011). Diversity and educational gains: A plan for a changing county and its schools. Civil Rights Project, University of California Los Angeles. Retrieved from http://civilrightsproject.ucla.edu/research/k-12-education/integration-and-diversity/diversity-and-education-gains-a-plan-for-a-changing-county-and-its-schools/Louisville-report-9-12d-final.pdf

Ravitch, D. (2014). *Reign of error: The hoax of the privatization movement and the danger to America's public schools*. New York, NY: Vintage Books.

Reardon, S. F. (2011). The widening academic achievement gap between the rich and the poor: New evidence and possible explanations. In G. J. Duncan & R. J. Murnane (Eds.), *Whither opportunity? Rising inequality, schools, and children's life chances* (pp. 91–116). New York, NY: Russell Sage Foundation.

Renter, D. S., Scott, C., Kober, N., Chudowsky, N., Joftus, S., & Zabala, D. (2006). From the capital to the classroom: Year 4 of the No Child Left Behind Act. Center on Education Policy. Retrieved from www.cep-dc.org

Romero, A., Arce, S., & Cammarota, J. (2009). A Barrio pedagogy: Identity, intellectualism, activism, and academic achievement through the evolution of critically compassionate intellectualism. *Race Ethnicity and Education*, *12*(2), 217–233.

Sleeter, C. E. (2011). *The academic and social value of ethnic studies: A research review*. Washington, DC: National Education Association.

Stoskopf, A. (2007). An untold story of resistance: African-American educators and I.Q. testing in the 1920's and '30's. *Rethinking Schools*, *14*(1). Retrieved from www.rethinkingschools.org/archive/14_01/iq141.shtml

Thompson, G. L., & Allen, T. G. (2012). Four effects of the high-stakes testing movement on African American K-12 students. *Journal of Negro Education*, *81*(3), 218–227.

Toussaint, R. (2000). Manifest destiny or cultural integrity? *Rethinking Schools*, *15*(2). Retrieved from www.rethinkingschools.org/archive/15_02/Test152.shmtl

Valenzuela, A. (1999). *Subtractive schooling: U.S. Mexican youth and the politics of caring*. Albany, NY: State University of New York Press.

Ware, J. G. (2017, March 23). Ethnic studies courses break down barriers and benefit everyone—so why the resistance? *Yes! Magazine*. Retrieved from www.yesmagazine.org/peace-justice/ethnic-studies-courses-break-down-barriers-and-benefit-everyone-so-why-the-resistance-20170323

7

INCLUSIVE DIVERSITY AND ROBUST SPEECH

Examining a Contested Intersection

Carlos E. Cortés

Introduction

Multicultural educators and other diversity advocates face numerous challenging issues. One of the most complex issues is striking a balance between two noble but often competing principles: the championing of inclusive diversity and the defense of robust speech.

The intersection of these two principles raises problems that do not lend themselves to clear and simple solutions. Rather it poses unavoidable dilemmas that require nuanced consideration and continuous adaptation. Conversations about these challenges are complicated by two widespread myths: the myth of free speech and the myth of monolithic diversity.

The Myth of Free Speech

First, speech. Let me get right to the point. We do not have free speech in the United States. We never have. However, we do enjoy robust *constitutionally-protected* speech, for which we should be thankful. As one who lived for two years under a military dictatorship, I am grateful for our strong speech protections. But we also have numerous legal limitations on speech.

The public confusion starts with the First Amendment to the U.S. Constitution. As former Harvard law professor John Palfrey (2017) writes in his book, *Safe Spaces, Brave Spaces: Diversity and Free Expression in Education*, "The First Amendment is often assumed to do something that it does not: to grant an affirmative right to free expression to all people" (p. 69).

So what does the U.S. Constitution do? It restrains government. According to the First Amendment, "Congress shall make no law … abridging the freedom of speech." The Fourteenth Amendment later extended that protection by restraining state and other government entities.

In practice, this means that government entities cannot abridge freedom of speech. (In fact, they do, which I shall address later.) However, private entities can. Just ask people who have been fired because of something they said.

For example, take the case of U.S. higher education faculty. In *public* institutions, faculty enjoy strong constitutionally-based speech protections. But these protections are not required at *private* colleges and universities. Every year, faculty at private institutions, particularly religious institutions, get fired for saying and posting things that public university faculty can get away with. No free speech there.

Or consider the Foundation for Individual Rights in Education (FIRE), probably the nation's most passionate defender of so-called campus free speech. Yet FIREs website points out, "if a private college wishes to place a particular set of moral, philosophical, or religious teachings above a commitment to free expression, it has every right to do so" (FIRE, n.d.).

But while we do *not* have totally "free" speech, we do enjoy a complex system of robust speech. More than two centuries of laws, regulations, and court decisions have seen to that. Yet despite the First Amendment to the Constitution, government entities have actually created speech restrictions.

When I began my diversity-and-speech research as a fellow of the University of California National Center for Free Speech and Civic Engagement, I dove into the scholarly literature, replete with books showcasing "free speech" in their titles. Yet, without exception, each of those "free speech" books also points out laws and court decisions that have restricted speech. I began making a list and soon had nearly two pages of such government prohibitions. Those limitations include:

- slander
- libel
- defamation
- fraud
- vandalism
- pornography (including revenge porn)
- bias crimes
- true threats
- fighting words
- punishable incitement
- sanctionable harassment
- invasion of privacy
- facilitating criminal conduct
- incitement to unlawful action
- revealing national security secrets
- creation of an unsafe working environment

- in special purpose facilities
- restricted by time, place, and manner
- speech integral to already-criminal conduct
- specific imminent objectively ascertainable serious harm.

This led me to the unavoidable conclusion that, book and article titles notwithstanding, most speech celebrants were not actually defending "free" speech. Rather they were defending our constitutionally-based system that both protects robust *legally-permitted* speech but also *selectively restricts* other categories of speech. To address this non-free-speech conundrum, analysts employ various categorical dualities that finesse the idea of "free" and thereby contribute to public confusion:

- protected vs. unprotected speech
- restricted vs. unrestricted speech
- permitted vs. unpermitted speech
- punishable vs. non-punishable speech.

While opposing most speech regulations in his book, *Campus Hate Speech on Trial*, philosopher Timothy Shiell (2009) nonetheless indicates that "no serious participant in the hate speech debate believes all speech regulations must go" (p. 158). In his well-argued book, *Speak Freely: Why Universities Must Defend Free Speech*, political scientist Keith Whittington (2018) asserts, "free speech can thrive only under conditions of *appropriate regulation*" (p. 94). Appropriate regulation! In other words, our speech isn't actually "free."

In her intriguing book, *Hate: Why We Should Resist It with Free Speech, Not Censorship*, Nadine Strossen (2018), the former president of the American Civil Liberties Union, argues against hate speech codes. Yet, to support her argument she devotes chapter 3 to explaining that such codes are unnecessary partially because there are *already* numerous legal restrictions on speech. In other words, she affirms that our current speech is not actually "free."

Multicultural educators should applaud speech protections and help students appreciate the value of robust speech, which includes their right to criticize injustice and speak truth to power. However—and a huge "however"—there are many good reasons to champion selected limits on speech. The diversity movement of the past half-century has highlighted some of those reasons. Yet diversity advocates, including multicultural educators, do not speak with a single voice when it comes to speech. This brings me to the second confounding myth: the myth of a diversity monolith.

The Myth of a Diversity Monolith

The diversity movement, including multicultural education, is a lock-step monolith governed by, well, whomever. So goes the oft-repeated narrative, repeated and disseminated continuously within the anti-diversity echo chamber (Wilson, 1995). Moreover, according to critics of diversity, the diversity thought police try to restrict speech and other forms of expression by applying the rules of political correctness. The problem is: this narrative is stereotypical nonsense.

Have excesses occurred in the name of diversity? Absolutely. I have continuously written and spoken out against these excesses, including in my diversity workshops and in my column in the monthly e-zine, *American Diversity Report.*

However, the diversity movement is no monolith. It has no agreed-upon set of rules, politically correct or otherwise. And it has no all-powerful thought police. If anything, the diversity movement is a case study in creative anarchy. So let's start by examining the diversity movement.

I use the umbrella term, diversity movement, to refer to the totality of separate individual and group efforts to reduce societal inequities that penalize people because of their membership in and identification with certain groups. Creatively pluralistic, the diversity movement has no all-encompassing organizational structure, no official leadership, no precise date of origin, and no agreed-upon founding documents that definitively express the multi-faceted movement's beliefs, values, and goals, including about speech. In fact, within the diversity movement, guiding principles are continuously evolving while also being constantly contested.

Some elements of the diversity movement emphasize themes; for example, civil rights, environmental justice, and, of course, multicultural education. Other movement elements focus on inequities faced by specific societal groups; for example, groups based on race, sex, ethnicity, age, religion, sexual orientation, ability/disability, gender identity, or language.

Because it is continually evolving, the diversity movement refuses to pose for a definitive snapshot. Much of its momentum comes from its continuous dynamism. There are constantly new sectors of action, new scholarly challenges, and new diversity "start ups." For example, in recent years the diversity movement has found new resonance in such expressions as "me, too" and "Black lives matter." Ten years ago few people were indicating their preferred pronouns, while airlines were not issuing detailed guidelines on comfort animals.

To help clarify this complex trajectory, I have framed the diversity movement as four basic currents, each of which takes a distinct approach to the issue of speech. While distinct, these currents often intersect, sometimes clash, and at other times cross-fertilize. Moreover, most diversity advocates do not sort themselves neatly into one and only one of these categories. Some participate in all four historical diversity currents:

- intercultural diversity
- equity-and-inclusion diversity
- critical theory diversity
- managerial diversity.

Intercultural Diversity

The intercultural strand of the diversity movement dates back to at least the 1920s, beginning with such entities as the Institute of International Education, formed in 1922. That field emphasizes intercultural relations, perceptions, understanding, and communication, focusing on the interaction of people from diverse *world* cultures (Pusch, 2017). However, with the arrival of the ethnic revitalization movement in the 1960s, some interculturalists expanded their attention to the domestic scene by addressing such issues as intergroup relations and cultural (or intercultural) competence.

Concerns about interculturalism inevitably involve issues of speech (Renteln, 2004). The intercultural movement has emphasized the importance of becoming more cognizant of language as well as non-verbal expression, particularly where cultural differences are involved.

In their training efforts, interculturalists tend to focus on helping people become more responsive to cultural otherness and *voluntarily* adapt their communication patterns in order to better relate to those who come from other cultural backgrounds, both internationally and within the United States. The intercultural premise: if people develop cross-cultural understanding and skills, they will likely modify their communication styles in order to build better relationships. The interculturalist emphasis is on *voluntary* action.

But this raises a fundamental issue. Isn't such voluntary self-restraint and conscious speech adaptation to otherness a form of self-censorship? Maybe so, at least in today's polarized atmosphere, with its penchant for knee-jerk labeling. But growing up in the Midwest in the 1940s, I learned that such self-restraint (today sometimes called self-editing) was common courtesy. Interculturalism adds another dimension: that varying ways of expressing courtesy and respect (as well as insult) are rooted in different cultural traditions.

Equity-and-Inclusion Diversity

Parallel to interculturalism runs the second and far more visible diversity strand, most commonly known today as Diversity and Inclusion (D&I), sometimes Diversity, Equity, and Inclusion. Because I am using diversity as the umbrella term for the overall movement, for clarity I refer to this strand as Equity and Inclusion. It developed out of the U.S. civil rights movement during the 1960s, although the D&I label would not appear until later.

At first the equity-and-inclusion current of the diversity movement primarily addressed the issue of race, focusing on such issues as segregation, denial of voting rights, and other race-based inequities. The movement also spread into the struggle for equity by other marginalized groups, such as women, gays and lesbians, transgenders, people with disabilities, and some religious minorities.

Activists in these different areas often struggled in parallel. Yet there was something more: a psychic contagion (a term that arose in the early 1970s) that connected these individual group struggles as part of a broader movement. Such contagion involved mutual inspiration, the transmission of ideas and energy, and the creation of alliances among people involved in different types of group-based advocacy. Among many things, it brought pedagogical reforms that ultimately contributed to the emergence of fields like multicultural education.

The intertwining of these different strands of group advocacy later led to the popularization of the concept of intersectionality. That term has nineteenth-century roots, when black feminists challenged white domination of the women's movement and criticized the movement's core narrative that focused almost entirely on white women. The idea gained greater traction in the 1980s when proponents of intersectionality argued that specific attention should be paid to the different experiential patterns of women of color and other non-dominant groups (Crenshaw, 1989). Intersectionality ultimately became a basic concept of inclusionist thinking: no person belonged to a single social category.

Somewhere in the fog of war involving these disparate group-based efforts and intergroup psychic contagion, the word diversity emerged. As the term gained wider usage, inevitably there came efforts to give diversity a more specific movement meaning. However, since the diversity movement had no central governing body, there could be no "official" definition. Diversity simply became a widely-accepted, multiply-defined umbrella term, distinct from synthetic dictionary definitions. For that reason I usually begin my workshops by explaining how I will be using the word (see Appendix), but pointing out that others use that word in different ways.

Equity and inclusion drew upon the ideas and language of interculturalism, for example, within the development of multicultural education. Yet tensions remained. Many inclusivists saw interculturalists as insufficiently concerned with issues of equity, power differentials, structural impediments, and social justice. Interculturalists sometimes viewed inclusivist efforts as insufficiently grounded in an understanding of intercultural dynamics.

Historically speaking, higher education's general support of robust speech has often contributed to equity and inclusion efforts. On college campuses, diversity advocates have benefited from speech protections—the right to express challenging and contentious ideas with vigor and even acerbic language. For example, in aggressive challenges to traditional white-centered, male-centered, and straight-centered curricula.

But as inclusionists examined issues of expression, they also argued that equitable diversity was not just a matter of knowledge and sensitivity. Other questions needed to be addressed. What inequities are built into historical and current language use? In what respects can language use actually undermine equity and inclusivity? How might changes in language use help to broaden inclusivity and deepen equity?

In addressing speech, interculturalists and inclusionists sometimes diverge. Interculturalists tend to focus on such topics as intergroup understanding and empathy as avenues toward *voluntary* speech restraint. Equity and inclusion advocates are more likely to apply such lenses as prejudice, power differentials, privilege-based advantages, and structural obstacles (Stewart, 2017).

In contrast to voluntarism-oriented interculturalists, some inclusionists have moved to a position of supporting speech prohibitions and favoring sanctions for language use deemed oppressive. At least one major university has considered punishing employees for using the wrong gender pronouns.

Critical Theory

In the 1980s emerged still a third strand of the diversity movement, critical theory. Like the first two diversity movement currents, its roots stretch back historically, in this case to the Institute for Social Research at Goethe University Frankfurt in the 1920s.

Like inclusionists, current critical theorists are involved in the pursuit of greater equity. However, they argue for a deeper, more skeptical analysis of the structures of inequality, dominance, and oppression. This can be seen, for example, in scholarship on critical race theory (Delgado & Stefancic, 2012).

Critical theorists refuse to bow to the idea of free expression as an assumed virtue. To them, all elements of society—laws, structures, and cultural practices—need to be examined in order to discover whether, deep down, they contribute to the maintenance of group-based inequities. Speech and other forms of expression cannot escape inspection (Lawrence, 1990; Matsuda, Lawrence, Delgado, & Crenshaw, 1993).

As critical theory began to infuse and sometimes even question other areas of the diversity movement, some traditional diversity organizations built critical theory into their operations. Indeed, the National Association for Multicultural Education now provides an award for *Critical* Multicultural Educators.

Beyond that, diversity advocates have developed a wide range of concepts that open new avenues for critical analysis. Not all of these new ideas may properly fall within the "official" scope of critical theory. However, they draw, at least indirectly, from critical theory and provide new analytical lenses for examining diversity and inequity in society. I call this the *penumbra* of critical theory. Take two examples.

Peggy McIntosh did not invent the term privilege, which has numerous dictionary definitions and common cultural meanings. However, in her penetrating 1988 article, "White Privilege and Male Privilege: A Personal Account of Coming to See Correspondences through Work in Women's Studies," McIntosh provided a very precise spin to the word. In the process she captured a simple but elusive idea: that members of certain societal groups receive *unearned advantages* that are supported by institutions and cultural practices. More insidiously, individuals can benefit from privilege even if they fail to recognize their unearned advantages. Indeed, part of the power of privilege is that it often operates under the radar.

A more recent addition to the diversity lexicon is the term microaggression. Developed by psychiatrist Chester Pierce and popularized by psychologist Derald Wing Sue (2010), microaggression refers to often subtle actions or remarks that have a cumulative negative impact on other individuals. Such actions or remarks may occur out of habit and without harmful intent. However, they may have a deleterious impact, usually the result of relentless if unnoticed repetition.

Of the four diversity currents, critical theorists and their followers have most vigorously challenged the concept of "free" speech. For them, an examination of speech cannot be divorced from a thorough analysis of inequitable outcomes built into language use. Many critical theorists view arguments for free speech as a regressive strategy for reifying inequitable group power differentials.

In *Must We Defend Nazis? Hate Speech, Pornography, and the New First Amendment*, Richard Delgado and Jean Stefancic (1997) throw down the gauntlet by strongly advocating greater legal restrictions on and punishment for certain forms of expression. Likewise, legal restrictions have been championed by critical theorists like Andrea Dworkin and Catharine MacKinnon (1988).

Managerial Diversity

Even as the intercultural, inclusivist, and critical theory strands of the diversity movement developed historically, a fourth diversity thrust gained traction in the 1980s. This was the concept of *managing diversity*, a term often credited to organizational theorist R. Roosevelt Thomas, Jr. (1991). Managing diversity supporters sought to create *systems* through which organizations and institutions could draw on diversity to support organizational goals.

Diversity managers might be rooted in ideas of equity, inclusion, and interculturalism. They might even be adherents of critical theory. But they also had to accept one other imperative of employment. Part of their job was to protect their institutions. Managing diversity within organizations necessarily became a delicate balancing act.

With each new managing diversity initiative, organizations and institutions, including in education, have amplified the message that diversity should be a core value. Things that inhibit equity, inclusivity, intergroup understanding, and a healthy institutional or organizational experience need to be addressed. Various forms of personal expression, including speech, inevitably became objects of examination.

This has led to tensions between diversity in its many manifestations and the defense of robust personal expression. For example, some 400 colleges and universities have adopted speech codes, mainly restricting hate speech. Although courts have generally ruled these codes to be unconstitutional, the issue of campus speech restrictions remains a contested topic (Gould, 2010).

Anti-diversity expressive acts continue to occur regularly in educational settings. Hardly a week goes by without the display of a noose, a charge of sexually-inappropriate remarks, a swastika drawn on a residence hall door, or Build the Wall scrawled upon some campus structure. In such cases, diversity managerialists find themselves caught in the crossfire of personal inclusionist values, legal limitations on action, and responsibilities for institutional protection.

Some managerialists have tried to find a sustainable middle ground. They often follow the course of taking a public stand against expressions of hate while at the same time defending the constitutional right of "free" expression. But such neither-fish-nor-foul strategies, particularly in the Internet age, are increasingly ringing hollow, especially to diversity advocates.

Fundamental Questions

Each of these four strands of diversity raises a particular set of challenges to speech and other forms of expression. Let me propose one fundamental speech question that each diversity strand raises.

Interculturalism: With their emphasis on voluntarism and the self-editing of speech, interculturalists raise the question: How can we create a more respectful organizational climate by educating people to become more cognizant of their language use and by appealing to voluntary action?

Equity and Inclusionism: With their stronger focus on historically-rooted inequality, equity-oriented inclusionists pose the question: What steps can be taken to create more equitable and inclusive living and working environments, even if this involves certain restrictions and sanctions on expression?

Critical Theory: With their deeper, more skeptical analysis of the structures of inequality, critical theorists pose the question: What legal actions can be taken, including modifying the current legal system and challenging the rigid defense of group power-maintaining "free" speech?

Managerialism: Given their necessary role in protecting their institutions, diversity managerialists must address the question: How can we balance the imperatives of diversity and the existence of a constitutional system that, at least currently, restricts some of their preferred courses of inclusive action?

Exploring the Changing Context

Multicultural educators face two challenges: to become better informed about the diversity–speech intersection; and to become more effective in helping students grapple with its complexities and nuances. This also means developing a greater understanding of the rapidly-changing context in which we live. Particularly in the last decade, diversity-driven challenges to certain types of speech have taken on added heft as a result of other forces, such as neuroscientific research and the Internet.

Breakthroughs in neuroscientific research have provided continuously greater insight into speech. This includes its power to wreak emotional, psychological, and even physical havoc on individuals and groups (Barrett, 2017). Conversely, such research has provided insight into ways for using speech to create greater equity and inclusivity (Carey & Robinson, 2017).

Then there is the development of the Internet. With its lightly-monitored easy access and its algorithm-driven reinforcement of beliefs and emotions (Noble, 2018), the Internet has led to an unprecedented torrent of often-anonymous, rapidly-disseminated vicious speech, which has upended lives. This has led to a variety of efforts to limit Internet speech, sometimes referred to as "deplatforming."

In an effort to scrub hate speech and other types of extremism from its sites, Facebook has developed more than 1,400 pages of content rules, which are applied to posts by some 15,000 "moderators" (Fisher, 2018). Even Twitter (n.d,), which previously branded itself as the epitome of free expression, has now adopted guidelines that users:

- "may not engage in the targeted harassment of someone, or incite other people to do so."
- "may not promote violence against, threaten, or harass other people on the basis of race, ethnicity, national origin, sexual orientation, gender, gender identity, religious affiliation, age, disability, or serious disease" (Twitter, n.d., p. 5).

Perhaps one of the most illuminating cases of the changing diversity-speech conversation involves debates within the American Civil Liberties Union (ACLU), historically one of the nation's foremost defenders of robust speech. Following the 2017 Charlottesville incident, 200 of the ACLU's full-time employees signed a letter criticizing the organization's policy of defending all speech. The letter stated, "Our broader mission—which includes advancing the racial justice guarantees in the Constitution and elsewhere, not just the First Amendment—continues to be undermined by our rigid stance" (Hemingway, 2018). Furthermore, the ACLU online document, "Speech on Campus," states the following: "To be clear, the First Amendment does not protect behavior on campus that crosses the line into targeted harassment or threats, or that creates a pervasively hostile environment for vulnerable students" (American Civil Liberties Union, 2018, p. 2).

Conclusion

Speech issues are not going away. Neither is diversity. Their intersection is fundamentally challenging our multicultural paradigms. As a former professional journalist and long-time media analyst (Cortés, 2000), I have a deep belief in the vital importance of robust expression. As a half-century participant in the diversity movement (Cortés, 2002), I also believe in the importance of inclusivity and the need to consider the challenges to speech raised by diversity advocates.

How can multicultural educators help in unpacking the intersection of robust speech and inclusive diversity? They can do so by simultaneously addressing two basic questions that I regularly pose in my diversity classes and workshops:

(1) In order to foster greater equity and inclusion, what additional limitations on speech should be considered?
(2) In order to foster abundant and robust speech, in what respects should personal and group discomfort, offense, and maybe even pain be recognized as inevitable aspects of life?

I am not suggesting that multicultural educators try to imitate law school dissections of free expression, civics class discussions of the First Amendment, or managerial workshop examinations of free speech within specific institutions. Rather multicultural educators should address the topic aspirationally: In striving to create a better world, how can we foster a society that honors both equitable inclusivity and robust speech?

My two questions may create discomfort and lead to difficult dialogues. However, by grappling with these questions, multicultural educators can help students develop a deeper and more nuanced understanding of the inevitable tensions and future possibilities of building upon these two noble imperatives: inclusive diversity and robust speech.

I wish to thank the University of California National Center for Free Speech and Civic Engagement and the University of California, Riverside, Academic Senate, for supporting my diversity and speech project.

Appendix: Components of Diversity

1 *Groupness*—People are *both* individuals and members of *multiple* groups.
2 *Impact*—Those groups *influence* (but do not *determine*) the lives of people who belong to them.
3 *Intersectionality*—All individuals are *partially* shaped by the *constellation* of groups to which they belong.
4 *Patterns*—Because groups have *patterns* (often known as group *culture* or *experience*), members of different groups have *patterned differences* (sometimes known as *cultural regularities*).
5 *Positionality*—Because of those patterns, members of groups *tend* to *view* the world and *approach* different situations from the perspectives of those groups.
6 *Generalizations*—Learning about group *patterns* provides *clues* to (but they should not become *assumptions* about) individuals who belong to these groups.
7 Concerning diversity:
   - Think in *generalizations*, not *stereotypes*.
   - Use generalizations as *clues*, not as *assumptions*.
   - Think in *intersections*, not *silos*.

References

American Civil Liberties Union (ACLU) (2018). Speech on campus. Retrieved from www.aclu.org/other/speech-campus

Barrett, L. F. (2017). *How emotions are made: The secret life of the brain.* Boston, MA: Houghton Mifflin Harcourt.

Carey, M. E., & Robinson, S. M. (2017). *Neuroscience of inclusion: New skills for new times.* Parker, CO: Outskirts Press.

Cortés, C. E. (2000). *The children are watching: How the media teach about diversity.* New York, NY: Teachers College Press.

Cortés, C. E. (2002). *The making—and remaking—of a multiculturalist.* New York, NY: Teachers College Press.

Crenshaw, K. (1989). Demarginalizing the intersection of race and sex: A Black feminist critique of antidiscrimination doctrine, feminist theory and antiracist politics. *University of Chicago Legal Forum, 1989*, 139–168.

Delgado, R., & Stefancic, J. (1997). *Must we defend Nazis? Hate speech, pornography, and the new First Amendment.* New York, NY: New York University Press.

Delgado, R., & Stefancic, J. (2012). *Critical race theory: An introduction* (3rd ed.). New York, NY: New York University Press.

Dworkin, A., & MacKinnon, C. (1988). *Pornography and civil rights: A new day for women's equality.* Minneapolis, MN: Organizing Against Pornography.

Fisher, M. (2018, December 27). Inside Facebook's secret rulebook for global political speech. *New York Times*, p. 13.

Foundation for Individual Rights in Education (FIRE) (n.d.). Private universities. Retrieved from www.thefire.org/spotlight/public-and-private-universities/

Gould, J. B. (2010). *Speak no evil: The triumph of hate speech regulation.* Chicago, IL: University of Chicago Press.

Hemingway, M. (2018, June 29). Want to defend civil liberties? Don't look to the ACLU. *The Weekly Standard*, p. 4.

Lawrence, C. R., III (1990). If he hollers let him go: Regulating racist speech on campus. *Duke Law Journal, 1990*(3), 431–483.

Matsuda, M. J., Lawrence, C. R., III, Delgado, R., & Crenshaw, K. (1993). *Words that wound: Critical race theory, assaultive speech, and the First Amendment.* Boulder, CO: Westview Press.

McIntosh, P. (1988). White privilege and male privilege: A personal account of coming to see correspondences through work in women's studies. Wellesley, MA: Wellesley College Centers for Research on Women. Retrieved from https://wcwonline.org/

Noble, S. U. (2018). *Algorithms of oppression: How search engines reinforce racism.* New York, NY: New York University Press.

Palfrey, J. (2017). *Safe spaces, brave spaces: Diversity and free expression in education.* Cambridge, MA: MIT Press.

Pusch, M. D. (2017). *The development of the field of intercultural communication.* Portland, OR: Intercultural Communication Institute.

Renteln, A. D. (2004). *The cultural defense.* New York, NY: Oxford University Press.

Shiell, T. C. (2009). *Campus hate speech on trial* (2nd ed., Rev. ed.). Lawrence, KS: University Press of Kansas.

Stewart, D.-L. (2017, April 4). Colleges need a language shift, but not the one you think. *Inside Higher Ed*, p. 4.

Strossen, N. (2018). *Hate: Why we should resist it with free speech, not censorship.* New York, NY: Oxford University Press.

Sue, D. W. (2010). *Microaggressions in everyday life: Race, gender, and sexual orientation.* New York, NY: Wiley.

Thomas, R. R., Jr. (1991). *Beyond race and gender: Unleashing the power of your total workforce by managing diversity.* New York, NY: AMACOM.

Twitter (n.d.). The Twitter rules. Retrieved from https//help.twitter.com/en/rules-and-policies/twitter-rules

Whittington, K. E. (2018). *Speak freely: Why universities must defend free speech.* Princeton, NJ: Princeton University Press.

Wilson, J. K. (1995). *The myth of political correctness: The conservative attack on higher education.* Durham, NC: Duke University Press.

8

EDUCATION IN TIMES OF MASS MIGRATION

Angela M. Banks

Multicultural education is an educational reform movement to make the total school environment more equitable for all students. Scholars have identified numerous school "practices related to race, ethnicity, language, and religion [that] are harmful to students and reinforce many of the stereotypes and discriminatory practices in Western societies" (Banks, 2019a, p. 1). One school practice that has received significant attention within the multicultural education literature is the social studies curriculum and the coverage of race, ethnicity, nationality, language, religion, gender, gender identity, and sexual orientation. At the advent of multicultural education these types of difference were rarely acknowledged within schools and students did not learn about contributions made by individuals from these various groups. Multicultural education scholars problematized the status quo theoretically and offered an alternative approach. As laid out in James A. Banks' (2019a) five Dimensions of Multicultural Education, the reform movement addresses: content integration, the knowledge construction process, prejudice reduction, equity pedagogy, and empowering school culture and school structure. As multicultural education has worked successfully to transform schools, one form of difference that has escaped focus is difference based on immigration status. This chapter contends that immigration status is an important form of difference that should be more explicitly incorporated into multicultural education.

In 2017 approximately 45 million foreign-born individuals were residing in the United States (Radford, 2019). Around 20 million of these individuals naturalized and became United States citizens (Passel & Cohn, 2018). This leaves approximately 25 million non-citizens residing in the United States. Of these individuals 10.5 million are unauthorized migrants (Passel & Cohn, 2018). Within the unauthorized migrant population there are 1.1 million children between the ages of 3 and 17. One million, or 97%, of these children are enrolled in K–12 schools

(Profile of the Unauthorized Population—US, n.d.). In addition to school children who are themselves unauthorized migrants there are another 3.5 million United States citizen children who have at least one unauthorized migrant parent (Passel & Cohn, 2018). Together these children represent 8% of K–12 students (National Center for Education Statistics, n.d.). Thus, 8% of school children are unauthorized migrants or have at least one parent who is, and they are invisible in the social studies and civic education curricula.

Status Matters

Within the non-citizen population there are a variety of immigration statuses. Each status carries different rights to reside in the United States, access to education, access to employment, and opportunities for political participation. It is important for educators to understand the varied positions that non-citizen students may be in and it is equally important for students to understand that an individual's ability to participate in society is shaped by their immigration status. Within the United States there are three major categories of non-citizens: **immigrants**, **non-immigrants**, and **unauthorized migrants**. While the term immigrants is often used to refer to all foreign-born individuals, it is a term of art within the law. **Immigrants**, also referred to as *lawful permanent residents* ("LPR") or *green card holders*, are individuals who have been granted permission to reside in the United States indefinitely. Immigrants can be deported if they run afoul of a statutorily enumerated deportation ground. The most applicable deportation grounds for immigrants are those that make criminal behavior and terrorist activities deportable offenses. Absent engaging in these activities, immigrants have rather secure residence rights. Immigrants also have rather robust access to employment and opportunities to participate in American society. For example, they face very few employment limitations. These individuals are authorized to work in the United States and their immigration status rarely disqualifies them. One of the few limitations is that states *can* prohibit immigrants from holding jobs that "go to the heart of representative government" (Sugarman v. Dougall, 1973). The United States Supreme Court has concluded that jobs such as state troopers, peace officers, and school teachers fit this description (Romero, 1997). *Immigrants' ability to attend primary, secondary, and post-secondary school is not restricted.* Immigrants face limitations on their ability to participate in American political life, but amongst non-citizens they have the most opportunities to participate. For example, only citizens can vote in state and national elections and run for office, but immigrants are able to volunteer with political campaigns, make financial contributions, and participate in non-election-related political activity.

Non-immigrants are non-citizens who are granted permission to enter the United States for a specific purpose and to reside for a specified period of time. For example, Jacques could be hired as a software engineer by Google as a temporary worker. Jacques would be admitted as a non-immigrant for the purpose of working at Google as a software engineer for three years. Sometimes the non-immigrant visa can be extended and sometimes it cannot. Non-immigrants are deportable not only on the criminal and terrorist activity deportation grounds, but also for violating the terms of their non-immigrant visa. This could happen if Jacques stopped working at Google and took a job at Starbucks as a barista. The non-immigrant visa granted to Jacques was only to work as a software engineer not as a barista. Therefore, Jacques would be deportable. Similarly, if Jacques stayed in the United States for five years without getting his visa extended, he would be deportable because he stayed longer than he was authorized to stay. Non-immigrants have more limited access to employment than immigrants. As noted above, Jacques is only allowed to work in the sector that is stated on his visa. Certain non-immigrants can apply to change employers, but they have to stay in the same job category that is stated on the visa. *Non-immigrants have access to primary, secondary, and post-secondary education. Access to education is thus the same for immigrants and non-immigrants.* In the area of political participation, non-immigrants' opportunities are similar to those of immigrants but non-immigrants are not able to make financial contributions to political campaigns. Non-immigrants are, however, able to volunteer with political campaigns and engage in other non-election-related political activity.

Unauthorized migrants are individuals who do not have permission to reside in the United States. There are two main ways that an individual becomes an unauthorized migrant. First, the individual entered the United States at a place other than a port of entry and was never admitted. This is the most common understanding of why an individual would be an unauthorized migrant. Second, the individual entered as a non-immigrant and did not depart when their visa expired. This is referred to as overstaying a visa. A recent study by the Center for Migration Studies of New York found that from 2016 to 2017 people who overstayed their visas accounted for 62% of the newly undocumented, while 38% had crossed a border illegally (Warren, 2019). Unauthorized migrants have the least secure ability to reside in the United States because they are deportable at any time. One of the statutorily enumerated deportation grounds is being present in the United States in violation of the law; therefore, any contact with local, state, or federal government officials can be viewed as risky for fear that one's lack of immigration status will be detected.

Unauthorized migrants' access to education, employment, and opportunities for political participation are the least robust. However, access to K–12 public schools is a significant exception. *Based on the 1982 Supreme Court case Plyler v. Doe unauthorized migrants cannot be denied a free K–12 public school education. Despite a robust right to free K–12 public education, access to public post-secondary education is more complicated. Plyer did not address post-secondary school and access to post-secondary education varies state to state.* As of September 2019, 19 states have provisions that allow unauthorized migrants to pay in-state tuition rates if they meet specific criteria. The criteria generally require the student to have attended high school in the state for a specified period of time (one to three years) and to have graduated or obtained a General Educational Development certificate (GED). Access to in-state tuition is an important issue because the cost of post-secondary education often plays a critical role in students' decisions to pursue higher education. Unauthorized migrant students are not eligible for federal financial aid, but some states (e.g., California, Colorado, Minnesota, New Mexico, Oregon, Texas, and Washington) allow these students to receive state financial aid. At the other end of the spectrum, three states—Arizona, Georgia, and Indiana—actually prohibit in-state tuition rates for unauthorized migrants regardless of how long they have lived within the state. Alabama and South Carolina have gone further and prohibit unauthorized migrant students from enrolling in any public post-secondary institution (National Conference of State Legislators, 2019). Access to post-secondary school is touted as the key to upward mobility in the United States and denying unauthorized migrant youth access or making costs prohibitive has implications for their future earning potential if they have access to Deferred Action for Childhood Arrivals (DACA) or a pathway to citizenship is enacted.

DACA or a pathway to citizenship are important for unauthorized migrants' employment options because unauthorized migrants are not authorized to work in the United States. Employers are required to have all employees complete an I-9 form in which the employee provides proof of identity and authorization to work in the United States. Evidence of authorization to work in the United States includes a United States passport, which is evidence of U.S. citizenship and thus authorization to work. Alternatively, a social security account number, LPR identification card, or employment authorization issued by the Department of Homeland Security are also evidence of authorization to work in the United States. Unauthorized migrants are able to obtain employment in the United States if they work for an employer that does not require completion of the I-9 form, or the unauthorized migrant provides fraudulent documents that indicate authorization to work. Despite increasing efforts to crack down on the employment of unauthorized migrants in the 1986 immigration reforms, unauthorized migrants are able to find employment in the United States. That employment can be precarious as they are vulnerable to poor working conditions, low wages, wage theft, and inconsistent hours.

Unauthorized migrants work in a variety of industries and hold a number of different occupations. Recent data from the Pew Research Center (Passel & Cohn, 2018) reveals that unauthorized migrants account for meaningful percentages of major occupations in the United States. For example, the significant share of the workforce in farming are unauthorized migrants but, only 3.7% of unauthorized migrants have this occupation (Passel & Cohn, 2018). It is the service occupation where most unauthorized migrants work, with 31% of this population working in service occupations (Passel & Cohn, 2018). When we look at American industries we similarly see the industries with the greatest share of unauthorized migrant workers are agriculture and

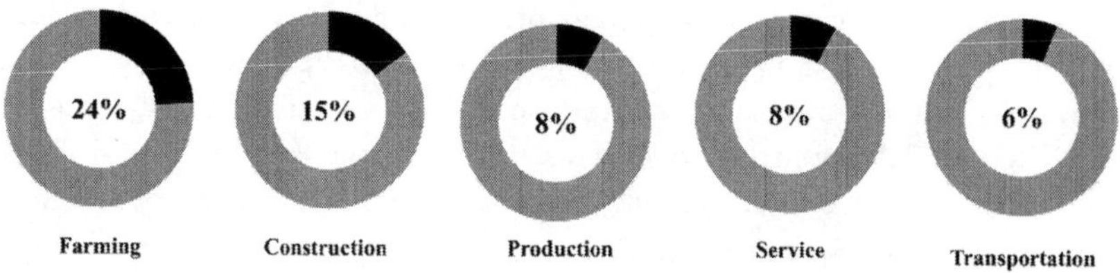

FIGURE 8.1 Unauthorized migrant share of occupations (2016)

Source: J. S. Passel & D. Cohn (2018). U.S. unauthorized immigrant total dips to lowest level in a decade. Pew Research Center. www.pewresearch.org/hispanic/wp-content/uploads/sites/5/2019/03/Pew-Research-Center_2018-11-27_U-S-Unauthorized-Immigrants-Total-Dips_Updated-2019-06-25.pdf

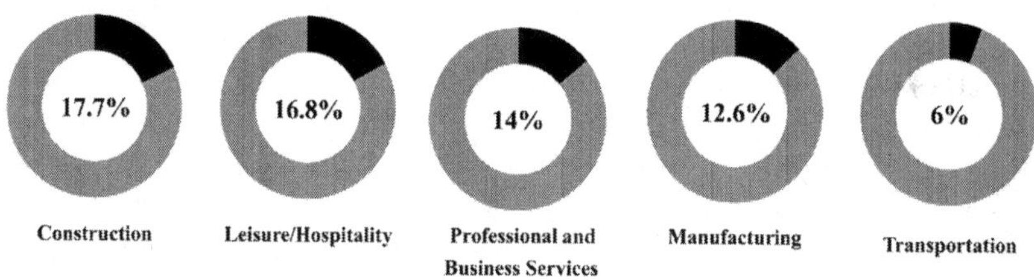

FIGURE 8.2 Unauthorized migrant share of industries (2016)

Source: J. S. Passel & D. Cohn (2018). U.S. unauthorized immigrant total dips to lowest level in a decade. Pew Research Center. www.pewresearch.org/hispanic/wp-content/uploads/sites/5/2019/03/Pew-Research-Center_2018-11-27_U-S-Unauthorized-Immigrants-Total-Dips_Updated-2019-06-25.pdf

construction (Passel & Cohn, 2018). Yet, most unauthorized migrants work in construction, leisure/hospitality, and professional and business services (Passel & Cohn, 2018).

Unauthorized migrants have limited opportunities for formal political participation, but they have been very effective at using social movement techniques to influence political decision making. As non-citizens, unauthorized migrants do not have the right to vote in national and state elections. They similarly are not eligible to run for national or state political offices. Unauthorized migrants are also not allowed to make financial contributions to political campaigns, but they can work as volunteers. Despite these formal limitations, unauthorized migrants have been incredibly active in mobilizing and lobbying for immigrant rights. Young people who are unauthorized migrants have organized marches, lobbied government officials, and engaged in civil disobedience to encourage the public and government officials to enact legislation and policies that provide a pathway to lawful immigration status for unauthorized migrants or in the alternative increase opportunities for post-secondary education and access to employment.

Whether a non-citizen is an immigrant, non-immigrant, or an unauthorized migrant often depends upon their family relationships and job skills. Access to immigrant and non-immigrant status is contingent on satisfying specific substantive criteria and the availability of the relevant visa. Immigrant visas are available to individuals who have specific family relationships or employment opportunities. The family-based requirements are being the spouse, parent, child, or sibling of a United States citizen or the spouse or unmarried child of an LPR. Without one of these family relationships a non-citizen must qualify for LPR status based on employment. The major categories for obtaining an employment-based green card are being a professional, an executive, or a skilled worker. Unskilled workers can also qualify for an employment-based green card, but there is a 10,000 person cap on these admissions each year, and a tremendous backlog for some countries (Immigration & Nationality Act, 1952). For LPR admissions in 2015, 2016, and 2017 the 10,000 person cap accounted for approximately 1% of all LPR admissions. With regard to the backlogs, in March 2020 citizens of China who had applied for LPR status based on being an unskilled worker in 2008 were being admitted and citizens from India who applied in 2009 were being admitted (United States Department of State, 2020). These individuals had waited approximately 12 and 11 years respectively. Another limitation on the ability of individuals to obtain LPR status based on being an unskilled worker is that all non-citizens seeking admission have to be admissible. Federal law specifies which individuals are not admissible and the grounds generally relate to criminal behavior or previous violations of immigration law. However, another inadmissibility ground is likely to become a public charge. This is a bit of an arcane term, but it means unable to support one's self. There are factors that are used to determine whether or not an individual is likely to become a public charge and individuals with low incomes are more likely to be deemed inadmissible (Immigration & Nationality Act, 1952).

There are a variety of non-immigrant visas available and they generally fall within the areas of high-skilled employment, tourism, low-skilled employment, and education. The key for all of these non-immigrant visas is that the individuals have to have a job offer from an employer in the United States or an acceptance from an educational institution and the non-citizen must be admissible, including not being likely to become a public charge.

In addition to obtaining admission to the United States as an immigrant or a non-immigrant, non-citizens can also obtain admission by getting asylum (Refugee Act, 1980). Asylum is available to individuals who are outside their country of nationality who are unable or unwilling to return due to having been persecuted or having a well-founded fear of persecution on account of race, religion, nationality, political opinion, or membership in a particular social group (Convention Relating to the Status of Refugees, 1951; Protocol Relating to the Status of Refugees, 1967). Persecution is generally understood to be a threat to life or freedom or other serious violations of human rights. The persecution must be because of one of the five identified reasons. If an individual was jailed because they burned down a building and everyone who committed the same act was imprisoned this would not be the basis for asylum. Many individuals fleeing persecution or other difficult circumstances do not have a visa to enter the United States. Such individuals are allowed to present themselves at the border and indicate that they would like to seek asylum. If they are determined to have a credible fear of persecution they are put in immigration proceedings in which an immigration judge will evaluate their claim. Many asylum seekers in this situation remain detained while their case proceeds through the system.

Challenges for Educators

Access to the United States is not available to all who are interested and a variety of factors cause individuals to enter or remain in the United States without authorization. A growing number of unauthorized migrants are school-aged children or U.S. citizen children with one or more unauthorized migrant parents. This presents unique challenges for educators. These challenges include access to education, immigration enforcement at school, and curriculum decisions.

Access to Education

Despite the Supreme Court decision in *Plyer*, public school enrollment practices can unintentionally prevent or discourage the enrollment of unauthorized migrant children or U.S. citizen children with unauthorized migrant parents or guardians (Banks, 2013a). In 2014 the United States Department of Justice and the United States Department of Education sent a letter reminding K–12 public school officials of their obligations under *Plyer* because these federal agencies had become "aware of student enrollment practices that may chill or discourage the participation, or lead to the exclusion, of students based on their or their parents' or guardians' actual or perceived citizenship or immigration status" (Lhamon, Rosenfelt, & Samuels, 2014, p. 1). School officials were reminded that they cannot prevent a student from enrolling in school "because he or she lacks a birth certificate or has records that indicate a foreign place of birth, such as a foreign birth certificate," or fails to provide a social security number (Lhamon, Rosenfelt, & Samuels, 2014, p. 2). Additionally, federal officials explained that "[p]recipitous drops in the enrollment of any group of students in a district or school may signal that there are barriers to their attendance that you should further investigate" (Lhamon, Rosenfelt, & Samuels, 2014, p. 3). It is important for school officials to be aware of the unique circumstances of unauthorized migrant students and students from mixed-status families so that policies are not adopted that unnecessarily require students or their families to reveal their immigration status.

Immigration Enforcement at School

Another challenge for K–12 educators is that unauthorized migrant students or students from mixed-status families may fear immigration enforcement actions at schools. Students and families may fear an immigration checkpoint en route to school, or federal immigration officers arresting individuals or engaging in surveillance at schools. In 2011, then Immigration and Customs Enforcement Director John Morton issued a memo explaining immigration enforcement action and sensitive locations. A sensitive location was defined as including, but not limited to, schools, hospitals, places of worship, e.g., churches, synagogues, and mosques, the site of a wedding, funeral or other public religious ceremony, and a site during a public demonstration, e.g., a march, rally, or parade (Morton, 2011). Enforcement actions are not to occur at these sensitive locations unless one of three conditions exists. First, exigent circumstances exist, second, "other law enforcement actions have led officers to a sensitive location," or third, prior approval for the action is obtained (Morton, 2011, p. 1). The enforcement actions that are covered by this memo are: arrests, interviews, searches, and immigration-related surveillance. Based on this policy, students and their families should not worry that schools could be sites for immigration enforcement because it would be rare and exceptional circumstances when one of the exceptions would be satisfied. While this policy was issued in 2011, as of November 2018 Immigration and Customs Enforcement stated that the sensitive locations policy was still in effect (U.S. Immigration & Customs Enforcement, 2018).

Curriculum

Unauthorized migrant students have a constitutional right to a free K–12 public school education and it is highly unlikely that immigration enforcement actions would take place at school. Yet the curriculum that students encounter when they are at school can be alienating and fail to acknowledge, for all students regardless of immigration status, the long-term residence and profound connections that unauthorized migrants have in the United States, and the valuable role that they have played and continue to play in American society (Banks, 2019b). Civic education provides a powerful example of the ways in which the failure to acknowledge immigration status as a meaningful difference limits the ability of educators to achieve the goals of civic education.

A key goal of civic education is to prepare students for responsible participation in a democratic society. To achieve this goal the curriculum often focuses on the structure and function of government, the various ways in which they can participate in economic, political, and social life, and the values and norms needed for living in a democratic society (McDonnell, 2000; Parker, 2001). Civic education scholars and teachers face two major challenges with a growing number of unauthorized migrant children and children from mixed status households attending K–12 schools. The first challenge is acknowledging that how one is able to participate in society is shaped by one's immigration status. Opportunities for employment, education, and political participation are all shaped by an individual's immigration status. The second challenge is providing students with the skills and knowledge to think critically about how democratic societies should determine who is qualified for membership within their society.

The aspects of civic education that focus on economic, political, and social participation within democratic societies can be alienating to unauthorized migrant students or students from mixed-status families. Failure to acknowledge that the types of participation discussed are only available to citizens or individuals with particular immigration statuses can leave students feeling invisible and/or that their lack of opportunity to participate is not worth discussing. Education scholar Dafney Blanca Dabach (2014, 2015; Jefferies & Dabach, 2014) has done important research examining how social studies teachers navigate teaching civic education in mixed-status classrooms. Dabach's research finds that explicitly acknowledging immigration status differences provides opportunities for civics educators to enable a range of students to find their political voice and to broker "different kinds of knowledge across contexts" so that students are not "left to navigate disjunctures on their own, which could form barriers to civic learning and action" (Dabach, 2015, p. 406).

Acknowledging immigration status difference creates an opportunity for educators to provide students with the knowledge and skills necessary to determine how membership and belonging is conceptualized within their society, to decide whether or not that conceptualization is just, and to offer alternative conceptualizations. One significant way that membership and belonging is conceptualized in American society is citizenship. Citizens have the most robust bundle of rights within the United States, which corresponds with the idea that citizens are the core members of the society. In order to assist students in analyzing whether or not citizenship is an under- or over-inclusive approach to membership students must understand the historical and contemporary rules governing access to citizenship, the various ways in which rights have been allocated to different groups of citizens, and the historical and contemporary barriers to accessing citizenship. This foundation will enable students to think critically about who is included and excluded and whether or not such exclusions are just. To the extent students conclude that current approaches to citizenship and belonging are under-inclusive, civics classrooms can provide opportunities for reimagining that connection or offering new ways to conceptualize membership in a democratic society.

Access to Citizenship

Many individuals are unaware of the fact that citizenship is not available to all individuals residing in the United States who desire it. Much like access to LPR status, access to citizenship status is limited. There are two main pathways to citizenship in the United States: birthright citizenship and naturalization. Birthright citizenship in the United States is available based on two principles—the *jus soli* principle and the *jus sanguinis* principle. The *jus soli* principle extends citizenship to individuals who are born within the territory of the country. The *jus sanguinis* principle grants citizenship to individuals who have at least one parent who is a United States citizen. Pursuant to the Fourteenth Amendment of the United States Constitution all individuals born within the United States are citizens. This reflects the *jus soli* approach to birthright citizenship. The *jus sanguinis* principle is the basis for federal statutory law that extends United States citizenship to individuals born outside of the United States if they have at least one U.S. citizen parent. Until 2017 if an individual was born outside of the United States to one U.S. citizen parent the rules about their citizenship at birth varied depending on whether the U.S. citizen parent was their mother or father. That year the Supreme Court ruled that the differential requirements were a violation of the Equal Protection Clause of the United States Constitution (Sessions v. Morales-Santana, 2017).

For individuals born outside of the United States to non-U.S. citizen parents naturalization provides the process for acquiring United States citizenship. There are a variety of requirements for naturalization but an important one for educators to understand is that the individual must be a lawful permanent resident for five years (or three years if they are married to a U.S. citizen). Therefore non-citizens who are non-immigrants or unauthorized migrants are not eligible to naturalize. Even if they meet the other requirements regarding residence, good moral character, and knowledge of U.S. history and civics, lacking LPR immigration status prevents them from accessing U.S. citizenship. Once students are provided with the opportunity to gain this knowledge about access to citizenship they are well positioned to think critically about whether or not this approach to citizenship is the best strategy for identifying members of American society. Engaging in this inquiry enables students to sharpen their analytical skills because they are required to identify a definition or understanding of membership and determine how well our current citizenship regime operationalizes that understanding of membership. This exercise also requires students to compare and contrast different definitions or understandings of membership, whether or not there are ways to explain why such differences exist, and what interests or perspectives are advanced by the differences. Additionally it would be useful for students to examine whether or not our current citizenship regime operationalizes some definitions or understandings of membership better than others. Providing students with knowledge about access to citizenship and the opportunity to compare the legal rules regarding access with normative understandings of membership allows students to think critically about the relationship between immigration status and membership.

Allocating Rights

Exploring the relationship between citizenship status and legal rights is another tool that can help students gain important knowledge that will be useful for thinking about the relationship between membership and immigration status. There are a number of rights that are exclusively available to United States citizens. For example, the right to vote in state and federal elections, to run for state or federal office, and an absolute right to live in the United States (Banks, 2017). Yet, historically and today there are a number of rights that are technically available to all individuals based on their personhood and presence in the United States, but in practice have only been available to a subset of citizens. For example, the Equal Protection Clause of the Fourteenth Amendment states that no state shall "deny to any person within its jurisdiction the equal protection of the laws" (U.S. Const.). Yet it took decades of litigation before the Supreme Court ruled that race-based school segregation and gender discrimination were violations of the Equal Protection Clause (Brown v. Board of Education, 1954; Reed v. Reed, 1971). In these cases characteristics other than citizenship (race and gender) were prioritized for understanding who was a full member of the society and entitled to the most robust set of rights. It took significant social movements for those perspectives to change and for the Supreme Court to conclude that this differential treatment was a violation of the U.S. Constitution (Kluger, 2004).

At other moments in U.S. history conceptions of membership have been broader than citizenship status. For example, in the 1800s there were a number of rights reserved for citizens that non-citizens who filed a declaration of intent to become a citizen had access to. At that time individuals who were interested in naturalizing had to file a declaration of intent to become a citizen three years before they would be eligible to naturalize. The declaration could be filed at any time after their arrival in the United States. Filing this declaration gave the individual access to voting and the ability to obtain property pursuant to the Homestead Act of 1862 (Motomura, 2007). Congress specifically allowed non-citizens who had filed this declaration to vote in the Dakota, Kansas, Minnesota, Nebraska, Nevada, Oklahoma, Oregon, Washington, and Wyoming Territories (Motomura, 2007). These non-citizens had to meet the other voting requirements, which sometimes had race and gender requirements. Access to voting and land ownership for non-citizens who filed the declaration of intent was an alternative way of operationalizing membership. It allowed those who desired to be citizens and were willing to declare that interest to be considered members. In the voting context this approach to membership recognized this subset of non-citizens as members of the community who were entitled to have a say about how it was governed.

Providing students with this type of history regarding legal rights and membership illustrates that citizenship status does not have to be the only way of conceptualizing membership. Historical approaches to the application of deportation grounds are another example of information that conveys a variety of understandings of membership and belonging that are not tied to citizenship status. Certain deportation grounds only applied during a non-citizen's first few years of residence in the United States. After that time period the non-citizens are viewed as members of the polity for whom deportation would be unjust (Banks, 2013b). This type of knowledge is useful for students to have as they analyze the current relationship between immigration status and membership in the United States.

Barriers to Citizenship

Finally, students should have knowledge about historic and contemporary barriers to citizenship status. Analyzing the justness of the current relationship between citizenship and membership would be incomplete without an understanding of whether or not there are barriers to citizenship and whether or not those barriers are legitimate. Historically race has been a significant barrier to obtaining citizenship in the United States. For example, in 1857 the United States Supreme Court declared that African Americans were not citizens of the United States in Scott v. Sanford. It was not until 1866 when Congress passed the Civil Rights Act that African Americans were formally recognized as United States citizens. Two years later the Fourteenth Amendment of the U.S. Constitution was ratified, which provides that "All persons born or naturalized in the United States, and subject to the jurisdiction thereof, are citizens of the United States and of the state wherein they reside" (U.S. Const.). Despite the seeming broad conception of citizenship adopted in the Fourteenth Amendment in 1884 the Supreme Court held that this provision did not grant birthright citizenship to American Indians (Elk v. Wilkins). It would be another 40 years before all American Indians would be recognized as United States citizens (Indian Citizenship Act, 1924).

A similar story of race-based exclusion exists in the history of U.S. naturalization law. The country's first naturalization law stated that only "free white persons" were eligible to naturalize (Naturalization Act, 1790). That requirement was extended to include "aliens of African nativity and to persons of African descent" in 1870 (Naturalization Act, 1870). The 1965 Immigration and Nationality Act finally eliminated all racial requirements for naturalization. For 175 years access to naturalization was limited based on race (Haney-López, 2006). Therefore opportunities for membership in American society were limited based on race in large part because of ideas about the cultural identity of American society and the ability of various racial groups to assimilate to mainstream American values, norms, and practices. This history of race-based exclusion is valuable knowledge for students evaluating the relationship between citizenship and membership because it demonstrates that this relationship is dynamic as conceptions of membership change over time. It also illustrates that legal approaches to membership can be unjust. The enshrinement of a particular approach in law does not mean that it is beyond reproach.

Increasing numbers of non-citizen students with varying immigration statuses presents a variety of challenges for educators. Challenges include access to education, immigration enforcement at school locations, and how to approach curriculum, particularly in social studies or civics courses. Paying attention to immigration status provides an important opportunity for students to think critically about conceptions of membership and belonging in their society. Gaining knowledge about access to citizenship, the allocation of citizenship rights, and barriers to accessing citizenship provides an indispensable foundation for analyzing whether or not the current coupling of citizenship status and membership is just. In other words, does it fairly identify the individuals within our society that have the characteristics of members. Such characteristics could include long-term residence and significant personal and economic connections to their local, state, and national communities.

Multicultural education offers important theory and practice for making the total school environment more equitable. Expanding the focus of multicultural education scholars and practitioners to include immigration status enables our society to adopt more equitable approaches to membership so that all those with the substantive characteristics of members are formally recognized as members.

References

Banks, A. M. (2013a). Closing the schoolhouse doors: State efforts to limit K-12 education for unauthorized migrant school children. In J. K. Donnor & A. Dixon (Eds.), *The resegregation of schools: Race and education in the twenty-first century* (pp. 63–81). New York, NY: Routledge.

Banks, A. M. (2013b). The normative and historical cases for proportional deportation. *Emory Law Journal, 62*, 1243–1307.

Banks, A. M. (2017). Bringing culture back: Immigrants' citizenship rights in the twenty-first century. *Santa Clara Law Review, 57*, 315–365.

Banks, J. A. (2019a). *An introduction to multicultural education* (6th ed.). New York, NY: Pearson.

Banks, J. A. (2019b). Civic education for noncitizen and citizen students: A conceptual framework. In M. M. Suarez-Orozco (Ed.), *Humanitariansim and mass migration: Confronting the world crisis* (pp. 232–251). Berkeley, CA: University of California Press.

Brown v. Board of Education of Topeka, 347 U.S. 483 (United States Supreme Court 1954).

Civil Rights Act of 1866 (An Act to protect all Persons in the United States in their Civil Rights, and furnish the Means of their Vindication), 14 Stat. 27 (1866).

Convention Relating to the Status of Refugees, 19 U.S.T. 6259 (1951).

Dabach, D. B. (2014). "You can't vote, right?" When language proficiency is a proxy for citizenship in a civics classroom. *Journal of International Social Studies, 4*(2), 37–56.

Dabach, D. B. (2015). "My student was apprehended by immigration": A civics teacher's breach of silence in a mixed-citizenship classroom. *Harvard Educational Review, 85*(3), 383–412. https://doi.org/10.17763/0017-8055.85.3.383

Elk v. Wilkins, 112 U.S. 94 (United States Supreme Court 1884).

Haney-López, I. (2006). *White by law: The legal construction of race* (Rev. and updated, 10th anniversary ed.). New York, NY: New York University Press.

Immigration & Nationality Act of 1952, 8 United States Code § 1101 (1952).

Immigration & Nationality Act of 1965 (To amend the Immigration and Nationality Act, and for other purposes), Pub. L. No. 89–236, 79 Stat. 911 (1965).

Indian Citizenship Act of 1924 (An act to authorize the Secretary of the Interior to issue certificates of citizenship to Indians), Pub. L. No. 175, 43 Stat. 253 (1924).

Jefferies, J., & Dabach, D. B. (2014). Breaking the silence: Facing undocumented issues in teacher practice. *Association of Mexican-American Educators, 8*(1), 83–93.

Kluger, R. (2004). *Simple justice: The history of Brown v. Board of Education and Black America's struggle for equality* (First Vintage ed.). New York, NY: Vintage.

Lhamon, C. E., Rosenfelt, P. H., & Samuels, J. (2014). Dear Colleague. U.S. Department of Justice & U.S. Department of Education.

McDonnell, L. M. (2000). Defining democratic purposes. In L. M. McDonnell, P. M. Timpane, & R. Benjamin (Eds.), *Rediscovering the democratic purposes of education* (pp. 1–20). Lawrence, KS: University Press of Kansas.

Morton, J. (2011). Enforcement actions at or focused on sensitive locations. United States Immigration & Customs Enforcement. Retrieved from www.ice.gov/doclib/ero-outreach/pdf/10029.2-policy.pdf

Motomura, H. (2007). *Americans in waiting: The lost story of immigration and citizenship in the United States.* New York, NY: Oxford University Press.

National Center for Education Statistics (n.d.). Digest of Education Statistics, 2017. Retrieved from https://nces.ed.gov/programs/digest/d17/tables/dt17_203.20.asp

National Conference of State Legislatures (2019). Undocumented student tuition: Overview. Retrieved from www.ncsl.org/research/education/undocumented-student-tuition-overview.aspx

Naturalization Act of 1790 (An Act to establish an uniform Rule of Naturalization), 1 Stat. 103 (1790).

Naturalization Act of 1870 (An Act to amend the Naturalization Laws and to punish Crimes against the same, and for other Purposes), 16 Stat. 254 (1870).

Parker, W. C. (2001). Educating democratic citizens: A broad view. *Theory into Practice, 6*, 6–13.

Passel, J. S., & Cohn, D. (2018). U.S. unauthorized immigrant total dips to lowest level in a decade. Pew Research Center. Retrieved from www.pewresearch.org/hispanic/wp-content/uploads/sites/5/2019/03/Pew-Research-Center_2018-11-27_U-S-Unauthorized-Immigrants-Total-Dips_Updated-2019-06-25.pdf

Plyler v. Doe, 457 U.S. 202 (United States Supreme Court 1982).

Profile of the Unauthorized Population—US (n.d.). Migrationpolicy.org. Retrieved from www.migrationpolicy.org/data/unauthorized-immigrant-population/state/US

Protocol Relating to the Status of Refugees, 19 U.S.T. 6223 (1967).

Radford, J. (2019). Key findings about U.S. immigrants. Pew Research Center. Retrieved from www.pewresearch.org/fact-tank/2019/06/17/key-findings-about-u-s-immigrants/

Reed v. Reed, 404 U.S. 71 (United States Supreme Court 1971).

Refugee Act of 1980 (An Act to amend the Immigration and Nationality Act to revise the procedures for the admission of refugees, to amend the Migration and Refugee Assistance Act of 1962 to establish a more uniform basis for the provision of assistance to refugees, and for other purposes), Pub. L. No. 96–212, 94 Stat. 102 (1980).

Romero, V. C. (1997). The congruence principle applied: Rethinking equal protection review of federal alienage classifications after Adarand Constructors, Inc. v. Peña. *Oregon Law Review, 76*, 425.

Scott v. Sanford, 60 U.S. 393 (United States Supreme Court 1857).

Sessions v. Morales-Santana, 137 S.Ct. 1678 (United States Supreme Court 2017).

Sugarman v. Dougall, 413 U.S. 634 (United States Supreme Court 1973).

United States Department of State (2020). Visa Bulletin for March 2020. *Visa Bulletin, X*(39), 1–9.

U.S. Const., § amend. XIX.

U.S. Immigration & Customs Enforcement (2018, November 25). FAQ on sensitive locations and courthouse arrests. Enforcement and Removal Operations. Retrieved from www.ice.gov/ero/enforcement/sensitive-loc

Warren, R. (2019). US undocumented population continued to fall from 2016 to 2017, and visa overstays significantly exceeded illegal crossings for the seventh consecutive year. Center for Migration Studies. Retrieved from https://doi.org/10.14240/cmsesy011619

9

TRANSFORMING CITIZENSHIP EDUCATION IN GLOBAL SOCIETIES

James A. Banks

Conceptions of citizenship and citizenship education are being challenged by a number of historical, political, social, and cultural developments that are occurring in societies around the world. Worldwide immigration, the challenges to nation-states that have been wrought by globalization, and the tenacity of nationalism and national borders have stimulated debate, controversy, and rethinking about citizenship and citizenship education (Banks, 2017a, 2020; Gutmann, 2004; Kymlicka, 2017; Suárez-Orozco, 2019).

Assimilationist, *liberal*, and *universal* conceptions of citizenship education are synonyms in this chapter. I describe why these concepts should be interrogated, and argue that citizenship and citizenship education should be expanded to include cultural rights for citizens from diverse racial, cultural, ethnic, and language groups. I also state why citizenship education should incorporate the recognition of group-differentiated rights (Fraser, 2000; Young, 1989). Liberal assimilationist notions of citizenship assume that individuals from different groups have to give up their home and community cultures and languages in order to attain inclusion and participate effectively in the national civic culture (Greenbaum, 1974; Kymlicka, 2004; Wong Fillmore, 2005). These conceptions of citizenship also view the rights of groups as detrimental to the rights of the individual. I argue, using the civil rights movement of the 1960s and 1970s in the United States as an example, that groups can help individuals to actualize their rights and opportunities to participate fully in the nation-state.

An effective and transformative citizenship education helps students to acquire the knowledge, skills, and values needed to function effectively within their cultural community, nation-state, region, and the global community. It also helps students to acquire cosmopolitan perspectives and values needed to work to attain equality and social justice for people around the world (Appiah, 2006; Nussbaum,

2002; Osler, 2016). In the final part of this chapter, I argue that schools should implement a transformative and critical conception of citizenship education that will increase educational equality for all students. A transformative citizenship education also helps students to interact and deliberate with students from diverse racial, ethnic, and cultural groups.

Conceptions of Citizenship and Citizenship Education

A citizen is an individual who lives in a nation-state and has certain rights and privileges as well as duties to the state, such as allegiance to the government (Lagassé, 2000). Citizenship is "the position or status of being a citizen" (Simpson & Weiner, 1989, p. 250). Koopmans, Statham, Guigni, and Passy (2005) define citizenship as "the set of rights, duties, and identities linking citizens to the nation-state" (p. 7). These basic definitions of citizen and citizenship are accurate but do not reveal the complexity of citizen and citizenship as these concepts have developed in modernized nation-states.

Marshall's (1964) explication of three elements of citizenship—*civil, political*, and *social*—has been widely cited and influential in the field of citizenship studies (Bulmer & Rees, 1996). He conceptualizes citizenship as developmental and describes how the civil, political, and social elements emerged in subsequent centuries. The civil aspects of citizenship, which emerged in England in the eighteenth century, provide citizens with individual rights, such as freedom of speech, the right to own property, and equality before the law. The political element of citizenship was an outcome of the nineteenth century. It gives citizens the franchise and the opportunity to exercise political power by participating in the political process. The social element arose in the twentieth century. It provides citizens with the health, education, and welfare needed to participate fully in their cultural communities and in the national civic culture. Marshall viewed the three elements of citizenship as interrelated and overlapping and citizenship as an ideal toward which nation-states work but never totally attain.

Cultural Rights and Multicultural Citizenship

Assimilationist, liberal, and universal conceptions of citizenship require citizens to give up their first languages and cultures in order to become full participants in the civic community of the nation-state (M. M. Gordon, 1964; Young, 1989, 2000). Most cultural, social, and educational policies in nation-states throughout the world, including the United States, were guided by an assimilationist policy prior to the ethnic revitalization movements of the 1960s and 1970s (Banks, Suárez-Orozco, & Ben-Peretz, 2016; Graham, 2005). Beginning in the 1800s, missionaries in the United States established boarding schools to assimilate and Christianize Native American youth (Deyhle & Swisher, 2012). Mexican Americans were punished in school for speaking Spanish during the 1940s and 1950s (Crawford,

1999). The histories and cultures of groups such as African Americans, Mexican Americans, and American Indians were rarely discussed in textbooks. When they appeared in textbooks, they were most frequently stereotyped. The depiction of ethnic minorities in textbooks was characterized by invisibility or stereotypes (Banks, 1969). School policy and practice, as within other institutions, were guided by Anglo-conformity (M. M. Gordon, 1964).

Since the ethnic revitalization movements of the 1960s and 1970s marginalized racial, ethnic, and language groups have argued that they should have the right to maintain important aspects of their cultures and languages while participating fully in the national civic culture and community (B. M. Gordon, 2001; Carmichael & Hamilton, 1967; Sizemore, 1973). These groups have demanded that institutions such as schools, colleges, and universities respond to their cultural identities and experiences by reforming their curriculum so that it will reflect their struggles, hopes, dreams, and possibilities (B. M. Gordon, 2001; Nieto, 2009). They have also demanded that schools modify teaching strategies so that they are more culturally responsive to students from different racial, ethnic, cultural, and language groups (Gay, 2018; González, Moll, & Amanti, 2005; Paris & Alim, 2017).

During the 1960s and 1970s, leaders and scholars within ethnic minority communities in the U.S. borrowed some of the concepts and language that had been used by advocates and scholars of White ethnic communities during the first decades of the 1900s when large numbers of immigrants were entering the United States from Southern, Central, and Eastern Europe. Drachsler (1920) and Kallen (1924)—who were immigrants and advocates for the cultural freedom and rights of the Southern, Central, and East European immigrants— argued that *cultural democracy* is an important characteristic of a democratic society. Drachsler (1920) and Kallen (1924) maintained that cultural democracy should co-exist with political and economic democracy, and that citizens in a democratic society should participate freely in the civic life of the nation-state and experience economic equality. They should also have the right to maintain important aspects of their community cultures and languages, as long as they do not conflict with the shared democratic ideals of the nation-state. Cultural democracy, argued Drachsler, is an essential component of a political democracy.

In the early decades of the twentieth century, Woodson (1933/1977) made a case for cultural democracy when he argued that a curriculum for African American students should reflect their history and culture and harshly criticized the absence of Black history in the curriculum. Woodson argued that Black students were being "miseducated" because they were learning only about European and not African cultures and civilizations. In the 1970s, Ramírez and Castañeda (1974) maintained that cultural democracy required that teaching methods used in the schools reflect the learning characteristics of Mexican American students as well as help them become bicognitive in their learning styles and characteristics.

Kymlicka (1995), the Canadian political theorist, and Rosaldo (1997), the U.S. anthropologist, make arguments today that are similar in many ways to those made by Drachsler and Kallen in the early 1900s and in later decades by Woodson and Ramírez and Castañeda. Both Kymlicka and Rosaldo maintain that immigrant and ethnic groups should be able to participate fully in the national civic culture while retaining elements of their cultures. The dominant culture of the nation-state should incorporate aspects of their experiences, cultures, and languages, which will enrich the mainstream culture as well as help marginalized groups to experience civic equality and recognition (Gutmann, 2004).

Expanding Marshall's Citizenship Typology

Expanding Marshall's (1964) conception of citizenship to include *cultural democracy* and *cultural citizenship* is consistent with his view that citizenship evolves to reflect the historical development of the times and expands to increase equality and social justice. Ethnic and language minority groups in societies throughout the world are denied full citizenship rights because of their languages and cultural characteristics, because they regard maintaining attachments to their cultural communities as important to their identities, and because of historic group discrimination and exclusion (Castles & Davidson, 2000; Koopmans et al., 2005; Kymlicka, 1995; Young, 1989). Consequently, citizenship in a modern democratic nation-state should be expanded to include cultural rights and group rights within a democratic framework.

Multicultural Citizenship

Global immigration and the increasing diversity in nation-states throughout the world challenge liberal assimilationist conceptions of citizenship and raise complex and divisive questions about how a nation-state can deal effectively with the problem of constructing civic communities that reflect and incorporate the diversity of its citizens and yet have an overarching set of shared values, ideals, and goals to which all of its citizens are committed (Banks, 2007). In the past, the liberal assimilationist ideology guided policy related to immigrants and diversity in most nation-states.

The liberal assimilationist conception regards the rights of the individual as paramount and group identities and rights as inconsistent with and inimical to the rights of the individual (Patterson, 1977). This conception maintains that identity groups promote group rights over the rights of the individual and that the individual must be freed of primordial and ethnic attachments in order to have free choice and options within a modernized democratic society (Patterson, 1977; Schlesinger, 1991). Strong attachments to ethnic, racial, religious, and other identity groups promote divisions and lead to ethnic conflicts and harmful divisions within society. Liberal scholars such as Patterson and Schlesinger also assume that group attachments will die of their own weight within a modernized, pluralistic democratic society if marginalized and excluded groups are given the opportunity to attain structural inclusion into the mainstream society. Liberal scholars argue that the survival of primordial attachments in a modernized democratic society reflects a "pathological condition," i.e., marginalized groups have not been provided opportunities that enabled them to experience cultural assimilation and structural inclusion (Apter, 1977). If Mexican Americans are structurally integrated into mainstream U.S. society—argues the liberal assimilationist—they will have neither the desire nor the need to speak Spanish.

A number of factors have caused social scientists and political philosophers to raise serious questions about the liberal analysis and expectation for identity groups within modernized democratic nation-states. These factors include the rise of the ethnic revitalization movements since the 1960s and 1970s which demand recognition of individual as well as group rights by nation-states and institutions such as schools, colleges, and universities; the structural exclusion of many racial, ethnic, and language groups in the United States and other Western nations (Banks, 2017a; Benhabib, 2004; Castles & Davidson, 2000; M. M. Gordon, 1964); and increasing global immigration throughout the world that has made most nation-states multinational and polyethnic (Kymlicka, 1995). Estimates indicate that "the world's 184 independent states contain over 600 living language groups and 5,000 ethnic groups. In very few countries can the citizens be said to share the same language, or belong to the same ethnonational group" (Kymlicka, 1995 p. 1).

Identity Groups in a Multicultural Democratic Society

Identity groups can both obstruct the realization of democratic values or facilitate their realization (Gutmann, 2003). Non-mainstream groups, such as Canadian Sikhs and Mexican Americans, as well as mainstream groups, such as mainstream Canadians and the Boy Scouts of America, are all identity groups. Democracies should treat individuals as civil equals and give them equal freedom (Gutmann, 2003). Identity groups can try to force their identity on individuals. However, they also can enhance the individual freedom of individuals by helping them to attain goals that are consistent with democratic values that can only be attained with group action.

Identity groups can provide opportunities for their members to freely associate and express themselves culturally and politically (Gutmann, 2003). Individuals can more successfully attain goals through the political system when working in groups than when working alone. Important examples are the political, cultural, and educational goals that African Americans gained from their participation in the civil rights movement during the 1960s and 1970s as well as the momentous changes that this movement initiated within U.S. society that gave significant benefits to other racial, ethnic, cultural, and language groups, to women, and to groups with disabilities.

The Immigration Reform Act of 1965 (which became effective in 1968) was a consequence of the civil rights movement of the 1960s and 1970s. This act abolished the national origins quota system and liberalized American immigration policy (Bennett, 1988). Immigration to the United States from Asian and Latin American nations increased substantially after this act was passed. Primarily because of the passage of this act, the nation's racial and ethnic texture has changed significantly and continues to become more diverse. Before 1968, most of the immigrants to the U.S. came from Europe. Today, most come from nations in Asia and Latin America. A significant number also come from nations in the West Indies and Africa. The U.S. is now experiencing its largest influx of immigrants since the late nineteenth and early twentieth centuries. The U.S. Census (2015) projects that ethnic groups of color—or ethnic minorities—will increase from 40% of the nation's population in 2019 to 54% in 2050.

During the course of U.S. history, marginalized groups have organized and worked for their group rights, which resulted in greater equality and social justice for all groups of Americans. This was the case with the civil rights movement, the women rights movement, as well as with the movement to enable all citizens to have a right to speak and learn their own languages in the public schools. Groups in the margins of U.S. society have been the conscience of America, and the main sites for the struggles to close the gap between American democratic ideals and institutionalized racism and discrimination (Okihiro, 1994). Through their movements to advance justice and equality in America, marginalized groups have helped the U.S. come closer to actualizing the democratic ideals stated in its founding documents—the Declaration of Independence, the Constitution, and the Bill of Rights (Okihiro, 1994).

Universal and Differentiated Citizenship

Group differences are not included in a universal conception of citizenship. Consequently, the differences of groups that have experienced structural exclusion and discrimination—such as women and people of color—are suppressed. A *differentiated* conception of citizenship, rather than a universal one, is needed to help marginalized groups attain civic equality and recognition in multicultural democratic nations (Young, 1989). Many problems result from a universal conception of citizenship which assumes that "citizenship status transcends particularity and difference" and which results in "laws and rules that are blind to individual and group differences" (Young, 1989, p. 250). A universal conception of citizenship within a stratified society results in some groups being treated as second-class citizens because group rights are not recognized and the principle of equal treatment is strictly applied.

When universal citizenship is determined, defined, and implemented by groups with power and without the interest of marginalized groups being expressed or incorporated into civic discussions, the interests of groups with power and influence will become defined as universal citizenship and as the public interest. Groups with power and influence usually define their interests as the public interest and the interests and goals of marginalized groups as "special interests." This phenomenon occurs in the debate over multicultural education in the nation's schools, colleges, and universities. Critics of multicultural education such as D'Souza (1991) and Schlesinger (1991) define the interests of dominant groups as the "public" interest and the interests of people of color such as African Americans and Latinxs as "special interests" which endanger the nation-state.

The Challenges of Global Citizenship

Cultural and group identities are important in multicultural democratic societies. However, they are not sufficient because of worldwide migration and the effects of globalization on local, regional, and national communities (Banks, 2004, 2017a). Students also need to develop the knowledge, attitudes, and skills needed to function in a global world society. Globalization affects every aspect of communities, including business and trade, health, beliefs, norms, values, and behaviors. Worldwide migration is increasing diversity in most nation-states and is forcing nations to rethink citizenship and citizenship education. National boundaries are being eroded because millions of people live in several different nations and have multiple citizenships (Castles & Davidson, 2000). Millions of other people have citizenship in one nation and live in another. Other people are stateless, such as millions of refugees around the world (Suárez-Orozco, 2019). There were 258 million people living outside their original homelands in 2017, which was a 49% increase since 2000. International migrants make up about 3.4% of the world population (United Nations, 2017).

National boundaries are also becoming more porous because of international human rights that are codified in the Universal Declaration of Human Rights (1948) and by the European Union. The Universal Declaration of Human Rights and the European Union codify rights for individuals regardless of the nation-state in which they live and whether they are citizens of a nation or not. The rights explicated in the Universal Declaration of Human Rights include the right to freedom of expression, the right to privacy and of religious beliefs, and the right to be presumed innocent if charged with a crime until proven guilty (Banks et al., 2005; Osler & Starkey, 2005). There are serious tensions between international human rights and national sovereignty. Despite the codification of international rights by bodies such as the United Nations, nationalism is as strong as ever (Benhabib, 2004; Calhoun, 2007). In his speech to the United Nations General Assembly on September 25, 2019, Trump stated a strong "America First" message, which echoed nationalistic messages that were also being made by politicians in other nations such as France and Hungary (Oprysko & Kumar, 2019).

The Challenge of Unity and Diversity

Balancing unity and diversity is a continuing challenge for multicultural nation-states. Unity without diversity results in hegemony and oppression; diversity without unity leads to Balkanization and the fracturing of the nation-state (Banks, 2020). How to recognize and legitimize difference and yet construct an overarching national identity that incorporates the voices, experiences, and hopes of the diverse groups that compose it is a major problem facing nation-states throughout the world (Banks, 2017a). Many ethnic, language, and religious groups have weak identifications with their nation-state because of their marginalized status and because they do not see their hopes, dreams, visions, and possibilities reflected within the nation-state or within the schools, colleges, and universities (Ladson-Billings, 2004; Osler & Vincent, 2002). These groups experience what I call "failed citizenship" (Banks, 2017b) and consequently have ambivalent and complex identities with their nation-states.

The diversity brought to European nations such as the United Kingdom, the Netherlands, and France by immigrants from their former colonies increased racial, ethnic, and religious tension and conflict throughout Europe (Koopmans et al., 2005). A bitter controversy arose in France regarding the wearing of the *hijab* (headscarf) by Muslim girls in state-supported schools. In March 2004, the French parliament passed a law that prohibits the wearing of any ostensibly religious symbols in state schools. Although this law prohibits the wearing of the Jewish yarmulke as well as large Christian crosses, its target was the *hijab*. The French policy is a contentious and divisive attempt by a nation with a strong assimilationist ideology to deal with religious expression in the public sphere in a way that is consistent with its ideals of equality, liberty, and republicanism (Bowen, 2008).

As worldwide immigration increases diversity on every continent and as global terrorism intensifies negative attitudes toward Muslims, schools in nation-states around the world are finding it difficult to implement policies and practices that respond to the diversity of students as well as foster national cohesion (Banks et al., 2005). The four Muslim young men who are suspected of being responsible for the bombings of the London Underground on July 7, 2005 had immigrant parents but were British citizens who grew up in Leeds. However, they apparently were not structurally integrated into British mainstream society and had weak identifications with the nation-state and other British citizens. The immigrant background of most of the suspects and perpetuators of worldwide violence has contributed to the rise of Islamophobia and racial tensions in Europe (Suárez-Orozco, 2006).

Schools and Citizenship Education in Multicultural Nations

The nuanced, complex, and evolving identities of the youth described in the studies by Abu El-Haj (2007), Nguyen (2011), and Maira (2004) indicate that the liberal assimilationist notions of citizenship are ineffective today because of the deepening diversity throughout the world and the quests by marginalized immigrant, ethnic, and racial groups for cultural recognition and rights. These researchers found that the immigrant youths in their studies did not define their national identity in terms of their place of residence, but felt that they belonged to national communities that transcended the boundaries of the United States. They defined their national identities as Palestinian, Vietnamese, Indian, Pakistani, and Bangladeshi, even though they valued their U.S. citizenship. Schools need to work to implement multicultural citizenship (Kymlicka, 1995, 2017), which recognizes the right and need for students to maintain commitments to their cultural communities, to the transnational community, and to the nation-state in which they are legal citizens.

Citizenship education should also help students to develop an identity and attachment to the global community and a human connection to people around the world. Global identities, attachments, and commitments constitute *cosmopolitanism* (Nussbaum, 2002). Cosmopolitans view themselves as citizens of the world who will make decisions and take actions in the global interests that will benefit humankind. Nussbaum states that their "allegiance is to the worldwide community of human beings" (p. 4).

Cosmopolitans identify with peoples from diverse cultures throughout the world. Nussbaum contrasts cosmopolitan universalism and internationalism with parochial ethnocentrism and inward-looking patriotism. Cosmopolitans "are ready to broaden the definition of public, extend their loyalty beyond ethnic and national boundaries, and engage with difference far and near" (W. C. Parker, personal communication, July 18, 2005). Cosmopolitans view social justice and equality globally, and are concerned with threats to the world community such as global warming, global epidemics such as SARS and Covid-19, and war. Students can become cosmopolitan citizens while maintaining attachments and roots to their family and community cultures. Both Nussbaum (2002) and Appiah (2006) view local identities as important for cosmopolitans.

The schools should help students to understand the ways in which cultural, national, regional, and global identifications are interrelated, complex, and evolving. These identifications are interactive and interrelated in a dynamic way. Each should be recognized, valued, publicly affirmed, and thoughtfully examined in schools. Students should be encouraged to critically examine their identifications and commitments and to understand the complex ways in which they are interrelated and constructed.

Citizenship education should help students to realize that "no local loyalty can ever justify forgetting that each human being has responsibilities to every other" (Appiah, 2006, p. xvi). The strong connections and interrelationships of all of the humans on earth were painfully indicated by the Covid-19 global epidemic that devastated people and nations worldwide during 2019 and 2020. Students also need to develop a deep understanding of the need to take action as citizens of the global community to help solve the world's difficult global problems and to make decisions and take actions that will enhance democracy and promote equality and social justice in their cultural communities, nation, region, and the world.

The increasing diversity throughout the world today and the increasing recognition of diversity—as well as the intractable problems that the world faces—require a re-examination of the ends and means of citizenship education if it is to promote inclusion, civic equality, and recognition (Gutmann, 2004). Liberal assimilationist conceptions of citizenship education that eradicate the cultures and languages of diverse groups will be ineffective in a transformed "flat" world of the twenty-first century (Friedman, 2005). Citizenship education in the U.S.—as well as within other Western nations—should be reinvented so that it will enable students to see their fates as intimately tied to that of people throughout the world and to understand why a "threat to justice anywhere is a threat to justice everywhere" (King, 1963/1994, pp. 2–3).

Mainstream and Transformative Citizenship Education

Citizenship education must be reimagined and transformed to effectively educate students to function in the twenty-first century (Banks, 2020). The knowledge that underlies citizenship education must shift from *mainstream* to *transformative* academic knowledge in order to reform citizenship education. Mainstream knowledge reinforces traditional and established knowledge in the social and behavioral sciences as well as the knowledge that is institutionalized within the popular culture and within the nation's schools, colleges, and universities (Banks, 1993). Transformative academic knowledge consists of paradigms and explanations that challenge some of the key epistemological assumptions of mainstream knowledge (Collins, 2000; Harding, 1991). An important purpose of transformative knowledge is to improve the human condition. Feminist scholars and scholars of color have been among the leading constructors of transformative academic knowledge (Collins, 2000; Harding, 1991; Takaki, 1998).

Mainstream citizenship education is grounded in mainstream knowledge and assumptions and reinforces the status quo and the dominant power relationships in society. It is practiced in most social studies classrooms in the United States (Rubin, 2012) and does not challenge or disrupt the class, racial, and gender discrimination within the schools and society. It either does not include each of the four elements of citizenship identified in the first part of this chapter—*civil, political, social,* and *cultural*—or includes them at superficial and limited levels. It does not help students to understand their multiple and complex identities or the ways in which their lives are influenced by globalization, or what their role should be in a global world. The emphasis is on memorizing facts about constitutions and other legal documents, learning about various branches of government, and developing patriotism to the nation-state (Westheimer, 2015). Critical thinking skills, decision-making, and action are not important components of mainstream citizenship education.

Transformative citizenship education needs to be implemented within the schools in order for students to attain clarified and reflective cultural, national, regional, and global identifications, and to understand how these identities are interrelated and constructed (Banks, 2020). Transformative citizenship education also recognizes and validates the cultural identities of students. It is rooted in transformative academic knowledge, and enables students to acquire the information, skills, and values needed to challenge inequality within their communities, their nations, and the world, to develop cosmopolitan values and perspectives, and to take actions to create just and democratic multicultural communities and societies. Transformative citizenship education helps students to develop decision-making and social action skills that are needed to identify problems within society, to acquire knowledge related to their home and community cultures and languages, to identify and clarify their values, and to take thoughtful individual or collective civic action. It also fosters critical thinking skills and is inclusive of critical citizenship education (DeJaegherre, 2007).

Conclusion

Students experience democracy in classrooms and schools when transformative citizenship education is implemented. Consequently, they are better able to internalize democratic beliefs and values, and to acquire thoughtful cultural identifications and commitments. The total school, including the knowledge conveyed in the curriculum, needs to be reformed in order to implement transformative citizenship education. Inequality and stratification within the larger society are challenged and are not reproduced in transformative and democratic classrooms and schools. Transformative citizenship education helps students to develop reflective cultural, national, regional, and global identifications and to acquire the knowledge and skills needed to take action to make their communities, nation, and the world just places in which to live and work.

References

Abu El-Haj, T. R. (2007). "I was born here, but my home, it's not here": Educating for democratic citizenship in an era of transnational migration and global conflict. *Harvard Educational Review,* 77(3), 285–316.

Appiah, K. A. (2006). *Cosmopolitanism: Ethnics in a world of strangers.* New York, NY: Norton.

Apter, D. E. (1977). Political life and cultural pluralism. In M. M. Tumin & W. Plotch (Eds.), *Pluralism in a democratic society* (pp. 58–91). New York, NY: Praeger.

Banks, J. A. (1969). A content analysis of the Black American in textbooks. *Social Education, 33*(8), 954–957, 963.

Banks, J. A. (1993). The canon debate, knowledge construction, and multicultural education. *Educational Researcher, 22*(5), 4–14.

Banks, J. A. (Ed.) (2004). *Diversity and citizenship education: Global perspectives.* San Francisco, CA: Jossey-Bass.

Banks, J. A. (2007). *Educating citizens in a multicultural society* (2nd ed.). New York, NY: Teachers College Press.

Banks, J. A. (Ed.) (2017a). *Citizenship education and global migration: Implications for theory, research, and teaching.* Washington, DC: American Educational Research Association.

Banks, J. A. (2017b). Failed citizenship and transformative civic education. *Educational Researcher, 46*(7), 366–377.

Banks, J. A. (2020). *Diversity, transformative knowledge, and civic education: Selected essays.* New York, NY: Routledge.

Banks, J. A., Banks, C. A. M., Cortés, C. E., Hahn, C. L., Merryfield, M. M., Moodley, K. A., Murphy-Shigematsu, S., Osler, A., Park, C., & Parker, W. C. (2005). *Democracy and diversity: Principles and concepts for educating citizens in a global age.* Seattle, WA: Center for Multicultural Education, University of Washington.

Banks, J. A., Suárez-Orozco, M. M., & Ben-Peretz, M. (Eds.) (2016). *Global migration, diversity, and civic education: Improving policy and practice.* New York, NY: Teachers College Press.

Benhabib, S. (2004). *The rights of others: Aliens, residents, and citizens.* Cambridge, UK: Cambridge University Press.

Bennett, D. H. (1988). *The party of fear: From nativist movements to the New Right in American history.* Chapel Hill: University of North Carolina Press.

Bowen, J. R. (2008). Republican ironies: Equality and identities in French schools. In M. Minow, R. A. Shweder, & H. Marcus (Eds.), *Just schools: Pursuing equality in societies of difference* (pp. 294–324). New York, NY: Russell Sage Foundation.

Bulmer, M., & Rees, A. M. (Eds.) (1996). *Citizenship today: The contemporary relevance of T. H. Marshall.* London: UCL Press Limited.

Calhoun, C. (2007). *Nations matter: Culture, history, and the cosmopolitan dream.* New York, NY: Routledge.

Carmichael, S., & Hamilton, C. (1967). *Black power: The politics of liberation in America.* New York, NY: Vintage.

Castles, S., & Davidson, A. (2000). *Citizenship and migration: Globalization and the politics of belonging.* New York, NY: Routledge.

Collins, P. H. (2000). *Black feminist thought: Knowledge, consciousness, and the politics of empowerment.* New York, NY: Routledge.

Crawford, J. (1999). *Bilingual education: History, politics, theory, and practice* (4th ed.). Los Angeles, CA: Bilingual Education Services.

DeJaeghere, J. G. (2007). Intercultural and global meanings of citizenship education in the Australian secondary curriculum: Between critical contestations and minimal construction. In E. D. Stevick & B. A. Levinson (Eds.), *Reimagining civic education: How diverse societies form democratic citizens* (pp. 293–316). Lanham, MD: Rowman & Littlefield.

Deyhle, D., & Swisher, K. G. (2012). Connecting the circle in American Indian education. In J. A. Banks (Ed.), *The Routledge international companion to multicultural education* (pp. 265–275). New York, NY: Routledge.

Drachsler, J. (1920). *Democracy and assimilation.* New York, NY: Macmillan.

D'Souza, D. (1991). *Illiberal education: The politics of race and sex on campus.* New York, NY: Collier Macmillan.

Fraser, N. (2000). Rethinking recognition: Overcoming displacement and reification in cultural politics. *New Left Review, 3,* 107–120.

Friedman, T. L. (2005). *The world is flat: A brief history of the twenty-first century.* New York, NY: Farrar, Straus and Giroux.

Gay, G. (2018). *Culturally responsive teaching: Theory, research, and* practice (3rd ed.). New York, NY: Teachers College Press.

González, N., Moll, L. C., & Amanti, C. (2005). *Funds of knowledge: Theorizing practices in households, communities, and classrooms*. Mahwah, NJ: Erlbaum.
Gordon, B. M. (2001). Knowledge construction, competing critical theories, and education. In J. A. Banks & C. A. M. Banks (Eds.), *Handbook of research on multicultural education* (pp. 184–199). San Francisco, CA: Jossey-Bass.
Gordon, M. M. (1964). *Assimilation in American life: The roles of race, religion, and national origin*. New York, NY: Oxford University Press.
Graham, P. A. (2005). *Schooling in America: How the public schools meet the nation's changing needs*. New York, NY: Oxford University Press.
Grant, S. G. (2001). An uncertain lever: Exploring the influence of state-level testing in New York State on teaching social studies. *Teachers College Record, 103*(3), 398–426.
Greenbaum, W. (1974). America in search of a new ideal: As essay on the rise of pluralism. *Harvard Educational Review, 44*(3), 411–440.
Gutmann, A. (2003). *Identity in democracy*. Princeton, NJ: Princeton University Press.
Gutmann, A. (2004). Unity and diversity in democratic multicultural education: Creative and destructive tensions. In J. A. Banks (Ed.), *Diversity and citizenship education: Global perspectives* (pp. 71–96). San Francisco, CA: Jossey-Bass.
Harding, S. (1991). *Whose science? Whose knowledge? Thinking from women's lives*. Ithaca, NY: Cornell University Press.
Kallen, H. M. (1924). *Culture and democracy in the United States*. New York, NY: Boni and Liveright.
King, M. L., Jr. (1994). *Letter from a Birmingham jail*. New York, NY: HarperCollins. (Original work published 1963)
Koopmans, R., Statham, P., Giugni, M., & Passy, F. (2005). *Contested citizenship: Immigration and cultural diversity in Europe*. Minneapolis: University of Minnesota Press.
Kymlicka, W. (1995). *Multicultural citizenship: A liberal theory of minority rights*. New York, NY: Oxford University Press.
Kymlicka, W. (2004). Foreword. In J. A. Banks (Ed.), *Diversity and citizenship education: Global perspectives* (pp. xiii–xviii). San Francisco, CA: Jossey-Bass.
Kymlicka, W. (2017). Foreword. In J. A. Banks (Ed.), *Citizenship education and global migration: Implications for theory, research, and teaching* (pp. xix–xxv). Washington, DC: American Educational Research Association.
Ladson-Billings, G. (2004). Culture versus citizenship: The challenge of racialized citizenship in the United States. In J. A. Banks (Ed.), *Diversity and citizenship education: Global perspectives* (pp. 99–126). San Francisco, CA: Jossey-Bass.
Lagassé, P. (Ed.) (2000). *The Columbia encyclopedia* (6th ed.). New York, NY: Columbia University Press.
Maira, S. (2004). Imperial feelings: Youth culture, citizenship, and globalization. In M. Suárez-Orozco & D. B. Qin-Hilliard (Eds.), *Globalization, culture, and education in the new millennium* (pp. 203–234). Berkeley, CA: University of California Press.
Marshall, T. H. (1964). *Class, citizenship, and social development: Essays of T. H. Marshall*. Westport, CT: Greenwood Press.
Nguyen, D. (2011). *Vietnamese immigrant youth and citizenship: How race, ethnicity, and culture shape sense of belonging*. El Paso, TX: LFB Scholarly Publishing LLC.
Nieto, S. (2009). *The light in their eyes: Creating multicultural learning communities* (10th anniversary ed.). New York, NY: Teachers College Press.
Nussbaum, M. (2002). Patriotism and cosmopolitanism. In J. Cohen (Ed.), *For love of country* (pp. 2–17). Boston, MA: Beacon Press.

Okihiro, G. Y. (1994). *Margins and mainstreams: Asians in American history*. Seattle, WA: University of Washington Press.

Oprysko, C., & Kumar, A. (2019, September 24). Trump pushes aggressive 'America First' message to world leaders. *Politico*. Retrieved from www.politico.com/story/2019/09/24/trump-america-first-unga-1509356

Osler, A. (2016). *Human rights and schooling: An ethical framework for teaching social justice*. New York, NY: Teachers College Press.

Osler, A., & Starkey, H. (2005). *Changing citizenship: Democracy and inclusion in education*. New York, NY: Open University Press.

Osler, A., & Vincent, K. (2002). *Citizenship and the challenge of global education*. Stoke-on-Trent, UK: Trentham Books.

Paris, D., & Alim, H. S. (Eds.) (2017). *Culturally sustaining pedagogies: Teaching and learning in a changing world*. New York, NY: Teachers College Press.

Patterson, O. (1977). *Ethnic chauvinism: The reactionary impulse*. New York, NY: Stein and Day.

Ramírez, M., III, & Castañeda, A. (1974). *Cultural democracy, bicognitive development, and education*. New York, NY: Academic Press.

Rosaldo, R. (1997). Cultural citizenship, inequality, and multiculturalism. In W. V. Flores & R. Benmayor (Eds.), *Latino cultural citizenship: Claiming identity, space, and rights* (pp. 27–28). Boston, MA: Beacon Press.

Rubin, B. C. (2012). *Making citizens: Transforming civic learning for diverse social studies classrooms*. New York, NY: Routledge.

Schlesinger, A. M. (1991). *The disuniting of America: Reflections on a multicultural society*. Knoxville, TN: Whittle Direct Books.

Simpson, J. A., & Weiner, E. S. C. (Eds.) (1989). *The Oxford English dictionary* (2nd ed., Vol. 3). New York, NY: Oxford University Press.

Sizemore, B. A. (1973). Shattering the melting pot myth. In J. A. Banks (Ed.), *Teaching ethnic studies: Concepts and strategies* (43rd Yearbook, pp. 72–101). Washington, DC: National Council for the Social Studies.

Suárez-Orozco, M. M. (2006, March 13). Commentary: A question of assimilation. *U.S. News and World Report, 34*, 36.

Suárez-Orozco, M. M. (Ed.) (2019). *Humanitarianism and mass migration: Confronting the world crisis*. Oakland, CA: University of California Press.

Takaki, R. (1998). *Strangers from a different shore: A history of Asian Americans* (Rev. ed.). Boston, MA: Little Brown.

Universal Declaration of Human Rights (1948). Retrieved from www.un.org/Overview/rights.html

United Nations (2017, December 18). *The international migration report 2017 (Highlights)*. Retrieved from www.un.org/development/desa/publications/international-migration-report-2017.html

United States Census Bureau (2015, March 3). Projections of the size and composition of the U.S. population: 2014 to 2060. Retrieved from www.census.gov/library/publications/2015/demo/p25-1143.html

Westheimer, J. (Ed.) (2015). *What kind of citizen? Educating our children for the common good*. New York, NY: Teachers College Press.

Wong Fillmore, L. (2005). When learning a second language means losing the first. In M. M. Suárez-Orozco, C. Suárez-Orozco, & D. Qin (Eds.), *The new immigration: An interdisciplinary reader* (pp. 289–307). New York, NY: Routledge.

Woodson, C. G. (1977). *The mis-education of the Negro*. New York, NY: AMS Press. (Original work published 1933)

Young, I. M. (1989). Polity and group difference: A critique of the ideal of universal citizenship. *Ethics, 99*(2), 250–274.

Young, I. M. (2000). *Inclusion and democracy*. New York, NY: Oxford University Press.

AFTERWORD

Bette Rose Tate-Beaver

Executive Director, National Association for Multicultural Education

> *Education leads to enlightenment. Enlightenment opens the way to empathy. Empathy foreshadows reform.*
>
> Derrick A. Bell, 1992, *Faces at the Bottom of the Well: The Permanence of Racism*

While reading *Visioning Multicultural Education: Past, President, Future*, Derrick Bell's quote came to mind. His words on education, empathy, and reform certainly fit with the vision of Multicultural Education. However, after reading the contributions of the esteemed scholars in the book, I would add that in education, reform is the beginning of the journey to educational revolution. Education as we know it, especially education of the colonizers, was never intended to be inclusive. Multicultural Education has led and continues to lead the necessary education revolution that the United States and the rest of the world needs.

The National Association for Multicultural Education (NAME) has been part of advancing education reform and revolution forward since 1990. This was the vision of Rose Duhon-Sells and NAME's founding members. If not for the contributions of Dr. Duhon-Sells and NAME's founding members, including Cherry Ross-Gooden, H. Prentice Baptiste, who each served as NAME presidents, G. Pritchy Smith, Lesley Baptiste, Marjorie Kyle, Glenn Doston, and Cornel Pewewardy, the vision of NAME would not have advanced.

Additional early scholars of Multicultural Education joined in to help expand and further the vision of NAME and its contribution to Multicultural Education. The early advocates whom Dr. Duhon-Sells called on included Carl Grant, Geneva Gay, Philip Chinn, Donna Gollnick, James A. Banks, Cherry McGee Banks, Rita Robinson, and Jill Moss Greenberg. They were just a small part of the army of scholars, educators, and activists who saw Multicultural Education as the way toward revolutionary reform in education.

These visionaries saw Multicultural Education as the way to truly improve schools so that they would include and address the unique needs of the invisible and marginalized populations. The way to revolutionize education was to recreate it, and these individuals hoped to make that happen. At the time Multicultural Education was a radical concept. In some ways it still is considered radical and probably always will be. Multicultural Education and NAME are large umbrellas. The umbrellas must be large to be truly inclusive of all of the aspects of education requiring reform, while including and embracing all marginalized populations.

The visions of Multicultural Education and NAME have progressed and in some ways have been adopted, but as the book's contributors tell us, there is much more to be done. The visions, the concepts continue to grow, develop, and move forward. So, the work *must* continue.

Over years many Multicultural Education scholars, educators, community activists, and NAME have continued to forge change in education. These change agents include visionaries like Sonia Nieto, Carlos Cortés, Patricia Marshall, Jeanette Haynes Writer, Tchet Dorman, Christopher Knaus, Kevin Roxas, Lynne Aoki, Christine Clark, Wayne Au, Alyssa Dunn, Brian Wright, and many others. As we continue to look forward, we see Kristen French, Angela Banks, Patrick Camangian, Omarthan Clarke, Miguel Zavala, Bre Evans-Santiago, plus many more working to continue and advance the Multicultural Education movement.

It is fortunate that there are far too many past, present, and emerging Multicultural Education reformists and revolutionaries to name. All of their work is vital to effect real and lasting education reform. The National Association for Multicultural Education is honored that some of them have shared their scholarship, determination, and vision in this book.

Going back to Derrick Bell's quote, enlightenment flows from education and creates a path for empathy and empathy leads to reform. In order for that to happen in the twenty-first century, the schools of tomorrow must not be shaped around models of the past. Multicultural Education can light the way to the future. To this end, it is important that the Multicultural Education movement consider the Sankofa Directive, which instructs us to know and accept the realities of the past, so we are able to chart the best course into the future. It is vital that today's revolutionary multicultural scholars make a path for tomorrow's education innovators so Multicultural Education keeps ahead of society's changing needs.

Finally, I must ask, now that you have read this book, how are you willing to contribute to the futuring of Multicultural Education and revolutionary education reform? To paraphrase Mahatma Gandhi, you must be the change you wish to see in Multicultural Education, education reform, and the world.

CONTRIBUTORS

Wayne Au is a former public high school teacher and currently is a Professor in the School of Educational Studies at the University of Washington Bothell. He is a long-time Rethinking Schools editor, and he has edited or co-edited several Rethinking Schools books, including *Rethinking Ethnic Studies*, *Teaching for Black Lives*, and *Rethinking Multicultural Education*. As an academic and an activist he remains involved in local and national struggles over racial justice in schools, and his most recent scholarly book is *A Marxist Education: Learning to Change the World*.

Angela M. Banks is the Charles J. Merriam Distinguished Professor of Law at the Sandra Day O'Connor College of Law at Arizona State University. She is an immigration and citizenship expert whose research focuses on membership and belonging in democratic societies. Her scholarship has appeared in leading American law review journals. Prior to joining the Sandra Day O'Connor College of Law faculty, Professor Banks was a Professor of Law at William & Mary School of Law. She has also served as the Reginald F. Lewis Fellow for Law Teaching at Harvard Law School; a legal advisor to Judge Gabrielle Kirk McDonald at the Iran-United States Claims Tribunal; an associate at Wilmer, Cutler & Pickering in Washington, DC (now WilmerHale); and a law clerk for Judge Carlos F. Lucero of the U.S. Court of Appeals for the Tenth Circuit. She received a B.A. in Sociology from Spelman College *summa cum laude* and a Master of Letters in Sociology from the University of Oxford, where she was a Marshall Scholar. Professor Banks is a 2000 graduate of Harvard Law School, where she served as an editor of the *Harvard Law Review* and the *Harvard International Law Journal*.

James A. Banks is Kerry and Linda Killinger Endowed Chair in Diversity Studies Emeritus at the University of Washington, Seattle. He was the Russell F. Stark University Professor at the University of Washington from 2000 to 2006 and founding director of the Center for

Multicultural Education from 1992 to 2018, which has been renamed the Banks Center for Educational Justice. He is a past president of the American Educational Research Association and the National Council for the Social Studies. He is a member of the National Academy of Education and a Fellow of the American Educational Research Association. His most recent book is *Diversity, Transformative Knowledge, and Civic Education: Collected Essays*.

H. Prentice Baptiste is a Regents and Distinguished Achievement Professor at New Mexico State University, Las Cruces, New Mexico. In 2014 he was awarded the first College of Education Diversity Award at New Mexico State University. He was President (2016 to 2018) of the National Association for Multicultural Education (NAME), a premier organization advocating for equity and social justice, which he helped found in 1990. His research interests include the conceptualization of multicultural education, the process of multiculturalizing educational entities, and culturally diversifying science and mathematics instruction. Baptiste has authored or edited seven books, as well as over 125 articles, papers, and chapters on multicultural and science education. He has presented papers and conducted workshops in Nigeria, Egypt, Germany, Jamaica, Kenya, Morocco, and the Netherlands. As President of NAME, he was co-leader of two educational cultural groups to Cuba.

Carlos E. Cortés is the Edward A. Dickson Emeritus Professor of History at the University of California, Riverside, and a former fellow of the University of California National Center for Free Speech and Civic Engagement. His books include: *The Children Are Watching: How the Media Teach about Diversity*; *The Making—and Remaking—of a Multiculturalist*; and his memoir, *Rose Hill: An Intermarriage before Its Time*.

Kristen B. French (Amskapi Pikuni-Blackfeet/Gros Ventre/Eastern Band Cherokee) is Professor of Elementary Education and Director of the Center for Education, Equity and Diversity (CEED) at Western Washington University. Kristen's engaged scholarship includes Indigenous education, decolonizing theory, critical land-based history and pedagogy, multicultural teacher education, and critical performative pedagogy. Kristen's current research is situated at the intersections of Indigenous futurities and Multicultural Education.

Geneva Gay is Professor Emeritus of Education at the University of Washington. She is a recipient of the Distinguished Scholar Award from the American Educational Research Association; the first Multicultural Educator Award presented by the National Association for Multicultural Education; the 2004 W. E. B. Du Bois Distinguished Lecturer Award presented by the Special Interest Group on Research Focus on Black Education of the American Educational Research Association; and the 2006 Mary Anne Raywid Award for Distinguished Scholarship in the Field of Education, presented by the Society of Professors of Education. She is internationally known for her scholarship in multicultural education, particularly as it relates to curriculum design, staff development, classroom instruction, and intersections of culture, race, ethnicity, teaching, and learning. Her writings are numerous, including the co-editorship of *Expressively Black: The Cultural Basis of Ethnic Identity* (Praeger,

1987); author of *At the Essence of Learning: Multicultural Education* (Kappa Delta Pi, 1994), and *Culturally Responsive Teaching: Theory, Practice, & Research* (Teachers College Press, 2000; 2nd edition, 2010; 3rd edition, 2018); and editor of *Becoming Multicultural Educators: Personal Journey Toward Professional Agency* (Jossey-Bass, 2003).

Carl A. Grant is Hoefs-Bascom Professor of Education, Department of Curriculum and Instruction, University of Wisconsin-Madison. He has authored/edited 40 books and written over 100 articles. Grant's books include: *Du Bois and Education* (2018) and *Black Intellectual Thought in Education* (Routledge, 2015) with Keffrelyn D. Brown and Anthony L. Brown; *Selected Works of Carl A. Grant* (Routledge, 2014); and *The Moment: Barack Obama, Jeremiah Wright and the Firestorm at Trinity United Church of Christ* (Rowman & Littlefield, 2013) with Shelby J. Grant.

Jeanette Haynes Writer (Tsalagi/Cherokee Nation citizen) is Professor of Curriculum and Instruction at New Mexico State University, Las Cruces, New Mexico. She has served in leadership and board positions for the National Association for Multicultural Education, the American Indian Studies Association, and the Association of Teacher Educators. Haynes Writer's areas of scholarship include Tribal Critical Race Theory; critical multicultural and social justice education; Indigenous education; Native American identity; and teacher education. She has published in journals such as *Action in Teacher Education, Anthropology & Education Quarterly, International Journal of Education & the Arts, International Journal of Multicultural Education*, and *Journal of Praxis in Multicultural Education*. Her recent work involves Native Science and the recruitment and retention of Native and other historically underrepresented faculty.

Patricia L. Marshall is a Professor at North Carolina State University. Her courses examine diversity and equity in schools and communities, and she has studied teachers' enactment of equity pedagogies with a focus on mathematics instruction. Her recent books include *When Critical Multiculturalism Meets Mathematics*, and *The Stories We Tell: Math, Race, Bias and Opportunity*. Currently, she is exploring cross-cultural competence stories of multicultural teacher educators and the multiculturalization of environmental education.

Christine E. Sleeter is Professor Emerita in the College of Education at California State University Monterey Bay, where she was a founding faculty member. She is past President of the National Association for Multicultural Education. Her research focuses on anti-racist multicultural education, ethnic studies, and teacher education. She has published over 150 articles and 24 books, including *Un-Standardizing Curriculum* (2nd edition with Judith Flores Carmona) and *Transformative Ethnic Studies in Schools* (with Miguel Zavala); she has also published two novels that feature teachers as main characters, *White Bread* and *The Inheritance*.

INDEX

Note: Entries in *italics* denote figures.